Three Women of Herat

Three Women of Herat

VERONICA DOUBLEDAY

University of Texas Press, Austin

for the people of Afghanistan

International Standard Book Number 0-292-78112-1
Library of Congress Catalog Card Number 90-70631
Copyright © 1988 by Veronica Doubleday
All rights reserved
Printed in the United States of America

First University of Texas Press Edition, 1990

Requests for permission to reproduce material from this work should be
sent to Permissions, University of Texas Press, Box 7819, Austin, Texas
78713-7819.

∞ The paper used in this publication meets the minimum requirements
of American National Standard for Information Sciences—Permanence of
Paper for Printed Library Materials, ANSI Z39.48-1984.

Contents

Illustrations

The author's pencil drawings were based on her own photographic material. They portray the women's environment without identifying specific women or breaking their code of modesty. The decorative borders are derived from geometric and floral patterns used in women's embroidery. The photos are all by the author except photos 9 and 14 (Oliver Doubleday).

Author's Note

It is common for anthropologists to mask the identity of their inform-
ants so as to avoid any betrayal of trust and, as the women I describe
observed purdah and hid their faces in public, I have felt this to be
necessary. I have changed all personal names, invented a few place
names, and not supplied exact details of where people lived. The
photographs and illustrative chapter headings are intended to provide a
visual atmosphere without establishing any particular individual's
identity.

As for pronunciation, 'Herat' has a long 'a' as in 'part'; so does
'Kabul', which rhymes approximately with 'marble'. Names like
'Shirin' and 'Karim' have a long 'i', sounding as in 'tureen', and the
name 'Nebi' rhymes with 'Debbie'. 'Kh' is like the 'ch' in 'Bach'. 'Gh'
and 'q' are similar to one another, uvular plosives, like 'k' produced
very far back.

Behind the Curtain

Night had fallen by the time we reached Herat city. Our dilapidated mini-bus, the only means of public transport from the Iranian border, rattled slowly along, now overloaded with tourists and Afghans crouching in the gangway. Small points of light twinkled in the distance ahead. Then, suddenly, rising from the darkness we made out the shape of the four tall minarets, remnants of a magnificent fifteenth-century mosque and university complex. The road ran between them, over an old bridge and down a pine-tree avenue to the site of the western gate of the once-walled city.

It was 1973, and the beginning of a year's stay in Herat. My husband John was embarking upon musical research and I was visiting Afghanistan for the first time. It was the start of a deep association with Herat and the Afghan people.

Our driver set us down in a side-street off the main tourist bazaar. We resisted the obsequious invitations of the hotel owner who had arranged for us to arrive at his door, and had our impressive pile of belongings wheeled on a hand-cart to another hotel. As we had spent the past eight months in Iran teaching English, learning Persian and preparing for our trip to Afghanistan, we had considerably more luggage than other Western visitors.

'You speak Persian! From Tehran?' asked our porter, immediately recognising our singsong accents.

Taking in the shadowy, archaic atmosphere of the bazaar, I felt we had stepped back centuries in time. The pavement was rough and uneven underfoot, and the street was barely lit. Traffic was minimal: there were almost no cars, just hand-carts, bicycles and *gadi*s – attractively festooned, jingling horse-drawn carriages that looked colourful and picturesque with their plumes and red pompons. Instead of the noise of engines, there were sounds of bells and clopping hooves. Although it was quite late, several shops were still open, raised above street level, like treasure caves stocked to the ceiling and lit by magical lamps. None of the buildings seemed to have perfect straight lines or right-angles, and surfaces were worn and softened with age, formed from natural materials such as sun-dried brick, wood and plaster.

A few men were milling around. They all wore traditional long shirts and baggy trousers with bulky white turbans. Those who were more affluent had fine skin hats of astrakhan fleece perched at a jaunty angle. Some wore magnificent striped coats around their shoulders, which had extremely long vestigial sleeves pressed flat on either side.

No women were to be seen. They remained at home, hidden behind high walls.

I paused to admire a shopkeeper sitting impassively among his wares, struck by the sheer beauty of the picture he presented. He had what I soon came to recognise as typically Herati features: dark slanting eyes, a long face and a pronounced aquiline nose. A single gas lamp hung above him, illuminating his white turban and his immobile head, and picking out the rich colours of the fruit piled around him – melons, limes, water-melons, green and purple grapes, apricots, aubergines and small green cucumbers.

Cement steps led up to the first-floor entrance of our hotel. A team of men was still working in a bakery below, moving fast and rhythmically like dancers. Their faces shone with sweat as they deftly shaped the flat oval loaves on to a board and slapped them against the hot walls of the clay oven.

We had to brush past a beggar who lay sleeping on a stone slab just outside the bakery. Something jolted inside me, focusing all my confused impressions of Herat into this single image. I realised that I had to accommodate the reality of poverty into my aesthetic appreciation of these strange, exotic surroundings. Poverty kept people chained to the past, free from the ugly accoutrements of twentieth-century life that I was so glad to escape, yet lacking some of the most basic and necessary facilities. However, I took comfort from people's tolerance of the sleeping figure and from the deeply relaxed expression on the old man's face.

The shock of arrival stayed with me for several days. After the hooting horns and traffic jams and the jostle of Iranian crowds, I delighted in the leisurely pace of Herat. Men stopped in the streets, uttering polite greetings, hand on heart, before sauntering on their way. They sat in shops drinking tea and chatting as though they had all the time in the world. The atmosphere was friendly and hospitable. Watches were worn as expensive ornaments, but rarely consulted. Instead, the days were punctuated by the movement of the sun and by the five calls to prayer at dawn, midday, mid-afternoon, dusk and late evening. Quite unselfconsciously men performed their ablutions and knelt and prayed in corners of their shops, with no sense of interrupting their activities.

The world of the women remained invisible and inaccessible to me. Very few Herati women had occasion to walk in the parts of the city frequented by tourists. Those who did moved silently and inconspicuously, closely veiled, impenetrable and faceless. I was appalled by my first sight of the Afghan *burqa* veil. It looked so stifling and anonymous, covering the face and body and with only a mesh window to see through. In Iran many women had worn the *chador* veil, but they draped it loosely, often casually, around themselves, and their faces were exposed. The *burqa* masked all public identity: eyes were covered and faces denied expression.

Herati men claimed they could tell a great deal from seeing a woman dressed in her veil, and later I became attuned to these subtleties. One noticed the style of shoe and the cut and cloth of the trousers that showed beneath the *burqa* hem, and one could appreciate a woman's posture and gait and judge her figure, especially if the veil was smart and tightly pleated. A woman's opulence and sense of fashion were revealed by the quality of her clothes, especially the veil itself. In those early days, however, I could apprehend only the extent to which a woman's body and personality seemed to be hidden.

I had no means of contact with the women. Occasionally I saw them pass through the bazaars of the old city, as if on sufferance, never lingering. They moved gently in groups, their veils billowing in the wind and their noses protruding like beaks from beneath. More than anything they reminded me of dark, wingless, sightless birds unable to fly to their destination.

During that first year in Herat I lived as a lone woman in a public world of men. John carried out his formal research, working with male professional and amateur musicians, and I sometimes accompanied him to musical events, or to visit musicians in their houses. At home I helped him by working upon the transcription and translation of Herati songs, struggling over tapes with a local schoolteacher who also gave us Persian lessons. Later I began studying miniature painting with a Herati master, trudging through the snow or blazing sun to his studio in the new city. I became very enthusiastic and worked hard, drawing intricate designs.

Gradually I learned my way around Herat. Landmarks became familiar: the towering mass of the citadel in the north-western corner of the city; the great Friday mosque covered with recently renovated mosaic tilework; the ruined walls which had once surrounded the city on four sides, enormous steep ramparts of dried mud; the four old bazaars that intersected at Char Su and cut the old city into four labyrinthine residential quarters. To the north and east of the old city there were newly built suburbs, the provincial Governor's administrative offices, schools, banks, a theatre and cinema and the recently developed tourist area, all collectively known as the new city.

Herat was steeped in history. Its most famous period was under Timurid rule from 1397, when Tamerlane's son, Shah Rukh, made it his capital, until the death of his successor, Sultan Hossein Baiqara, in 1506. Tamerlane had taken Herat and destroyed the city walls in 1381, but Shah Rukh was more interested in peaceful pursuits than his father, and he instituted a cultural renaissance. Many important monuments and shrines date from the Timurid period, in particular the mausoleum of Gohar Shad, Shah Rukh's wife, and the minarets of the ruined Musalla complex. A Golden Age of literature, philosophy, arts and science ended with the capture of Herat by the northern Uzbek people and the subsequent struggle for control between the Uzbeks, Persians and Afghans.

The majority of Heratis lacked precise information about the high achievements of the Timurids, although they were well aware of their city's ancient origins and felt a deep pride in their roots. They kept the past alive through traditions and beliefs, stories and songs, patterns and

designs, and they visited and revered the holy shrines of saints and poets that were dotted throughout the city and its surrounding valley. Herat was situated at a strategic oasis, and had been a cultural focus, market centre and political stronghold for many centuries. Founded by Alexander the Great, it had been devastated many times by invaders such as Genghis Khan and Tamerlane, only to be rebuilt anew.

The sounds and smells of the city became familiar to me. I recall the jingling and clopping of horse-drawn carriages and the cries of drivers shooing passers-by from their path; the slow, insinuating echo of the call to prayer sounding from the different mosques at prayer time; the melodious chants of street vendors; the blaring of Afghan popular music over cassette machines and loudspeakers in shops and tea-houses. Then there was the scent of the pines that lined many of the streets, and the pungent pine-smoke that blew through the city at dusk as women cooked out in their courtyards; the stench of stale urine and excrement in the alleys, for there was no sewage system and people used open latrines; the smell of horse manure, of baking bread, of aromatic spices, of sickly sweets being fried in confectioners' shops.

We rented a house in the residential area to the north of the city. The air was cleaner, and close by there were green fields of clover, a canal and quiet villages. Our landlord lived next door. Once his wife came through the gate that connected the two houses; half-hidden by a voluminous veil, she knocked timidly at our back door. I had often caught sight of her when she came to milk the cow that lived in our field, but we had hardly spoken. I had no private room for entertaining women and sensed her acute anxiety that at any moment my husband might appear, so I took her into the kitchen where I carried on chopping onions and tried to chat with her. After a moment she mumbled an excuse and retreated. Only later did I realise that by not offering her a place to sit down I had disobeyed the first rule of hospitality. Somehow it had hardly dawned on me that she had come on a social visit!

There were also awkward meetings with a woman who came to collect our washing. She used to stand nervously at our gate, afraid that a man might see her with the front panel of her veil thrown back so that she could talk. I should have asked her in, but knew no better.

Herati women were strange and curious to me then. I felt uncomfortable with them and did not go out to meet them. When we were invited to Herati houses I sat and ate with the men, nourished and refreshed by unseen hands. Trays of food and tea were carried in by men and children; the women remained out of sight. On our arrival at a house the men would call to them, '*kas nabasheh!*' – 'let no one be around!' – as was customary when bringing strange men to the house.

Guest rooms were always sited near the front door, and did not overlook the courtyard where women sat and worked or relaxed. These spotless rooms were used only for entertaining. Usually the walls were decorated with religious posters, embroidered wall hangings or framed photographs of men in formal poses. Often a high shelf would run round the room, where beautiful red or blue flower-painted Russian-style bowls or teapots were kept out of reach of the children. We would sit on the floor on narrow cotton-stuffed mattresses, our backs and arms supported by huge cushions or long bolsters which were covered with immaculately laundered embroidered slips.

Towards the end of a visit our host might suggest that I go into another room to meet the women, who wanted to see me. Only then did they have the leisure to sit and drink tea with me, since they had been working for us behind the scenes. I used to follow my host into the courtyard and enter a more modest family room, where the curtain hanging over the door would be grubby, the floor coverings of striped woven cotton faded and worn, and the walls finger-marked and scratched. Mattresses and cushions would be old and covered with serviceable cloth, not the velvets or delicate embroideries reserved for guests.

Taking me to visit their women, my hosts often visibly relaxed and stayed a while in the family room, laughing and joking. They would indicate their mothers, wives, sisters and sisters-in-law and pick up children and cuddle them, making a big display of affection. It was refreshing after the long hours of relative formality.

In this way I cut through the curtain of purdah, no longer an honorary male visitor. Nevertheless I found these early encounters with the women exhausting and even humiliating, as I was inevitably bombarded with questions and exposed to a mixture of delight, admiration and ridicule.

'Do look! How beautiful her skin is – so white! Are all your people fair like this?' they would ask. Light skin was a mark of beauty; dark skin was associated with villagers, nomads and labourers.

'What beautiful hands! How white and soft!' they exclaimed enviously. 'Just look at ours – they're ruined.'

They held out their hands, which were blackened and rough from scouring sooty pans and from the constant use of coarse soap. I heard them say that I did not work, but used machines, which made me feel undermined, as though housework accorded virtue and I was idle and ignorant.

Often they wanted to lift my dress and examine other parts of me. Did I wear pants? – look, they had pants beneath their loose trousers! They showed me, giggling. Underclothes were a new thing with them. Could they see my bra? Did we all wear bras? Mostly their breasts hung loosely beneath their dresses and younger women were constantly pulling them out to suckle. Nowadays new brides were supplied with bras from Iran or Kabul, heavily stitched and moulded to shape breasts into two pointed cones.

'Just look at that cloth!' they said incredulously to one another, fingering my coarse denim jeans with evident distaste.

I looked down at the faded and worn cloth, quite unable to explain why this should be regarded as fashionable at home. Their clothes were light and pretty, patterned with flowers and resplendent with colour. They wore shimmering brocades and glittering metallic fabrics: loosely waisted dresses over silky white trousers which had a deep border of lace. Often the trousers were slightly translucent, so that the line of a woman's legs showed against the light as she stood in a doorway. Even at home they took special care to cover their heads and wore a *qadifeh*, a long chiffon scarf edged with lace. Their hair was invariably long and plaited tidily beneath their scarves.

'Don't you have any gold?' they asked pityingly, casting implicit disapproval upon my husband. They all wore ear-rings of gold or amethyst and were adorned with necklaces, lockets, bangles and rings. Beside them I felt dowdy.

'Have you no children?' was always one of their first questions, one which I grew to expect and hate. I wanted children, but circumstances, not least the fact of living so far from home, had forced me to delay. Sometimes, seeing my age and childlessness, they would ask how long I had been married, and occasionally they even wondered whether John and I had learned to make love!

'I take pills,' I used to explain.

They were all deeply interested in birth control. I never met a Herati woman without having to answer questions about it. Many older women thought it was sinful: having babies was God's business and we should not interfere. They urged me to stop taking pills so I would get pregnant. Others, worn out from bearing and bringing up children, begged for information. They said they would try any medicine to prevent getting pregnant. They were all amazed that I should have reached my mid-twenties and not had a child, and that I should use contraception before having any children.

'Do you want to wait until you're thirty?' asked one woman incredulously, making me feel very embarrassed. Thirty! By that time a Herati woman would have grown-up sons and daughters. Children brought dignity and status: they could not understand why one should want to delay. In Herat girls married young, often as early as fourteen and usually by about eighteen, and they began producing children immediately. I felt awkward and ignorant beside these teenage mothers, having very little experience of babies myself. I found an answer which seemed to satisfy their own terms of reference, explaining that I was far from my mother and had no one who could help me. I knew that they extended enormous support to new mothers and would pity my plight as a traveller.

Often the women tired me. In addition to their avid curiosity they had a marked tendency to moan and grumble. Complaints focused around two related issues: sickness and the restrictions imposed by their seclusion. They complained of backaches, lack of energy and many other ailments, and said that sometimes their husbands would not let them go to a doctor. Occasionally they hoped I had medicine that might help, but I had no skill in prescribing cures and had to disappoint them. I could offer only sympathy, and sometimes even that wore thin.

Some women complained specifically about their seclusion, which they called *qeit*: 'confinement', 'imprisonment'.

'My husband's mean. He won't let me go anywhere,' they would say. 'Some husbands are all right; their wives can come and go as they please. Mine won't even let me visit my mother. I get sick of staying here all the time.'

I began to understand that purdah was not simply about being segregated and veiled; it meant that men had complete control over the movements of their women. The purpose of purdah was to protect women's honour, and thus the good name of the family, and it gave men ultimate power.

Ironically, many women also complained about their children, even though they chided my childlessness in the same breath. They said they felt worn down by the burden and responsibilities of motherhood, and that they could no longer think straight because their children were so mischievous and troublesome.

Often I came away from the women weary and confused, hurt by their ridicule and tired by their questions. I disliked being an object of curiosity, little understood as a person in my own right. It took some time for our differences to be smoothed out and for personal friendships to develop.

We spent two separate years in Herat, with a shorter visit in between. In 1976, before the beginning of our final year there, I made a decision to withdraw from public life and explore the world of Herati women, as by then I had become sufficiently attuned to make some close friendships. Although men treated me with respect and courtesy, I began to feel self-conscious and out of place in their company. I was attracted to the warmth and friendship the women offered and curious to discover their hidden world.

With some reluctance I abandoned my study of miniature painting because it kept me isolated at home or in the company of men at my teacher's studio. Instead I took up embroidery, a woman's art whose beautiful designs were related to the patterns in miniature painting. Having become increasingly interested in ethnomusicology, I also realised that I could make an invaluable contribution to John's work if I undertook my own complementary study of women's music, which was completely inaccessible to him. I knew that performance was an extremely useful research tool, and so decided to learn to sing women's songs as well as to research and write about Herati women.

What adaptations did I have to make? I could no longer sit on the fence: I had opted for the women's world and made a positive choice to be where they were. This meant accepting some of the limitations of purdah. There was no point in feeling outraged by customs such as veiling, as this would have emphasised our differences rather than brought us closer. When a friend suggested that I wear a *chador* I took that step 'to see what it was like', without questioning the morality of the practice. Wearing a veil in public initiated an important and subtle change in me, cultivating an aura of modesty and self-containment. It masked my foreignness, enabling me to join many women's outings where I would otherwise have attracted undue attention, and it brought a welcome privacy. It was also fascinating and salutary to discover that being invisible is addictive.

Purdah means 'curtain', and Moslem women live behind veils, walls and curtained doors. Many Herati compounds even have a small wall just inside the courtyard so that the family are screened from view when people come to the front door. The custom of veiling and secluding women has become a strongly reinforced Moslem cultural pattern, although there is in fact no statement in the Holy Koran explicitly requiring that women be kept hidden from public view, only an injunction for modesty of dress. Interpretations of purdah vary considerably within different societies. The *burqa* is an urban veil, used in Afghanistan, Pakistan and north India, and it is one of the most extreme forms of veiling as it brings total public anonymity. Nomads and village women wear veils similar to the Iranian *chador*, and leave their faces exposed.

Of course my own purdah was by no means complete. I did not hide my face from men; my husband placed no restrictions upon my movements; I talked freely to men in the various households I visited, as an honorary sister or daughter, and I received men who visited our house (although they would never come in unless John was at home). But gradually I ceased attending men's public gatherings, choosing instead to experience life from the women's point of view.

There were many things to learn. All my social communication with Afghan women was conducted in Persian; in fact I knew very few Heratis who spoke English. I had to learn to greet and thank people gracefully and to make speeches of goodwill. I had to become aware of ranking, to be careful about where I chose to sit and how I entered or left a room. The elaborate Afghan code of manners was common to men and women, but women were less able to make allowances for me. It is important to stress the degree of convention that governed people's behaviour. Heratis care deeply about what other people think or what would earn disapproval, so I had to be sensitive to their constraints.

Through becoming attuned to Heratis, I experienced unexpected changes in my own way of thinking. It became instinctive to avert the evil eye when I praised or admired something, just as we 'touch wood' when making a dangerously confident statement, and I learned never to tempt fate by speaking of the future without the qualifying phrase '*enshallah*' – 'God-willing'. I also found myself speaking quite naturally about God, who was constantly remembered in people's talk, an unseen force who sometimes took over quite dramatically, but who 'knew best'. I was cut down to size, a mere human. How could I pretend to rule my own destiny?

Learning to perform Herati music was enjoyable and challenging. In general the women play only one instrument, the *daireh*, a frame drum like a tambourine with bells and rings fixed inside the rim, used to lay down rhythms for dancing or to accompany singing. Herati voice production is also very different from our own, with a strained nasal quality. The vocal line is free and ornamented and texts are improvised from a bank of well-known quatrains. Aside from technical difficulties, there were also social pitfalls in conducting music research; the women's code of modesty placed constraints upon where and when music could be played.

Gradually I came to appreciate the strength and self-sufficiency of Herati women, and I began to see how arrogant and ill-informed our Western view of Moslem women is. What exactly is our stereotype? Women held in subjugation and imprisonment, ashamed to show their bodies; women treated as chattels, given in exchange for so many camels; women kept deliberately backward and subservient, walking ten paces behind their husbands, incapable of independent thought or decision; women in harems, scantily dressed, given up to the pleasure of indolent sultans. These ill-assorted images of exploitation and oppression are in reality only half-truths, based upon facts that have been jumbled and poorly understood. Western cameos of Moslem women in yashmaks toiling through Harrods had as little to do with Herati women as the colourful hippies trailing through Herat had to do with the sober reality of London's weary commuters dozing in a packed, grimy British Railways train.

I set out on my study with certain questions. How radically did women's beliefs and customs differ from men's? What freedom and power, if any, did women have, and what limitations were placed upon them? How did they feel about their own seclusion? More specifically, what outlets existed for their creativity – singing, dancing, story-telling, embroidery – and what was the context of these activities? In this book these issues are explored in detail. Generally women accepted the segregation of the sexes and their roles, but protested against gross limitations of their freedom. Some were strong and lucky enough to determine their own lives and social relationships, but others were less fortunate, suffering and struggling against enormous odds. There were certainly areas in which women's talents were buried, and the very confined nature of women's experience bred ignorance. Even so it is worth bearing in mind that men also lived very circumscribed and conventional lives, bowing to established authority, adhering to traditional values, and in most cases following in their fathers' professions.

What of recent events in Afghanistan? People often ask me how things have changed for Afghan women since the Soviet invasion. The Soviet-backed government claims to have instituted sweeping reforms in women's rights, but the dramatic changes they have promised have simply not materialised. On the contrary, the gradual process of emancipation that occurred during the past century has been disrupted by the total upheaval of war. Afghan men and women now live with the pressing daily concerns of economic shortages, bombardments, harass-ment by soldiers or secret police, curfews and a climate of hatred and fear, not to speak of the destruction of whole villages and agricultural areas. The issue of women's rights has been superseded by a far more immediate struggle for liberation, or relegated to a symbolic battle of ideologies. More than ever, Afghan women find themselves in the grip of powerful patriarchal forces, whether those of fundamentalist Islam or of a ruthless colonising power.

None the less, attitudes and customs change slowly, and there are distinct areas in which women still have power and responsibility. I found that they were at the heart of the kinship network that forms the basis of communal relationships, choosing brides for their sons and fostering new links that were useful to the whole family. Afghan women have considerable status as mothers. Men love and respect their mothers and listen to their advice. It is very different from the West, where women are made to feel insignificant if they cannot compensate for being simply 'mothers'. In Afghanistan once a woman has given birth she is then usually called by the more prestigious title 'Mother of . . .'

Many Western people pity Moslem women without real understanding, assuming the picture is completely black. In fact Afghan women are spared the shock and isolation so often experienced by Western mothers, who suddenly have to learn a new way of life, finding themselves marooned at home, unable to rest for the demands of toddlers, nappies, telephones, school schedules and evening meals. The extended Afghan family is very supportive, and women automatically help one another and share burdens.

Before the war Afghan women were free to grow old without anxiety, secure in the knowledge that they would be cared for by younger members of the family. Old age brings status and dignity, not disgust and ridicule. The elderly had no fear of being jettisoned in an old people's home, washed and fed by the capable hands of strangers and then propped up in front of a television. Old women rule their families, supervising the work of the younger women, giving advice, listening to the news of visitors and rocking babies. They are not unwanted or redundant. Women age naturally, under no pressure from the media to strive to be eternally youthful and slender.

In Afghanistan I also discovered that it is precious to have some privacy from men, an advantage which perhaps is hard to appreciate unless you have experienced it! Afghan women have a right to a social and cultural life of their own, and this is enjoyable. Western feminists have begun to make a forum for women to express themselves without domination by men – Greenham Common is a perfect example – but these new separatist creations tend to be exclusive; certainly they are very different in character from women's societies which have evolved traditionally. All the same, the communal spirit, the camp fires and the singing at Greenham struck an emotional chord that reminded me of Afghanistan.

Even before the war, life was not easy for many Afghan women, and the balance of power is still heavily weighted against them. The laws of marriage, divorce and inheritance continue to discriminate against them. Most women's lives are circumscribed within the domestic sphere. The hard work of nurturing children is left entirely in their control, and every mother knows how draining this is even when the load is shared. The various types of veil are cumbersome and restrictive to wear, and men have the final word as regards freedom of movement. Much suffering stems from poverty and ignorance, and now the war has given women an even deeper sense of vulnerability and powerlessness against oppressive outside forces.

I had originally planned to write generally about women, but later, long after I had left Afghanistan, I decided to focus upon three particular friends, each of whom had played a vital role in my understanding and experience of Herat. Although they were from dissimilar backgrounds, I feel they complement one another, and I also recognise that they represent different aspects of my own search for a personal identity in a foreign land.

Mariam satisfied my interest in the intricate social rules of family life and in the rituals and beliefs of Shiah Islam. She was a steadying influence, helping me to see most clearly how women functioned and exercised power within the community. Our friendship stemmed originally from a close relationship with her family. I first knew her father and brothers, who were wonderful musicians, and then discovered that the women were humorous, welcoming and affectionate. I enjoyed visiting their house and just feeling part of the family. Mariam understood my interest in the women; she included me in family outings and explained events to me as they took place.

Mother of Nebi provided a darker attraction. She had an unusual and painful history, having suffered a serious illness caused by spirit possession which had eventually been cured by a religious healer. She later became his disciple and practised as a diviner helping women who came to her with problems. Originally villagers, her clan had migrated to the city during the 1960s and had succeeded in improving their material circumstances. In our final year we lived next door to Mother of Nebi and I became a frequent visitor. She lived in strict seclusion, and in her I saw how damaging the psychological effects of purdah could be on women.

Shirin was my music teacher. Although I knew her for a much shorter time than either Mariam or Mother of Nebi, we became very close. (Mother of Nebi used her title as a mother according to custom, whereas Mariam still used her given name within the family and Shirin kept hers as a professional singer.) Of all three friends, Shirin had perhaps the most profound effect upon me, as she developed my career in singing. She came from a notorious clan known as the Minstrels, musicians and rivals to Mariam's family. Becoming her pupil was a daring act, one that could have been perpetrated only by an outsider such as myself. No Herati woman could have gone to her house for lessons: the Minstrels' work as entertainers at weddings so offended against the rules of propriety that they were regarded as loose women. When I accompanied Shirin to weddings as a member of her band, my own status in Herat was eventually threatened.

I do not claim that these three women provide a cross-section of Herati womanhood, let alone Afghan womanhood. Their stories, particularly those of Mother of Nebi and Shirin, are far too idiosyncratic. Nor should Herat be taken as a microcosm of Afghan culture. Afghanistan encompasses many ethnic and language groups, villagers and nomads as well as city-dwellers. Although Herat was a major Afghan city, whose population in 1976 was around a quarter of a million, it was poorly understood by other Afghans. Situated far from the capital, and until recently linked to other parts of the country only by road, Herat is often viewed as an extension of Iran, almost as another land. While the majority of Afghans are orthodox Sunni Moslems, Herat had a prosperous minority of Shiahs (the sect most strongly represented in Iran; since the war many of them have taken refuge there), and this was another reason for viewing Herat as 'different', if not alien.

Even within Herat there was a great diversity of culture, and there were communities with which I had little or no contact. Not all types of female society are described in this book: for instance, at the spearhead of change there was an interesting group of emancipated young female schoolteachers, almost the only women working in the public sector. They were not secluded and preferred to pursue their careers unmarried and unencumbered. However, my own interest focused upon traditional culture, specifically music, and this drew me to the poorer, disadvantaged sections of society.

My three friends had certain factors in common. All had a connection with music: Mariam's and Shirin's families were hereditary professionals and Mother of Nebi was a gifted amateur. All three were married to orphans, which meant that they did not have to live under the thumb of a mother-in-law. Women who married orphans were able to stay in their own homes, among people who cared for them. My friends were not overshadowed by more senior women and became heads of their own households at a relatively young age. Although they differed greatly in personality and background they were, in important and basic essentials, like almost all Afghan women: they were married, they were mothers and they had faith in Islam.

In Afghanistan all women and men know the *atan*, a group dance performed at weddings and on national days. The dancers form a circle and move in an anti-clockwise direction, bending their bodies and inclining to the centre to clap on the main beat, then turning outwards and holding a graceful pose, their arms delicately raised. Step, close, step, close . . . They dance, bending inwards to clap and then leaning outwards, arms aloft, wrists loose and heads proud.

I wish I could bring my three friends to dance together – as they never did in real life – and celebrate the beginning of their stories. I imagine myself drumming for them, playing joyfully on the *daireh*. We are together in Herat, in a courtyard, our bare feet on the warm brick floor, the bright sun casting slanting shadows on the side of some house. We are surrounded by women, girls and children all eagerly clapping the syncopated rhythm of the dance. It is a painful dream because since the war I have lost contact with all three women. I do not know where they are or whether they are alive or dead, and I miss them with all my heart.

Each woman is graceful, but perhaps the most beautiful is Mariam, with her slanting eyes and slender waist. I see her dancing with utmost concentration, self-aware, fluent and delicate. I see Mother of Nebi behind her, delighted at joining in. She is a small woman, swinging her plaits and dancing with great energy, swishing her dress from side to side. She dips to the centre and stamps her feet, wanting to steal attention from the others. I see my beloved Shirin, fat, self-confident and laughing. She moves lightly despite her weight, encouraging the girls to clap louder, whipping up enthusiasm. She dances effortlessly, flicking her hands coquettishly, her brown eyes twinkling.

I play faster and faster, with gathering intensity, and the dancers follow my beat. In my dream we are perfectly synchronised: I drum and they dance, clapping together at the centre. They point down to the earth and up to the sky. Their arms become the wings of birds; their transparent white scarves are feathers ruffling in the wind. We become one in the dance.

PART ONE

Mariam

1
First Meeting

Mariam's father, Latif Khan, was a hereditary musician and the established authority on classical music in Herat. All other musicians paid him respect and deferred to his knowledge and experience in music. Naturally he was a key informant in my husband's research, and it was through him that I came to meet Mariam and the women of the family.

I remember well my first sight of him, watching him enter a crowded

Ramadan concert room. He was in his early sixties, a handsome, striking man; erect, dignified and urbane, dressed in a fine silk turban and flowing striped *chapan* coat. Heads turned as he made his way to the front of the audience, greeting friends as he passed, and from the stage the singer pressed his hand to his heart and bowed to him as he sang. Later, encountering him by chance in the bazaar, I felt the bright conjunction of his fame and my own power to draw curious crowds: people stared as we exchanged greetings, and he held my hand for a long time, enjoying the experience of being seen in public with me.

I first met Mariam early in March 1974, when we were invited to a musical evening at her father's house. I had seen Latif Khan and his sons at various public events, but had not yet visited them at home. They lived in a predominantly Shiah neighbourhood in the old city, not far from the bazaar. The majority of the population of the city belonged to the orthodox Sunni sect and ranged from wealthy and powerful families to poor labourers, but there was also a strong minority of Shiah Moslems, who were affluent shopkeepers, business men or artisans.

The schism between the Sunni and Shiah sects dates from the first century of Islam when there was a struggle over the succession to the Prophet Mohammad. The Shiah religion has a Messianic doctrine and focuses strongly upon the mourning of martyrs who fell at the crucial battle of Karbala. In the past there had been sectarian disharmony in Herat city and many Sunnis still held misconceptions about Shiahs and openly disliked them. As a musician and a Shiah, Latif Khan's position in the community was doubly sensitive. Religious prejudice against music persisted: some *mullah*s taught that music was the work of the devil and that it distracted people from prayer and correct living. Proud and dignified as he was, Latif Khan knew well that people could still stab him in the back and abuse him for his Shiah faith or for his 'unclean' profession.

As this was our first visit to the house, we found Karim, Latif's son, waiting at the bottom of the alley, ready to show us the way. I already knew him quite well and loved his playing of the *rubab*, the wonderfully resonant Afghan short-necked lute. He led me straight across the courtyard to meet his mother and sisters, leaving his youngest brother, Hossein, to escort John upstairs to the guest room. Mother of Karim rose to greet me, apologising for the humble family room with a sweep of her hand, sighing as she surveyed its scratched walls and thin cotton carpet, but then she began talking and joking as if our surroundings really did not matter. She was small, cheerful and stooping, and very soon her relaxed manner put me at ease. Karim joined in our conversation, obviously delighted to have brought us together.

For some time Mariam was eclipsed by other members of her family;

by virtue of her role as a daughter she remained silent and in the shadows. Her father shone out, an important and famous man. Karim attracted me with his friendly jokes and his musical brilliance. Mother of Karim was humorous and delightful, and lacked the tendency to complain or criticise that had put me off other Herati women. I noticed the soft features and dark eyes of the girls, who sat quietly, not presuming to interrupt, and I saw the dirt on their clothes and hard calluses from housework on their hands. But my impressions were fleeting, and at that first meeting Mariam was just a face, merely one of several daughters; she was hardly a distinct person at all.

The guest room was on the first floor, and visitors were escorted upstairs by one of the sons: Karim, Zahir or Hossein. Apart from me, they were all men. Politely they ushered one another to their places on the mattresses that lined the room, urging each other to sit 'up' away from the door. Family friends and relatives insisted on taking inferior places, making important patrons or strangers such as ourselves sit in places of honour, according to the hierarchy of the occasion. Latif Khan greeted us all one by one, solicitously asking after our health. This exchange of *hawalporsi* – 'asking health' – always replaced conversation during the initial stage of a social encounter, and involved much formalised murmuring of polite questions and responses. When there was a lull between the arrivals of new parties of guests there were long relaxed silences, broken only by quiet whispering. I could not help comparing this gradual social interaction with our Western customs, where we speak for the sake of making conversation, and 'circulate' so as to avoid talking to anyone for too long, and where one is in danger of being stranded in a noisy crowd. Here we sat peacefully, getting used to one another, and not having to rack our brains for something to say.

Eventually, when all thirty or so of us were assembled, Zahir brought round the long-spouted metal ewer to wash our hands before eating, pouring warm water and offering the soap and towel with practised skill. Then an enormous plastic cloth was laid out and spread with a feast of steaming rice, long flat loaves of bread, bowls of lamb stew and delicious spinach with black-eyed beans. We gathered round and ate.

Afterwards, the guests relaxed against their cushions, chatting and drinking tea while the musicians began to tune their instruments. Latif Khan was to sing, accompanying himself on the portable Indian harmonium, Karim played *rubab*, and Zahir played *tabla*, the Indian drum pair. They were joined by Nader, who played the local lute (*dutar*) and was not part of the family.

Latif Khan amused a small group of guests with an anecdote while playing a long tuning note on his harmonium, pumping continuously with his left hand. Karim cocked his head to his *rubab*, adjusting each peg with the confident precision of a true professional, oblivious of other noises around him. Then, satisfied, he closed his eyes and began playing melodic phrases with the unmistakable enjoyment of a musician who is at one with his instrument and his music. His father began to play introductory improvisations on the harmonium, complementing Karim's fast *rubab* patterns, and gradually the others joined in, testing and retuning until they were all ready. Latif Khan fixed his eyes upon his audience, like a conjuror about to perform a trick, and began to sing. '*Wah wah!*' sighed his listeners, drinking in the beauty of the music and poetry, shaking their heads in appreciation.

Later I became all too conscious of the divisions that existed within the family, but that night father and sons played together harmoniously, providing me with an almost mythological image of unity through music. My first impressions of the family were untinged by the sadness of closer knowledge, and they are still very precious memories.

Towards midnight the instruments were packed away. The guests remained in their places, chatting contentedly, unwilling to break the circle of conviviality. Hossein took me downstairs to see his mother, lighting our way with a paraffin lamp. It had begun to pour with rain. I entered their kitchen, which opened on to the courtyard, brushing raindrops from my hair and, still elated by the music, excitedly thanked them for a wonderful evening. Mother of Karim agreed that the music had been '*por jush*' – 'boiling', 'exciting' – and told me that they had listened to some of it from the passage. Seeing scoured pans and piles of crockery on the floor, I hastened to praise their food, remembering their hours of slaving for our enjoyment. Water began to hiss from a large blackened kettle on the farthest of the two fireplaces, and wood burned brightly beneath: even now the women had not finished their work.

Mother of Karim laughingly commented upon my dress, which was very long, modelled on the loose nomad style. It was obviously quite alien to their concepts of fashion and she could not believe that the skirt came right to the ground. Then we heard voices on the stairs and Hossein called me, saying everyone was leaving.

'Come back soon!' said Mother of Karim, holding on to my hand as we parted.

'I'll come and improve my Persian with you!' I suggested, lifting my hem to avoid getting it wet.

'Yes, come and see us again,' she said, and Mariam and her sisters murmured goodbye as Hossein and I disappeared through the curtain of rain that fell across the doorway of their blackened kitchen.

2

Strangers on the Throne

After that, I began to visit the house regularly. The women always greeted me warmly and planted loud kisses on each of my cheeks. We would sit together drinking tea companionably, sometimes joined by one or other of the men, who were pleased that I had become a family visitor.

The women asked me about England. How far away was it? How

could it be so far by road and so close by plane? What were our houses like? What food did we eat? How could we bear to eat potatoes every day and not rice? Was it true we believed in free love? How could a boy and girl choose one another? Was it not better for a mother to choose a bride for her son?

They were lively and curious, yet narrow in their outlook. Like many Heratis they could not read or write and they had not attended secular school. Women seemed to evaluate events according to their own experience and hearsay. They did not read books or newspapers; at that time there was no television in Afghanistan; they did not go to the cinema or theatre; and they only listened to the radio or music cassettes when men played them. Their knowledge and entertainment came from visiting and being visited by other women, and from ritual gatherings, particularly weddings.

Sometimes they invited me to stay for lunch. The men came home to eat and were always served first, sitting apart from the women and children. I would be given a separate tray of food and thoughtfully supplied with a spoon, since I could not eat efficiently with my fingers. Mother of Karim used to urge me to eat up and 'fill my bag', laughing and pointing to my stomach. She gave me a nickname: Khaliteh, a joke name meaning 'bag'.

Gradually I made friends with all the family. Karim and Zahir were followed in age by Fereshteh, the eldest daughter. She had married a musician from Kabul, Mohammad Omar, and they lived separately from Latif Khan, although Fereshteh often visited the house. Mariam was the fourth child, in her mid-twenties and married to Hassan, her orphaned cousin. They lived at the house and had a small daughter, Simin. Next came Hossein and the two unmarried daughters, Parwaneh and Nassimeh. I spent most of my time with Mother of Karim, Mariam and Parwaneh.

I became used to the household tasks that filled the women's days. Sometimes they laboriously picked through a tray piled with uncooked rice, patiently cleaning out the unwanted husks and stones. I enjoyed helping, and would sit opposite Mariam or Parwaneh methodically sifting the grains through my fingers. They used to protest that guests should not work, laughing at the impropriety of my labours, but they were glad to let me feel at home.

Since they catered for such large numbers, cooking was a major production, a slow sociable process. They worked outside in the courtyard, drawing water from the well, cutting up meat and vegetables, sifting out the chaff from split beans. They kept a few hens, which grubbed around in the dust, and a watch-dog which was chained during the day and let off at night. In the summer they worked in shady corners, and in winter they sought the sun. People came and went and neighbours called and shared a smoke on the water-pipe. The pace of their lives was leisurely and unhurried.

During that summer I became closer to Mariam, and I began to appreciate her intelligence and willingness to talk seriously. Mother of Karim had a sunny personality and made gatherings amusing and light-hearted, but Mariam had the patience and application I needed to help me understand the women's world. I had already realised that the process of marriage was crucial to women's culture; firstly because its organisation and rituals were in the hands of women, and secondly because it affected young girls at the beginning of their maturity and formed the entire basis of their future lives. I enlisted Mariam's help in explaining the exact details of the marriage procedure.

I knew that the preferred marriage was between first cousins (particularly the children of two brothers, just like Mariam and Hassan themselves), and that cousins were often betrothed as children or even as babies. Cousin marriage was favoured because it strengthened kinship links and kept wealth within the family. Otherwise, it was the duty of a prospective bridegroom's mother to find a suitable girl and to make full enquiries about her family before setting out on a proposal.

'When a mother is convinced that the girl is right and that she has a good chance of a successful proposal, she calls on the senior women of her own family and together they go and visit the bride's house,' Mariam explained. She described everything in great detail, enumerating the family members who would make up the party and what would be said and done on each successive visit. We sat together in the doorway that overlooked the courtyard and I took notes. We laughed about some of the things she told me, such as the way the bridegroom's mother would delicately make it clear why she has come by saying she was 'thirsty' and would like a glass of water. Mariam said it took several visits before a bride's parents would agree to proceed with the wedding: no daughter would be given too hastily, and there were often prolonged negotiations concerning the payment of the bridewealth – a substantial sum of money paid by the bridegroom to the father of the bride in recompense for the loss of a member of the family. After the marriage had been agreed a preliminary contract would be signed, and the bride's family would send the groom a symbolic gift of acceptance called the 'needle and thread'. Later there would be the 'sweet-eating', the formal engagement party, followed by the religious wedding, or *nekah*, and the final celebrations, the *arusi*, during which the bride was taken to her new home.

Mariam's account was fascinating and rich in detail, describing the rituals and exchanges of gifts with great care, and it took several long visits to complete. She opened the trunk tucked behind the alcove curtain where she kept her possessions, and showed me her red brocade wedding dress and the triangular pieces of velvet which, on the eve of her wedding, had bound henna on to her feet and hands to dye them deep orange-red.

People from traditional cultures usually feel proud of the rituals and customs that give their ceremonies interest and life, and after Mariam's vivid description I felt embarrassed to admit that such matters were treated so perfunctorily in my own country. Even the most elaborate English wedding would seem simple and dull by comparison. To make matters worse I had personally been married in a registry office with only two witnesses: no one had begged for my hand; my father had not given me away; I had no engagement ring or gold jewellery apart from a wedding ring I had ceased to wear, and I had no dowry or battery of wedding presents. When Mariam asked about English wedding customs I was reduced to generalisations about what other people did – having their engagement announced in the newspaper, being showered with confetti and driving away in a car festooned with lavatory paper and old boots, or wearing a white dress and walking up the aisle to the Wedding March. It seemed inconsistent to be delighted with her account and yet to have rejected our own traditional customs.

Karim's engagement came as a complete surprise to me. I had no inkling that negotiations were taking place, but Mariam had told me that while a marriage was under consideration people kept it quiet for fear of public humiliation if things went wrong. One day I found two girls sitting with Mother of Karim, but she did not explain that she had chosen the elder, Tayereh, to become Karim's wife. They were sitting inside because some workmen had begun building an extension to the house.

'I'm very inconvenienced right now,' said Mother of Karim, jerking her head in the direction of the men. 'We can't sit out in the courtyard while they're here. We have to stay well inside, with our "prayer veils" close at hand.' Heratis used the Iranian *chador* as a veil in all-women gatherings or as a covering for ritual prayer. 'We have to cook so much meat and rice!' she added. 'It's our custom to feed our workmen, and we don't want to appear mean.'

Latif Khan had a spacious house with rooms arranged around a large courtyard. In addition to the existing rooms on the north side, there would now be an extension with two new south-facing rooms on the ground floor, divided by a sunny verandah, and two rooms on the first floor adjoining the existing guest room and connected by a balcony.

Two separate sets of steps led to the first-floor rooms and to the flat roof where Karim kept his pigeons, and from there one could see into the neighbouring courtyards, across the city roof-tops and out to the distant mountains that enclosed the valley. Although the women spent so much time at home, they were usually out in the open, but now they had to cover themselves with their prayer-veils each time they crossed the compound.

While we were chatting, Karim entered the courtyard, but saw that his mother had visitors and did not come near. Tayereh let out a squeak of panic and threw her veil right over her head, crouching under it like a stalked animal in hiding. I was quite astonished at her reaction, but after she had left Karim playfully intimated that they were engaged, and I realised why she was so afraid of being seen.

'Will she be good for me?' he asked, smiling, enjoying my surprise and delight at his news. 'Is she pretty?'

'She's beautiful,' I said, casting my mind back to the girl, whom I guessed to be about eighteen. She had a soft feminine body and dark wavy hair; her front teeth were capped with gold, which flashed when she smiled, and she had dimples in her cheeks. 'Your mother chose well,' I assured him.

Mariam told me that although Tayereh's father had now given his word of consent, the 'needle and thread' had not been sent to Karim. She said that Tayereh's mother had come to their house to see if it was acceptable, and that they had shown her the building work and explained that Karim and Tayereh would have two upstairs rooms to themselves.

'They're quite poor, you see,' she said softly. 'They know Tayereh will be better off with us. When they have sent the "needle and thread" our hearts will be at rest.'

I also discovered, from Parwaneh, that Tayereh had already been married: she had been a second wife to an old man who had recently died. I guessed that it had been difficult for Mother of Karim to find a family prepared to give their daughter to a musician. Tayereh provided a neat solution, as widows were quickly found new husbands and lower bridewealths were given for them. In deference to Karim, Tayereh's past marriage was never openly mentioned.

The following week we were invited to the engagement party and presentation of the 'needle and thread'. Until the actual wedding all celebrations would take place at the bride's house, so we were escorted to Tayereh's home, deep in the heart of the old city. I went inside, and John was taken to a neighbouring house where a small party of men was being entertained.

Hossein led me across a small courtyard and up some steep steps to the room where the women were celebrating. I had recently been ill and felt light-headed and feverish, and the crush of people and bustle of noise and colour quite took my breath away. Women and children pressed on me from all sides, dressed in the most vivid and sparkling clothes. The din of voices and laughter half drowned the singing and drumming of the musicians in one corner. Hossein lingered at my side, enjoying the excitement. Although he was still young enough to be admitted among the women, he clearly responded to their allure.

They sat me near an open window overlooking the courtyard, but there was very little breeze and the room was sweltering. I recognised Mariam, Fereshteh and their mother, all in splendid new dresses. Parwaneh joined me, trying to explain who everybody was, but I was too dazed to take much in. Tayereh, the bride, sat against the far wall. She looked tense and withdrawn and clutched a white handbag, which looked odd and out of place as Herati women did not as a rule carry handbags. Her breasts jutted out beneath her colourful dress like two mountain peaks, and I guessed that her bra had been one of the many gifts of clothes bought for her by Mother of Karim. I felt for her, sensing her dread at this first meeting with her new husband. I did not know that her silent passivity was the correct behaviour for a bride, and that she was not expected to smile and look around her, but to remain serious.

The women musicians sat by the door, partly obscured by a crowd of eager girls. One played harmonium, another *tabla* drums, and a third the *daireh*. I sipped my tea and watched them with fascination, wondering if they were really prostitutes, as was widely rumoured. Women were taking it in turns to dance. Fereshteh was performing in a small space in the centre of the floor, her arms raised, slightly shading her face. Her lips were parted and she looked dream-like, as if in a trance, a figure in shimmering silver. Then Mother of Karim danced, as was fitting for the mother of the bridegroom. She moved gently, gracefully framing her face with a scarf held behind her head. I found it strange to watch a woman of her age dancing alone, and was touched by the playful, mischievous expression on her face.

When I had finished drinking tea, the girls immediately begged me to dance, dragging me to my feet. I protested strongly, saying I had been ill, but felt obliged to dance for them. I did my best and then reeled to the floor, dizzy from the effort and from the clapping and the driving rhythm of the drums.

Some of the women began to get Tayereh ready in another room. Her white handbag was in fact a vanity case filled with make-up and toiletries. They asked me to make her up, seeing that I was familiar with the tubes of foundation cream, eye-shadow and eye-liner. She trembled as I applied beige cream all over her face. Her solemnity was no act; she was very apprehensive. The women urged me to paint her lips and eyes very boldly: brides were meant to look artificial like dolls; in fact 'bride' and 'doll' share the word *arus*.

The call came up that the men were entering the courtyard, so we hurriedly left Tayereh alone in the room, completely covered with a white veil. Through the window I saw four or five men walk up the steps to her room. What was happening? I began to suspect that this was more than a preliminary betrothal. No one explained at the time but I discovered later that this was the *nekah*, the religious marriage, and the men had come to witness and ratify the wedding vows. Often a bride did not attend her own *nekah*, but had her father act as her *wakil* or spokesman.

The men left and down in the courtyard a *takht* or 'throne' of cushions was prepared for the bridal couple. In front of it the gifts that Karim had brought for Tayereh were laid out for inspection by the guests. Women began crowding around, wanting to get a good view of the rituals that were about to take place.

'They're coming! They're coming!' the cry went up as the men re-entered the compound. Latif Khan, leading Karim by the hand and followed by several others, mounted the steps to Tayereh's room and minutes later emerged again, preceded by the musicians singing wedding verses and drumming loudly on the *daireh*s. These girls faced the men quite brazenly, freshly made-up and singing at the top of their voices, whereas many of the guests shielded their faces with veils.

Down the steps they came, hands linked like a chain: Latif Khan, proud and confident; Karim, solemn and unfamiliar in a Western suit; Tayereh, wearing a white veil fanning out around her head, her face utterly transformed by the bold make-up. I was afraid that she might trip in her white high-heeled shoes. The women craned forward, eager for their first sight of the new couple, who took their places on the magnificent throne of deep red velvet. The musicians stood drumming in front of them, singing to the bride that she should have no fear:

> *Bride, don't put your head on your knee and cry bitterly*
> *All this is God's wish, thanks be to God!*
> *O Mohammad, Prophet of God, solve our problems;*
> *Make difficult things easy for everyone!*

One of the musicians displayed the gifts, calling out each item as she held it up to the crowd, counting out dress lengths, pairs of shoes, clothes for Tayereh to wear in the *hamam* (the public baths), a new *burqa* veil, and even underwear: the basis of a complete new wardrobe.

Tayereh and Karim kept their eyes down. Their hands had separated and lay slackly in their laps. The 'needle and thread' and cakes and sweets were displayed on the ground directly in front of them.

Suddenly it was clear that the party was over. The musicians packed their instruments and women began putting on their veils. People took their leave, kissing Karim's and Tayereh's cheeks and offering them luck and blessings. Then the bridal couple were ushered into another room and the shutters closed solicitously after them. I watched in horror. What were they supposed to do now, alone and in the darkness? Were they expected to consummate the marriage, having just met?

We left, taking the sugared nuts that were distributed at all auspicious occasions. I felt shocked and confused. One image remained with me – Tayereh and Karim, side by side on their throne, nervous and uncommunicating; strangers locked in the most intimate of bonds.

Later I asked Mariam, 'Were they supposed to sleep together when you closed the shutters?'

'No. They just sat together and drank tea!' she laughed. 'After the *nekah* it's not a sin to make love, but it's very bad if a girl gets pregnant before the *arusi*. That was their 'needle and thread', engagement party and *nekah*. Some people have those parties separately.'

The *arusi* was postponed until the spring. Tayereh's mother needed time to assemble the dowry – a complete set of household goods customarily given to the bride by her own family. In the meantime Karim went to visit his wife and spent nights at her house: this 'engagement play' was an accepted period of courtship before the couple set up home together.

Their marriage turned out happily. Over the years I became accustomed to the sight of bridal couples stiffly enthroned together at weddings, and I learned that the impressions they gave were very unreliable indicators of future relationships. Girls who played at looking demure could later become powerful forces within their marriages, and couples who looked well together could later become incompatible. Mariam maintained that goodwill between the families and a similar background were very helpful in promoting successful marriages, and in this Karim and Tayereh were at an advantage. Mother of Karim had chosen well: Tayereh was a good-tempered, tolerant girl and she always seemed cheerful despite Karim's difficult moods and jealous authority over her.

3

Bitter and Sweet

Marriage was by no means the closest emotional bond. In fact husbands and wives spent little time together and had separate interests and social circles. In the Western family the tie between husband and wife is overemphasised – and greatly strained – in comparison with the extended family, where many relationships come into play and where there is more scope for mediation in conflicts. In Herat I found that links between siblings were very strong, although sometimes competitive, and that above all people loved their mothers and regarded them as precious. Unfortunately, the intensity of family relationships sometimes led to quarrels, particularly between men, which could be long and bitter. It would be known that certain people were on bad terms and might refuse to talk or sit together for months or even years.

While Karim was enjoying 'engagement play' with Tayereh, a conflict arose between him and Zahir. The reason was trivial: one day Zahir failed to arrive to play at a wedding engagement, but he maintained that he had not received a message about it. Karim was admonished by the band-leader and so took offence against Zahir. Mariam explained to me that the brothers were avoiding one another and would not eat together. Her mother was at her wits' end trying to effect a reconciliation. Mother of Karim was ill and she wept when she talked about it, both from bodily pain and from grief at seeing her sons quarrel.

I spoke to Karim and Zahir myself, vainly trying to intercede. Karim was angry with me and turned away at the mention of his brother's name, and Zahir shook his head sadly and refused to talk.

'It's no good,' said Mariam. 'Zahir knows Karim won't forgive him. He doesn't want the pain of rejection, otherwise he would have gone to him already.'

Undoubtedly hidden conflicts lay at the root of these fierce displays of ill-feeling. There was professional rivalry between Karim and his father, and the fact that he was newly engaged created jealousy between him and Zahir. It was a difficult period of adjustment for Karim, who was having to forge new relationships with his wife and parents-in-law. Mother of Karim pleaded with him but, much as he loved her, he was set on hostility and would not relent.

In such situations reconciliation was ritualised: the junior person had to approach the senior, no matter who had initiated the conflict. The best opportunity for peace-making was at the two annual religious festivals called Eid, one ending the pilgrimage to Mecca and the other ending the Ramadan fast. At Eid fighting should cease and enemies should embrace.

Later Mariam told me about a time when she and Karim had quarrelled.

'It was because of a little thing I said; he did not speak to me for months. At Eid I went to ask for a reconciliation, but he would not forgive me. He said, "You're not my sister."' Tears sprang into her eyes at the memory of his rebuff. 'I waited until the following Eid and asked him again. By that time Tayereh had come to live with us and she pleaded for me too. That time he agreed and let me kiss his hand.'

It was sad for me to leave Herat on a bitter note. Our year came to an end and I cried uncontrollably when we said goodbye. Mother of Karim was seriously ill and the brothers had not made up their quarrel. My tears were of sympathy for the unhappy household and of sorrow at parting without knowing when I might return.

The following year, 1975, we visited Herat for six weeks during the summer. Experiencing the familiar sights and sounds once more, we felt euphoric as we set foot in the bazaar. By chance the very first person we met was Latif Khan, who stopped us just as we were about to cross the road. As we had corresponded he was not surprised to see us, and we talked excitedly for five or ten minutes before he finally interrupted the flow of our conversation.

'I want to tell you something,' he said seriously. 'We didn't like to tell you in a letter, thinking you'd be upset . . . My wife has died.'

His news took my breath away. For a moment neither John nor I could speak. I could only gasp in disbelief, desperately searching for some phrase of sympathy. Seeing our numb reaction, he gently repeated the news. He touched his unshaven chin, indicating that he was still in mourning.

'The house is empty without her. It's been four months, but our hearts are sick with pain and we can't forget our loss.'

I stood amid the noisy traffic in shocked silence. Fond images of my forthcoming meeting with Mother of Karim flooded my mind, robbed of reality. I realised with horror that I had even forgotten to ask after her health, so completely had I forgotten my manners! I remembered that in their last letter they had mentioned taking her to Kabul, the distant capital, for treatment, a sure sign that her illness had been very serious. Yet I had never once considered that she might die.

'We didn't touch our instruments for forty days,' said Latif Khan, referring to the traditional mourning period. 'After that we had to accept work, but with her gone music gives us no pleasure. Our lives are ruined.'

I visited the house. Seeing me reminded the family of their mother and they cried, feeling their loss anew. Mariam told me that her father had taken Mother of Karim to the hospital in Kabul twice, but they had been unable to cure her. Her pain had been terrible. She had not been able to dance at Karim's wedding, but had lain suffering in another room, and Karim had been miserable at this. They showed me a blurred photograph of Karim garlanded with paper flowers, sitting with his kinsmen at the midnight ceremonies.

The new rooms were finished and he and Tayereh were living upstairs. Mariam had quietly stepped into her mother's place, making everyday decisions, supervising the cooking of meals and taking charge. So much had changed in the space of a few months.

'We still miss our mother very much,' said Parwaneh sadly. 'Now we can only see her in our dreams. We have to wait until night and then hope we might meet her. She can see us and follow us in our lives, but she must be apart.'

Of all the children Karim, the first-born, seemed to have mourned his mother most deeply. He had plunged into abject grief, lacerating his face with his fingernails. Mariam felt her loss equally painfully, but for the sake of the others she took up her new responsibilities, knowing that now she had to fulfil the role of mother.

We embarked upon our second full year of research in Herat in September 1976. We went immediately to visit Latif Khan's house and were invited to lunch the next day so that we could spend time renewing our friendship. The men entertained John upstairs and I stayed in the courtyard with the women, and was delighted to discover that Mariam had recently had another baby, a boy called Mahmood.

'Remember I was expectant last year?' said Mariam, who had become pregnant soon after her mother's death. 'I had a little girl, but she died at ten days. Her breathing became faint and she grew weak and died. Now, thank God, I have Mahmood. Today he's forty-three days old!' she said, proudly lifting her firmly swaddled infant, kissing him and crooning affectionately. She called him her heart, her liver, her life-breath, her body-and-soul. His birth had brought new hope and life into the household. She and her sisters tended him constantly, picking him up and comforting him when he cried. She fed him on demand, sitting cross-legged and pulling up her dress to expose one of her white breasts. She was not shy about doing this near her father or brothers; no one thought twice about the sight of a woman breast-feeding. Before giving him the nipple she used to squeeze out a tiny jet of milk to ensure it was flowing properly, or maybe to tempt him with its taste. In the sociable family time after meals, her brothers would often take Mahmood in their arms and play with him, talking baby-talk.

I caught up on all the family news. Fereshteh had been invited: she now had two small girls, and told me that her mother-in-law had been worried that she had been slow in conceiving and had given her a herb to promote pregnancy. Tayereh had become part of the household, although living and cooking upstairs. She informed me that Karim and Zahir had become reconciled, but Mariam commented that since his marriage Karim had grown apart from the family. I gathered that Karim and Tayereh regularly went to spend a few days at Tayereh's parents' house, and so their contact with Mariam was sporadic. I noticed a great change in Parwaneh, who had become fully secluded and spent her days at home working hard for the family. I marvelled that at fifteen she could cook a meal for so many of us without panicking, but I knew that it was normal for a girl of her age, 'in training' to be chosen as a bride.

I told them all about the new house we had found in the residential area where we had previously lived. They said the rent was too high and were amazed that we needed four rooms for two people: one for sitting, one for sleeping, one for working and one for guests. I also explained that I was hiring a man who would cook, clean, shop and draw water from the well. This would free me to go out and pursue my own interests.

Mariam advised me about moving house.

'The first things you take inside the house should be a broom and a mirror,' she said.

I forgot to ask why. Maybe these meant that the house would always be clean and its inhabitants would be as pure as their own reflection in the glass; certainly the mirror has an esoteric meaning in Islam, whereby the mystic aspires to reflect divinity. No doubt Mariam would have given her own reason for this particular choice of items. Heratis believe that starting a new project has special significance, and that it should be done mindfully. They say blessings at the beginning of a journey or when taking the first bite of a meal, just as they give out sugared nuts when some important work has been completed.

Mariam also told me to carry some burning seeds of rue three times around the rooms, when all our belongings had been taken inside. *Esfand*, or rue, was used to ward off supernatural influences and to protect against the evil eye. In particular its aromatic smoke would be wafted over new babies or brides, or anything young and beautiful that might excite jealousy or admiration. She went to her tin of spices and wrapped up some of the small, dull, brown seeds in a screw of paper, handing it to me with a smile.

I carried out her advice in a trusting spirit, willing to believe that such initiatory rituals could have some beneficial effect. I valued and respected her as a friend and wanted to follow her word. When we moved in I carefully wafted the sweet, pungent smoke into every corner of the house, wishing for good fortune during the coming year.

4

The Married Daughters

I drew support from my friendship with Mariam, and even wondered that when I first met the family I had not paid her much attention. Now that she had become the female head of the house she had a quiet self-confidence; she was intelligent and subtle, and I found beauty in her soft face, high cheek-bones and slanting eyes. I watched as she thoughtfully cared for her large family – her father, brothers and sisters, children, husband and sister-in-law. When they were sick they came to her for medicines – home remedies for stomach cramps or fevers – and when they had worries many of them went to her for advice. She was a nurturer and comforter.

I asked her advice myself. I wanted a baby and felt very much under pressure from Afghan women to get pregnant, but I knew the timing was bad. What should I do?

'You're not so old,' she said. 'How old are you? About my age:

twenty-six, twenty-seven? For us that's very late to begin having babies, but for your people maybe not. You say they have good doctors and free medicine there . . . It would be hard for you to be pregnant here: you go out so much. Sometimes when I was pregnant I'd feel sick and faint walking to the *hamam*. The baby moves about inside your belly; it's troublesome and heavy. And you have that long journey home in the Land Rover. Didn't you say it took twenty days? No, don't stop taking the pill because the women talk like that. Wait until you're in your own country and then have your baby, where your mother and kinswomen will be there to help you. It's not so long for you to wait.'

Very few Herati women would have given me such sensible, unselfish advice. Having babies of their own, they would have urged me to become a mother like them. Mariam did not take the pill herself and I had even heard her say that it was a sin, but she recognised that my needs and considerations were different from her own.

I could not help noticing a great gulf between Mariam and her sister, Fereshteh, that seemed to spring directly from their marriages. In contrast to Mariam, Fereshteh was severely restricted by her husband and she had become lonely and depressed. As Mariam grew more independent and assured, Fereshteh's self-confidence dwindled through sadness and isolation.

I discovered from Mariam how each sister had come to marry. Mariam's husband, Hassan, was her first cousin, and they had played together as children. Both his parents had died when he was quite young and he had been raised first by his grandmother and then by his paternal aunt. Mariam's parents watched him grow up and chose him as their son-in-law: Mariam said they loved him as their own son. He was hard-working, intelligent and good-natured, and he got on well with everyone. He never became a musician, but was apprenticed as a carpenter to his aunt's husband. This work had better status and a more regular income than music-making.

It was common enough for women to select orphans from their own families as sons-in-law. Mothers liked to arrange marriages which meant their daughters stayed at home with them. This matriarchal tendency existed within the predominantly patriarchal system, and I imagine that Mother of Karim promoted the marriage strongly. The only person who resisted was Latif's sister, the senior aunt, as she realised that Mother of Karim was proposing for Hassan to join their family, whereas she wanted Mariam to become her daughter-in-law and come to live with them. For a while she was upset with Hassan, who was happy to marry into his uncle's house, and she refused to attend the wedding.

Mariam was seventeen when they married. They had not seen one another for several years, ever since Mariam had begun hiding her face in public. She told me that when Hassan came to the room to lead her to the bridal throne he had hesitated before taking her hand.

'The women who were waiting with me expected him to recognise me – after all, we had grown up together. Poor Hassan, he was so nervous that he didn't know me! "Which one is my bride?" he said.'

She laughed. There was tenderness in that memory.

'It was because you were so beautiful. He couldn't believe his eyes!' I teased.

Mariam had an enormous advantage in her marriage. Until her mother's death she had the support of an older, experienced woman in the house, and yet she never had to undergo the discipline of a mother-in-law. Hassan placed no restrictions upon her. She always had a little change in her pocket and was free to make purchases when necessary. Sometimes she bought clothes for the children in the second-hand bazaar, close to the Friday mosque, or odd things from a neighbouring woman who traded around the houses. If a relative fell ill, for instance, she followed her duty and went to visit, taking a small gift. If a child was sick, she went straight to the holy man for healing prayers to be sung over the child's head. She had the help, love and respect of all the family, and for a woman of her age she had an unusual degree of independence.

'Hassan's a good husband – better than Karim,' Tayereh assured me. 'I can't go anywhere! Karim's quarrelled with so many people that often I can't join the others when they go visiting. He's mean with money too. I have to beg for everything I need.'

Romantic love did not enter into the question. I knew that Tayereh and Karim were fond of one another and had seen them laugh and joke together. I imagined that they were happy and sexually contented in their private love-nest upstairs. But Karim was grudging about Tayereh's freedom, and this made him a 'bad' husband.

Herati women's expectations of marriage were very different from our own. At first a husband was distant, even awesome, and he rarely became a close friend. Husbands and wives spent very little time together; they were not expected to form a lifelong partnership that acted as a focus of their social lives, as in the West. Within the family their roles remained separate. Marriage was primarily an economic arrangement which provided support for the production of offspring.

As for Fereshteh, I felt sorry for her. She chided me for never going to her house, saying I must love Mariam more than her, so I arranged for Hossein to take me there. One very cold afternoon we set out together from his house with the youngest daughters, Parwaneh and Nassimeh, and little Simin, Mariam's daughter. Mariam and Tayereh stayed at home. Mariam explained that Hassan would not be happy for her to go there, as Fereshteh's husband, Mohammad Omar, had spread some malicious rumours about him. No one in the family liked Mohammad Omar, and this was the root of Fereshteh's isolation. He was jealous and quarrelsome. Neither Karim nor Zahir had accepted his marriage to Fereshteh. They had not attended the wedding, or spoken to him since. Latif Khan tolerated him for Fereshteh's sake, knowing that a complete break would cause her even more pain.

Hossein led us deep into the old city, along a labyrinthine route of twisting alleys. The paths were slushy and we sometimes had to skirt round deep pools of mud. Winter had arrived and there had been several falls of snow. Simin cringed and had to be coaxed along, fearful of slipping. High walls screened the alleys on either side. Far from the bazaar it became quiet except for muffled sounds coming from within hidden courtyards; voices calling, children laughing, the rhythmical hammering of a mortar and pestle or the thud of wood being chopped for a kitchen hearth. Occasionally we passed the open courtyard of a shrine, usually with an old pine planted near the grave. There were many little shrines buried in the old city, places where women went to perform rituals and execute vows. We also passed under tunnels where first-floor rooms had been built across the alley, and sometimes went through massive gateways with hinges set in them. Long ago the doors that had sealed off that part of the old city had been removed. Parwaneh walked close to Hossein. I could not see her expression beneath her veil, but I sensed that she felt unsure in the outside world, even in those quiet anonymous alleys. Young Nassimeh marched confidently ahead, quite used to visiting Fereshteh alone.

We reached the house and climbed up to the two top rooms where Fereshteh lived. She was sitting alone and unoccupied, watching over her children as they took an afternoon nap. Straight away she sent Hossein out to get paraffin, nodding to an empty can and handing him some money. He left without a murmur.

'I've been waiting for you all morning!' she said, chiding us for not coming sooner. Apologetically she surveyed her humble dwelling with distaste: two dark rooms and a landing where she cooked. They had no water. Every day she had to pay a water-bearer five *afghanis* for a skinful of water, as the closest public tap was far away. Any Afghan woman would have found her isolation intolerable, conditioned to the support and companionship of others around the house. It would not have comforted her to know that many British women live a similarly marooned existence alone at home all day, albeit in greater comfort.

Her situation was not helped by their poverty. Mohammad Omar did not make a good living. Although he was intelligent and a versatile musician, he was too quarrelsome to last long in any band. Sometimes he gave music lessons and he also mended and dealt in musical instruments, but his income was very insecure. Nothing was fixed in their lives: plans were always changing and they never seemed to stay long in one place. Sometimes they lived at his mother's house in Kabul, but then there would be a crisis and they would return to some dismal lodgings in Herat. His father had died several years ago and there had been quarrels between the sons over the division of property.

'I'm sick of moving,' Fereshteh sighed. 'We're like travellers here. Half our things are packed in boxes in Kabul. Mohammad Omar says we'll move from this place – he's found somewhere else. At least I'll be nearer my father's house.' A flicker of hope passed over her face, but then it clouded again and she began pouring out her recent troubles to Parwaneh, whispering in a high, soft voice, and occasionally touching her knee to emphasise a point.

I got up to examine the other room. It was neat and tidy, but there was a hole in the corner of the roof which had been inadequately covered with a sheet of polythene. It was far too cold and draughty to sit in there. Who came to their house anyway, I wondered, examining the family photographs on the wall? I identified Mohammad Omar's brothers, but noted that there were no pictures of Fereshteh's family. When I sat down again, Fereshteh was still complaining about Mohammad Omar.

'He blames me for this life we lead. He says our ruin comes from the wrong done him by my father and brothers! I cry and cry, but he won't stop saying these things. He says terrible things against you all. I want to stop my ears.'

She puckered her forehead, leaning forward urgently to impress her pain upon us. I sensed in her an insatiable hunger for pity and sympathy. When I had first known her I had thought her prettier than Mariam, with her soft, gentle features and her modern fringe. Now her eyelids were heavy and her eyes wrinkled with lines of fatigue and sadness. She always looked dazed, as though the light was too strong. But during the two hours of our visit, she laughed and relaxed and we drank tea and chatted. A neighbour even came and joined us, entertaining us with stories. Nassimeh played with the children and time passed pleasantly. When we announced that we would have to go she sighed deeply, as though a curtain had come down over her happiness. Saying goodbye she looked forlorn, dreading her husband's return in the evening.

Mariam told me that Fereshteh's marriage had happened at the insistence of Ustad Sultan Khan, Mohammad Omar's father, a famous master of classical music from Kabul. As a young man Latif Khan had become his disciple.

'When Ustad Sultan Khan came to Herat to give concerts he used to stay for several months,' said Mariam. 'It was good for him here: there were many generous patrons. At that time there was no proper road between Herat and Kabul, so his visits were long. Well, it happened that he became ill, and his doctor in Kabul advised him to take a complete rest, so he came to Herat and stayed in our house for about a month, recovering his health. I was young at the time – maybe about twelve . . .

'It was impossible for us to hide ourselves from him. We didn't sit with him, but all the same he noticed us. He spoke directly to our mother and told her to give one of her beautiful girls to his son in marriage . . . In fact the one he originally chose was me,' she added shyly. 'My mother spoke very firmly and told him to forget the whole idea. She didn't want her daughter to live so far away. She told him I was engaged to Hassan, but she said she would never let Fereshteh go either.

'Then he sent his wife and daughter-in-law to Herat to plead with her. They came to our house every day asking for Fereshteh. She could do nothing to discourage them. Whatever she said, they still came. No one in the family wanted the marriage. They didn't want to lose Fereshteh and they didn't want Mohammad Omar in the family. Karim and Zahir were very strongly opposed, and because they had never learned anything from the *ustad* they could speak their minds more freely.'

Latif Khan was in a very awkward position. In refusing the request of his teacher, or *ustad*, he was placing his obligations as a father above those as a disciple. Many factors weighed against Mohammad Omar: his restless, unreliable character; a previous marriage and divorce; the fact that he came from a Sunni family; above all, the extreme distance of Kabul from Herat. In comparison with these serious disadvantages the question of the bridewealth was unimportant.

'My mother could do nothing to discourage the women. They still came and pleaded with her,' Mariam went on. 'They went to the shrines and made supplications and they bought written prayers to promote the marriage. They even told her that Mohammad Omar was threatening to kill himself if he did not get Fereshteh as his bride.'

'But he'd never seen her!' I gasped.

'No – only heard about her from the others . . .' She hesitated and then went on, lowering her voice a little. 'The only person who did not oppose the marriage was Fereshteh herself. She *wanted* to go, and she let our father see that, which made him waver. It was hard for him to keep refusing his *ustad*. Her willingness gave him the way to satisfy his *ustad*. She didn't say, "I want to marry him" – no girl could say that – but she said, "A bride has to go where her husband goes", meaning she was willing.'

Mariam could not hide her exasperation at what Fereshteh had done. Her action had been improper and foolish and she had undermined her parents' impulse to protect her from a marriage that they rightly feared would bring unhappiness. I imagined that Fereshteh's head had been turned, that she had been seduced by her future mother-in-law's flattery, swayed by the idea of Mohammad Omar as an impassioned lover, tempted by the glamour of life in the capital. Maybe she was also jealous of Mariam, her younger sister, who was already engaged.

I had always counselled Fereshteh to stand up to Mohammad Omar and defend her family against his vindictive talk, but one day I witnessed an outburst of his temper, and after that I saw things rather differently. I encountered him in the bazaar, quite by chance. Delighted, he insisted upon taking me to visit Fereshteh in their new lodgings, which were not far away. Latif Khan, Hossein and Nassimeh had faithfully helped them pile their belongings on to hand-carts and unload them in the new house. When we arrived Fereshteh jumped up nervously, still holding an onion she had been peeling, but then smiled with pleasure at seeing me. At first Mohammad Omar seemed glad to have brought us together, but then he left us abruptly, as though suddenly feeling unwanted. My eyes wandered, taking in the desolation of their new surroundings, which were if anything more confined and depressing than before. The walls were rough and unplastered, bare mud, crumbling away in places. Angry thudding noises came from the other room.

'He's fixing a drum,' Fereshteh explained, mechanically peeling her onion, but then she remembered herself and jumped up to put the kettle on. 'My mind's not functioning well,' she apologised. 'The little one's been ill and I had a bad night.'

Suddenly and quite unexpectedly Mohammad Omar burst into the room, worked up into a state of fury. He sat down opposite me and glared accusingly.

'What kind of a cow-shed do people expect us to live in here?' he shouted, gesturing angrily at the walls as though I were personally responsible for their state of decay. 'People in Herat are peasants! They don't know how to live decently. Look, there's not even any electricity. It's a shame I ever came here, a pity I ever married this woman. What help has her family ever given me? I've helped them all. They're all my students. My father taught them everything they know and now they treat me like this! Do they let me live in this pigsty because they think I'm some kind of an animal?'

His eyes bulged with passion. I was terrified, and remained silent lest the smallest remark should spark him to further violent excesses. He ranted against Latif Khan, Karim and the others: they had betrayed him, let him down, kicked him out of their family. I felt stunned by the torrent of abuse. Fereshteh cowered beside me, also keeping quiet.

'Call themselves professional musicians! They're illiterate. They can't even write,' he mocked, gesticulating wildly. His eyes glittered crazily and I felt afraid. Eventually he stormed out of the room.

'Now you can see what he's like,' Fereshteh whispered. 'You can't argue with him. He hates me. Can't you see it now? He hates us all.'

I remembered wryly how I had told her to stand up for herself, yet I myself had kept quiet under his attack. No wonder she had been worn down by him and reduced to tears and depression. She added softly that he no longer slept with her; she claimed to be indifferent, but I sensed her pain at this total physical rejection.

'What about divorce?' I asked, seeing things had become so hopeless.

'I could never do that,' she answered softly, looking over at her children. 'They'd take my children away. I could never let them go. You've never had children so you don't know how sweet and precious they are to a mother. I could never be parted from them.'

I winced at the extent of my own ignorance. The law was heavily weighted against women. Children belonged to the paternal blood-line and divorce meant renouncing them for ever. While still small they could stay with the mother, but after the age of seven they left, to be cared for by a grandmother, aunt or stepmother. Divorce was final: no visiting, no access. The two families were irrevocably parted. No matter what her grievance, a woman could not seek divorce without making this enormous sacrifice.

I often thought about the contrast between Mariam's and Fereshteh's lives. Was it a question of luck, or were they in some way responsible for the way their husbands treated them? Was there a fundamental difference in their characters that made Mariam strong and in control of her life while Fereshteh was a natural victim?

'Fereshteh has been ill-fated,' said Mother of Rahim, their aunt. 'You can see that, can't you? Mariam's luck has been "white" and Fereshteh's "black". They should never have given her to Mohammad Omar. When she was married she was bonny and plump, but now she's all skin and bone. But look at Mariam: see how she blossoms! Everything has turned out well for her. She lives in her father's house and her brothers and sisters help her in everything. She's the one with all the luck!'

For Mother of Rahim the matter was clear-cut: no credit or blame should be attached to the two sisters. It was simply a question of fate.

5

Ritual Food

The separation of women and men in everyday life applied even to their religious practice. Women not only worked, ate, socialised and often slept apart from men; they also prayed and worshipped separately, and in rather different ways. Whereas the spiritual life of men emphasised formal, communal observances, women were excluded from joining them for prayer in mosques, and had no public gathering-place such as the main mosque where men congregated on Fridays to hear a sermon and become inspired within a huge crowd of worshippers. As regards prayer, very few women regularly performed the *namaz*, the long Arabic recitations and formal prostrations at the five daily prayer times. *Namaz* requires a state of ritual cleanliness that was impractical for most Herati women, who were constantly being polluted with children's urine. During menstruation they were totally banned from prayer, as unclean, and unlike men they could neither take time to do the necessary ablutions, nor afford to keep changing their clothing as it became soiled. In practical terms they found themselves to some extent excluded from the prescribed observances of their faith. In compensation, their devotional life focused around local shrines, and involved bringing votive offerings or cooking ritual food. While they did not perform the *namaz*, they prayed through wishes and supplications known as *doa*, prayers expressed directly to God or through the intercession of saints.

One day Mariam sent us a message through Hossein, asking if we would like to drive out to the shrine of Seyed-i Mukhtar. As it was a perfect, sunny, windless afternoon, we made arrangements to set off immediately. We collected them at the end of their alley. Mariam, Parwaneh, Nassimeh and Simin piled into the back of the Land Rover, and Hossein sat in front next to John. They had also brought their neighbour Mother of Ghani with them, an old widow who had been a friend of Mother of Karim and midwife to their babies; they always included her in their religious activities. We were disappointed that Karim had not given Tayereh permission to come; I suspected that this was because he was jealous of my friendship with Mariam.

I pointed to the sack and various bundles that they had thrown down at our feet, and Mariam explained that they had brought things for cooking. She said that when she had been giving birth to Mahmood she had made a vow promising Seyed-i Mukhtar, the holy saint, that she would cook *halwa*, a sweet ritual food, at his shrine if the baby was born safely. Today they had finished all their housework and, seeing it was such a lovely afternoon, she had decided to visit the shrine and fulfil her vow.

We drove out of the west gate of the city, past the pine trees of the Women's Park where spring gatherings were held every year, between the four tall minarets, and straight towards the mountains at the edge of the valley. Mariam pointed out the Rolling Place, a shrine where pilgrims made their wishes and rolled on the ground of the courtyard. If they rolled right to the wall the augury was auspicious, but otherwise their wish was unlikely to be granted. I asked if women rolled too, finding it hard to imagine them rolling fully veiled in the dust, but Mother of Ghani assured me that they did.

We drove past fertile land criss-crossed with irrigation channels and rows of trees. Tall poplars lined the road, and pigeons flew ahead, as if showing us the way. Then I caught sight of the shrine, perched high on the edge of the cliff, its holy flags waving in the wind. The Land Rover began to climb and the women clung to their seats, muffling little shrieks of alarm as they saw the sheer drop out of the window.

We climbed the last stage on foot and slipped our shoes off at the top.

The tomb was set in the middle of a paved courtyard, shaded by a large spreading tree which grew from its centre. A long verandah faced out across the valley. The place was silent and deserted. The holy men who tended the shrine had retired to their underground room and John and Hossein left us to perform our devotions in privacy. I followed the others to the long tombstone, and kissed the stone and pressed my forehead to it as they did. Then we sat keeping our hands in contact with the stone for a long time, as though drawing strength and sustenance through our fingertips, quiet and absorbed in meditation. Even the children behaved reverently. Mother of Ghani kept her eyes tightly shut, moving her lips as she uttered her silent supplications.

Eventually Parwaneh broke the spell.

'Fereshteh came here to pray for a baby,' she said softly. 'She made a doll and tied it to the tree – and then two months later she found herself pregnant! Today we want to make a doll for Tayereh. Wouldn't it be marvellous if she had a little one like Mahmood.' Suddenly she had an idea. 'Shall we make a doll for you too?' she asked, delighted with her plan.

I protested that I was taking the pill, but she insisted that I wanted a baby one day. Mother of Ghani broke off her prayers and nodded in agreement, and I laughingly acquiesced. The old woman brought out some cloth and tore it into strips, some of which she then wound into a ball and tied to a twig, forming a head and body.

'There, a turban!' she said, winding more cloth around the doll's head. 'You want a boy first, don't you?'

'Whatever God gives,' I said, not resisting her confident management of my future.

'Pray for a boy first,' she advised: a son to satisfy my husband and continue the paternal blood-line. She tucked in the end of the turban and handed me the doll. 'Now, take it!' she said, waiting expectantly.

I did not understand what she meant me to do. Seeing them all waiting for me to act, I did the first thing that came into my head and placed the doll between my legs to imitate its birth. They giggled with delight.

'No, like this!' Mother of Ghani corrected, laughing. 'Cradle the baby on your lap.'

She put the doll on my knee. I now recalled the familiar image of Mariam sitting cross-legged with Mahmood, feeding him. It gave me the strangest feeling acting out motherhood in this way, nursing the featherlight effigy in my lap. She then put the doll to each of my breasts and made squeezing motions with her fingers, making me blush. The others smiled, enjoying the thoroughness of her ritual. Finally she made

a cradle with a large strip of cloth and laid my baby in it, swinging
between the branches of the holy tree.

'Now say "*Bismillah*" – "In the name of God" – and make a wish in
your heart for a baby boy,' she ordered.

I stood under the tree and wished, looking at the touchingly small
doll in its cradle. The branches were filled with many similar tokens:
rags, stones and metal hands pointing their five equal digits to the sky in
supplication. Parwaneh and Nassimeh made another cloth doll for
Tayereh and tied it up too. The tree was festooned with women's
wishes.

In one corner of the shrine's brick verandah a prayer niche faced west
towards Mecca. Mariam was preparing to light some candles on its
ledge, and had begun fixing them into the hot wax that she had dripped
out. She said that five of the candles were for her own wishes, and
handed me one to light. She left a silence and then told me that the other
five candles were from Zahir, who had asked her to light them on his
behalf.

'He told me to make a wish that we would find him a good wife,' she
said, leaving a silence for her words to sink in.

Until that day Zahir had insisted that he would not marry as he was
still mourning his mother. Mariam worried about him, wishing he had a
wife and insisting that their mother would have wanted it. All the
candles were now dancing points of flame: after two years he had finally
let Mariam know that the time had come for her to find him a bride.

At the other end of the verandah, Mother of Ghani had already begun
to light a fire in the brick range. The walls were black with soot from
other women's cooking. We gathered and watched her. First she made a
good fire and then, uttering a blessing, she scooped vegetable fat into
the heavy metal pot. It sizzled and melted. She squatted comfortably on
her haunches as she cooked, throwing in flour and stirring vigorously to
stop the mixture from catching and burning. Gradually it browned, and
after about ten minutes she removed the pot and with a loud hiss of
steam added a bowlful of sugar and water. After cooking it a little longer
she pronounced it ready, and Parwaneh unwrapped some flat loaves of
bread and spread them thickly with *halwa*. Nassimeh took them down
to the mendicants, to whom visitors always gave food or money.

Mariam told me to join John and Hossein to eat on the sunny
verandah step, but she and the others stayed in the shadows by the fire,
eating the *halwa* that remained in the pot. Our food was served on a
tray, and we sat chatting together, feasting on bread and warm, sweet
doughy *halwa*. I had noticed Hossein carrying a heavy ritual stone very
seriously many times around the saint's grave, and asked him what he
had wished. He said he wanted to travel: to Kabul, Iran or even India.

We packed up and prepared to leave, pausing to enjoy the view from the top of the steps. In the distance the mountains threw up jagged protective peaks against the sky, almost encircling the valley. Behind us, to the west, the valley opened out and one road led to Iran and another north to the Soviet Union, each only about two hours' drive away. In the east the mountains closed in, massing in front of the high ridges of the furthermost tip of the Hindu Kush, the vast range that spans Afghanistan like a backbone. From Herat the paved road led south-east to Kandahar, a day's drive away, and from there to the subcontinent. Across the mountains lay the old Silk Route to Central Asia and China.

We looked down at the fertile patchwork of fields fringed with irrigation ditches, and at the clustered city lying in a haze of its own wood-smoke below. It looked like a childish model sculpted from earth and water, the very same colour as the ground from which it had sprung. The strong ramparts of the citadel dominated, and we could clearly make out the tall minarets of the Friday mosque. Detached and calm, we looked across the valley, yet could hear no sound apart from the gentle flapping of the holy pennants of the shrine and the soft rustle of leaves.

We began to make our way down, encountering a party of about forty women and children toiling up the steep steps, panting heavily. They mumbled greetings as they passed, and judging from their numerous bundles I guessed they had come for a protracted visit. Two mini-buses had been parked in the clearing at the bottom of the steps. The drivers squatted patiently nearby, gazing out across the valley. One of them took out a tin of snuff and neatly tossed some under his tongue. They seemed contented, in no way perturbed at the prospect of several hours' wait.

'Who was Seyed-i Mukhtar?' I asked Mariam, once we had set off home.

'I don't know,' she replied, 'ask my father; he can tell you. We always come to this shrine. It's a special place for us.'

She knew nothing of the saint whose bones we had revered. The tradition of coming there, the peace and solace in doing so, the physical detachment from the house and from domestic worries, and the sense of executing vows and articulating wishes was sufficient.

'Now our hearts feel refreshed,' she added peacefully.

Religious festivities and observances followed the lunar calendar, and during the month of Safar women used to cook a ritual thanksgiving sweet, milky rice known as *nazr*, which means 'vow'. It was cooked at home on a Wednesday and sent out to friends and neighbours as a gesture of goodwill and an act of charity. I heard one woman jokingly call it 'the game of the plates' because it involved borrowing and returning so many plates. *Nazr* entailed making supplications and vows to the holy women of the family of the Prophet, and during difficult times women would undertake to cook extra *nazr* in the hope of resolving problems. *Nazr* was an annual obligation, and failure to honour the pledge brought misfortune to the family.

Mariam invited me to join them one Wednesday for *nazr* and said she was ordering a bucket of milk from a neighbour who kept a cow. She explained that over the years their family had built up an obligation to cook two *man*s of rice into *nazr*. (A *man* is a local weight, equivalent to forty *sir*s and equalling more than two kilos.) However the previous year they had gone to the *mullah*, who had reduced their obligation to one *man* since their mother had fulfilled all her vows and was now dead.

I was fascinated by Mariam's account of their family vows. When Karim and Zahir had been born, their mother had vowed ten *sir*s each time; she had vowed another ten when their father had kidney trouble, and another ten when they moved into their present house about twelve years ago. When Karim and Zahir had been drafted into military service, she had vowed another ten *sir*s each time, praying that they would be transferred to Herat, which they were. When she had fallen ill the family had vowed another ten *sir*s; and finally when Simin was born, Mariam had vowed ten *sir*s on her own behalf.

This struck me as an interesting charter of times of family crisis or thanksgiving, faithfully remembered over the years. Birth and illness, particularly of senior members of the family, were common reasons for making vows. Military service was another; understandably so, since it lasted for two years and was very hard for those who were drafted to distant parts of Afghanistan, cut off from the emotional and financial support of their families. Once women had made these vows, they said they had them 'on their necks', as the neck was where responsibility was borne.

Mother of Ghani arrived in the morning, greeting Latif Khan without hiding her face. She was sufficiently old and close to the family not to cover herself. She brought the big bronze cooking pot down from its shelf, and uttered a blessing as she began rinsing it out. Then she set it on the hearth and threw in a quantity of fat to melt. *Nazr* was made with round-grained rice; a large basinful was tipped into the hot fat and stirred, followed by almost the whole bucket of milk. Finally she added a bowlful of sugar and several cardamoms for flavour, firmly fixing on the lid and leaving the mixture to cook.

Amid a flurry of greetings Fereshteh arrived. We had not seen her for several months as she had been away in Kabul. A little later Mother of

Ghani took out the *ta degi* – 'the bottom of the pot', the crispy crust – and the children gathered around, eager for a share. She warned them that none of the *nazr* should fall to the ground, where it would be polluted. This was ritual food and they were to eat with care. Then she made a big hole in the centre of the rice with the handle of the spoon and poured in the rest of the milk and a cup of rosewater, smoothing the surface into a gently rising mound. She covered the pot and shovelled embers on to the lid so that the rice cooked through very slowly away from the fire. This process was called *dam* – 'steam' or 'breath' – and rice was always cooked in this way: the longer the steaming, the better.

Mariam and Parwaneh lit six small candles and stuck them on to a brick with their own hot wax. Mariam handed a candle to Fereshteh with a meaningful look; I assumed that she wanted Fereshteh to make a vow, knowing she was very unhappy in her marriage.

'Lady Fatimeh, grant the wishes of our heart . . .' they whispered, palms upturned. Then Mariam took the brick and placed it on the cooking pot, leaving the candles to burn out.

We left the kitchen and went to sit in the sunny window of the family room, well away from Latif Khan and Hossein so that we could talk in private. Nassimeh brought the water-pipe and Fereshteh recounted her recent months in Kabul to Mariam and Mother of Ghani. They spoke in low voices, punctuated by the soft gurgle of the pipe. Then Mariam saw the blind *sheikh* enter the courtyard, and called Nassimeh to lead him into the room. He was a holy man who made a scanty living from singing *rowzeh*, Shiah mourning songs in memory of the dead. His visit today was a special occasion; normally he came every Thursday, the day on which Mother of Karim had died. He settled down next to Latif Khan, stiffly alert to his new surroundings, gradually becoming attuned to the presence of others in the room, staring blankly ahead as he murmured greetings in turn.

After a short silence he offered to begin the prayers, which were followed by *rowzeh*-singing. Without understanding many words of the song, I could tell that he was singing about the Battle of Karbala, the occasion on which Hassan and Hossein, the two sons of Ali, were martyred, suffering cruelly from thirst in the inhospitable desert. The martyrs had been fighting for Ali's claim to the Caliphate, which was ended decisively on the battleground of Karbala, in modern Iraq. Their martyrdom, the focal moment of Shiah consciousness which gave that form of Islam its particular intensity and passion, was dramatically commemorated during the month of Moharram. For forty days Shiahs had no wedding celebrations and allowed no playing of music; they did not cut their hair, buy clothes or use henna, and they washed and shaved less frequently than usual, practising bodily mortifications as a sign of outward grief. There were torchlight processions with men flagellating themselves with fine chains, chanting rhythmically, and public *rowzeh* gatherings where men and women would cry and sob as the story of Karbala was vividly recounted. Moharram had already passed, but the martyrs were remembered and mourned in every *rowzeh*.

Nassimeh nudged me with a giggle. Mother of Ghani had begun sobbing loudly and without restraint, which was the appropriate response to the *sheikh*'s singing. Fereshteh, Mariam and Parwaneh began to cry quietly too, wiping their tears with the edge of their scarves. I found myself weeping with them, flooded with confused feelings. I did not cry for the martyrdom at Karbala, which I suspect is often merely a focus for the unleashing of pent-up sadness. Maybe I cried for myself: for my rootlessness and for my love of these people. I was touched that Mariam had included me in their family circle.

The *sheikh* finished with a long prayer and we raised our palms again. Nassimeh and Parwaneh went to touch his hand, and then returned softly to their places.

'Today we have a guest from England,' Mariam said, after a silence. 'She often comes to our house. She knew our dear mother . . .'

'That is good,' said the *sheikh* benevolently, but I could think of nothing to say.

'It brings merit for us to have a non-Moslem in our midst,' said Mother of Ghani, beaming at me.

The concept of religious merit is as important to Moslems as the concept of sin, and provides a counterbalance to it. It brings merit to perform any pious act, and on the Day of Judgment counteracts the effect of sin. The most obvious ways of accumulating merit are in the observance of the 'Five Pillars of Islam', the core of Moslem practice: faith in God and his Prophet, prayer, fasting, giving charity, and if possible the pilgrimage to Mecca at least once during a lifetime. Merit can also be gained in smaller ways: by cooking and eating *halwa* at a shrine, for instance; by dyeing the hands and feet with henna for New Year's Day; or by uttering blessings upon the wearing of a new garment.

An easy silence settled in the room, and the *sheikh* stared blindly ahead, relaxed and immobile. The women went to the kitchen to serve out the *nazr*. A sweet milky steam arose when Mother of Ghani lifted the lid. Fereshteh scooped up some rice and ate it, saying, 'There's merit in taking the first rice from the pot.'

'Do you want to "borrow" some from the pot this year?' asked Mariam, inviting her to make her own vow. I sensed that she felt Fereshteh ought to undertake this obligation and pray for help.

'No, who knows where I'll be next year,' she replied. 'If God wills it I'll be here with you again.'

I guessed that Fereshteh was afraid to assert her own Shiah customs upon Mohammad Omar, a Sunni.

As female head of the house, it was Mariam's duty to serve and distribute the *nazr*. First she served the *sheikh*, her father and Hossein. Then she began to distribute the rice that would be sent out, starting with four large portions for her father's most important patrons. Smaller plates were for relatives and neighbours, and occasionally she asked Fereshteh if she had served enough, or added a little to be on the safe side. It was all right to send a small amount to close relatives, but one had to send more to others, for fear of appearing mean. She set aside a really large plate for myself and John, ignoring my protests and despite the knowledge that we were only two. Nassimeh and Simin carried the small plates out to the neighbours, holding them carefully inside knotted handkerchieves.

Eventually we sat down to eat. Karim and Zahir were not at home and Hossein, his father and the *sheikh* had already finished. Mariam reserved some *nazr* for her brothers and for the whole family to eat in the evening, and we had what remained. It was soft and sticky, and tasted like delicately flavoured rice pudding. When the men had gone to the bazaar, Mariam smoked a water-pipe with Mother of Ghani and Fereshteh: she kept her habit secret from Hassan and her father.

'When did you start smoking?' I asked.

'After my mother died. A woman suggested that the pipe might calm me. When I had nothing to do but grieve I'd light a pipe; it distracts you from your sadness.'

'Sometimes a pipe's a blessing,' agreed Mother of Ghani, who, like many Herati women, was addicted to the strong Afghan tobacco.

Fereshteh began nervously collecting her things, suddenly agitated. It was late, she said, obviously afraid Mohammad Omar would be angry. Mariam looked sad to see her so anxious, but she did not urge her to stay. Fereshteh was not a guest, who needed to be made to feel welcome, but a daughter of the house. She summoned her children and took Nassimeh home with her to help her start cooking supper. Mother of Ghani took her leave too, but I stayed on with Mariam and Parwaneh. I was working at my embroidery, which made me feel relaxed and disinclined to move.

'Mother of Ghani thinks you're getting ready to convert to Islam,' said Mariam.

'Because I wept when the *sheikh* sang? There's so much to be sad about when you think . . .' I said.

'Mariam, why is it that life gets sadder as you grow up?' asked Parwaneh.

'As you get wiser you become more aware,' Mariam explained. 'When you're young you have no cares, but then as you grow up you begin to learn.' She sighed. 'That's the second year we've cooked *nazr* without our mother. I miss her so much, you know. I've no one to turn to for support. Sometimes I pray for her guidance. At least this day we've fulfilled our obligation and thanked God for His mercy in all things, but it's hard for me. I have to find a wife for Zahir, which is no easy thing to arrange, and sometimes I worry about our father too. I know he gets depressed without her.'

I knew she sometimes felt overwhelmed by family responsibilities and I sympathised. I thanked her for inviting me, finished my sewing and packed up my threads, preparing to leave.

'Next year we'll miss you and remember this day,' she said. 'Your place will be empty.'

6

Women Who Miscarried

To everyone's delight Tayereh became pregnant. Nassimeh was jubilant, saying it was because we had tied the doll in the tree at the shrine of Seyed-i Mukhtar. It was not that she was under any illusions about the realities of sex, having seen Karim's pigeons mounting one another and stray dogs copulating in the alley: she simply meant that thanks to the intercession of the saint our wishes had been granted.

Tayereh began to take care what she ate, for pregnant women were supposed to avoid foods which were 'cold' or 'sour'. All food was classified in terms of a folk version of Greek humoral medicine, in which the four qualities (hot, cold, wet and dry) had been simplified into two dominant categories of 'hot' and 'cold'. The ideas of Greek theorists such as Galen and Hippocrates had been adopted by early Islamic thinkers, later percolating throughout the Moslem world. Until recently Greek medicine had flourished in Herat, practised by traditional healers known as *hakims*, but it had been superseded by Western medicine. (*Hakims* still practice in Pakistan, India and other areas in the Moslem world, even in British immigrant communities.) I learned to classify food myself. 'Hot' food was substantial, fatty, sweet and full of protein, whereas 'cold' food was watery and acidic. 'Sour' was a subsection of 'cold', and 'spicy' a subsection of 'hot'. Food with 'wind' could be either 'hot' or 'cold' and in certain conditions had to be avoided. Dietary rules aimed to maintain a healthy balance between 'hot' and 'cold' taking into consideration the condition of the body and the weather.

The winter became severe and, as there were no weddings during the cold weather, Karim had no work. He decided to make a trip to Kabul and Mazar-i Sherif, in the north of Afghanistan, and to take Tayereh with him. She was excited at the prospect of travelling, having never visited other parts of the country before, but Mariam was worried about her undertaking the journey while pregnant. However Karim did not listen to her and they set off.

I was visiting the house the day they returned from their trip. During winter Heratis kept warm by huddling around a *kursi*, a low table covered with a thick quilt which trapped the heat from a brazier of glowing embers. Parwaneh and I were snuggled cosily together and Mahmood was asleep, tucked under one corner of the quilt; Nassimeh was busily splitting pistachios to earn money from a local confectioner, laboriously hammering them open on a stump of wood, and Mariam had just returned from an outing to the *hamam*. Tayereh entered the room, smiling and self-conscious: we had not seen her for more than two weeks. After we had all kissed and greeted her, Mariam commented upon how thin and tired she looked, and she sat down to tell us about her adventures.

She seemed excited but exhausted, spilling out her impressions in a confused torrent. She had been terrified by the bus journey over the Salang Pass between Kabul and Mazar-i Sherif, which went through the highest tunnel in the world, and said the mountains had been so snowy and high that she was afraid they would never get through. She wondered how anyone could sleep in the beds in their hotel in Kabul: she had been unable to rest for fear of falling out. We listened intently as she babbled. I had never heard her talk at such length.

Karim interrupted us by calling her upstairs to sweep the snow from their roof so the whiteness would not dazzle his pigeons. It was inconsiderate of him to order her to do this chore, but Tayereh had already told us that he did not seem able to make any allowances for the fact that she was pregnant and feeling sick and queasy. She returned twenty minutes later, laughing that the very first thing he had done on his return was to tend his birds.

'Oh, it's so nice to be home!' she said, settling at the *kursi* again. She turned to Mariam. 'I wanted to tell you something: the night after crossing the Salang I took fright and woke with a shock, and the next morning I noticed a little blood in my trousers, so that made me anxious . . .'

'Losing even a little blood is serious,' said Mariam, immediately alert to the danger of miscarriage. She advised Tayereh to go to the *mullah* and ask him for a string to wear around her waist to protect the pregnancy. 'Don't be shy,' she said. 'Tell him you're three months pregnant and that you had a shock which endangered the baby.'

I asked Mariam what kind of string the *mullah* would give her. She said it would probably have seven threads of different colours. Some women attached a key to the string, which was blessed by the *mullah*. Mariam said that she had worn a protective string while she had been carrying Mahmood, and that she had broken it when she went into labour.

'You should sort out all your washing today,' she said to Tayereh. 'Tomorrow Parwaneh and I will do a big wash. We'll have it ready this evening so we can start on it first thing in the morning.' She brushed aside Tayereh's protests. 'You shouldn't do that work. You can never be too careful if you start losing blood. Don't worry; we can manage it all.'

Tayereh talked on, recounting the vivid dream that had shaken her after their journey across the Salang Pass.

'You got over-excited and frightened,' said Mariam, when she had finished. 'You haven't been able to sleep away from home. You need a good rest to regain your health.'

Tayereh lost her baby. The spots of blood had been the first signs of a miscarriage. As soon as I heard the news I visited her, bringing some home-baked biscuits made with 'hot' foods to build up her strength.

'I didn't have too much pain,' she said. 'We went to the *mullah* to get the string, but I didn't really think it could protect the baby: it was too late, I had already started to lose blood.'

Mariam came up and joined us, holding Mahmood in her arms. She admonished Tayereh in a childish lisp for losing the little baby that would have been Mahmood's wife.

'You've taken away my little wife: what can I do with my little cock?' she said, waving Mahmood's hand at her, making us all laugh.

'Could you tell if it was a boy or girl?' I asked.

'The top of its head was all wrinkled,' said Mariam. 'Mother of Ghani said a boy's head would have been smooth.'

Tayereh told me what had happened.

'That evening I went downstairs for a pee and I almost fainted. I couldn't climb the stairs back to my room, so I went to Mariam. She made me lie down and said she'd look after me.'

'I covered her with a quilt and went up to tell Karim to call Mother of Ghani,' said Mariam, 'but he refused to go, saying he had toothache! Just imagine a man refusing to call a midwife for his wife,' she said angrily. 'The other men were out, so Parwaneh and I had to fetch Mother of Ghani ourselves, leaving Nassimeh with Tayereh. She ordered us to make Tayereh a drink. Dill seeds would have been best, but we had to use cinnamon, cardamom and cummin instead, infused in tea.' These spices were all 'hot' and their action was supposed to speed the delivery.

'Then the blood came faster,' Tayereh went on. 'It came in big clots. They wouldn't let me go to the toilet to pee, because it would be a sin if the baby fell in that dirty place. I had to pee squatting in the courtyard. That was when the baby fell from me. It was only this big,' she showed us, marking off her wrist with her finger, 'and it had a layer of skin all around it. You couldn't really see its face at all.' She dropped her hands into her lap, smiling uncertainly, upset by the memories.

'Are you very sad?' I asked.

'No. It was God's will. In a way I'm relieved because I'd become very anxious about having a baby, seeing all that Mariam has to do for Mahmood. My mother told me not to grieve. It was fate that the baby died. In God's time I'll have another.'

Her mother had come to look after her and cook for them for three days, during which time her younger sister, who was Parwaneh's age, took charge of all their mother's housework. Now that her mother had gone, another sister was staying and helping with everything. In times of crisis the extended family offered great support: people stepped in and helped without any fuss, simply knowing their duty to one another.

During that time Mariam's aunt, Mother of Rahim, also miscarried: she lost so much blood that she had to spend five days in hospital. I went with Mariam to visit her as soon as she returned home. Tayereh wanted to accompany us, but she was under doctor's orders to stay at home for twenty days. We chatted on our way out and Tayereh told us that Karim had ordered her to start taking the pill: he did not want the bother of pregnancies and babies. Parwaneh smacked her cheek in astonishment, but Tayereh reassured us that she had tricked him by saying that now she could not get pregnant for three months. Mariam told her to sleep with Karim on the fortieth night after the miscarriage, when a taboo on sex after giving birth was lifted: this would be sure to bring a new conception. Supposing he was not in the mood, I asked, interested that women could initiate sex. 'After forty days?' said Mariam, dismissively. She also advised Tayereh to put a piece of sticky plaster on the small of her back to make it strong again: people believed this area of the body was the source of sexual energy and was weakened by childbirth. I could not help being amused at this novel use of a plaster.

We set off to visit Mother of Rahim. Mariam left Mahmood at home with Nassimeh and we made our way out to the bazaar, walking more or less in silence. Women felt ill at ease in the bazaar, even shrouded in their veils. This was the men's territory, where we had to remain anonymous and unnoticed. I saw that women sometimes picked their way over the ice on the shady side of the street so as to avoid the crowded, sunny pavement, where men sauntered like owners, their smoky breath billowing out in cold plumes. I was aware that I was attracting undue attention to our party, an outlandish figure in boots and a long navy cloak.

We found Mother of Rahim sitting huddled under the *kursi* quilt, propped up by cushions and surrounded by her family. Her head was completely swathed in a prayer veil to keep it warm. I was shocked at the change in her: her eyes were grey and hollow, her lips white and bloodless and her skin sickly pale, and she had the painful lassitude of an invalid. Mariam's uncle greeted us and then left the room, anxious to escape our talk of the intimacies of illness. Mariam recounted the story of Tayereh's miscarriage, evoking ejaculations of thanks to God for her survival from Mother of Rahim, who then went on to tell her own story.

She had been to visit the senior aunt, and had found her and her daughter-in-law finishing their washing. As they began hanging out the wet clothes she had pulled the washing line tight, and some fluid had escaped from between her legs, but she had been busy talking and had not thought about it or realised that her waters had broken. The membrane must have ruptured without her feeling anything.

'I woke in the middle of the night and found my mattress soaking wet,' she told us. 'Everything was sodden with blood and there was no way of stopping the flow.' One of her sons had sent for her mother and sisters, who lived a short distance away, but by the time they arrived she had begun to feel very strange. What was everybody doing? Why were they all there, clustering so close to her?

She paused for breath, panting slightly. Beads of sweat had collected on her face, and her hands moved in large circles as she spoke. The room was silent. No one tried to calm her, mesmerised as we were by her story. She said that she could tell from everyone's faces that they thought she was dying, and she even began imagining that she had already left this world. It seemed that they were in mourning, yet she was still there. Nothing seemed to make sense.

'The only thing I could focus on was little Zia's face' – Zia, her youngest child – 'so close to my pillow and so sad. I burst into tears. My heart went out to him, poor motherless child.'

She had obviously been deeply affected by her experience that night, and kept praising God loudly, thanking Him for saving her from death. Her eyes glittered with unnatural excitement as she told her story.

Shortly after her mother's arrival she had lost consciousness and remembered nothing until she awoke in hospital. The doctors told her she had been five months pregnant. There had been no need to operate: they had pulled out the foetus of the baby boy and shown it to her. He had been perfectly formed, but with a large head and tiny legs, she said. I asked if she grieved for him, but she said she already had seven children and did not want any more. She only felt grateful to be alive.

'What have you been giving Tayereh?' she asked, her thoughts turning to convalescence. 'When I came home they killed a chicken for me. That's very beneficial, you know. And green tea and saffron, with an egg: that's excellent too. Do they have miscarriages in England?' she asked, turning to me.

'Yes, it happens,' I answered. 'But if a woman is pregnant she visits her doctor regularly to check that everything is all right. Hospitals and doctors are free. The government pays their salaries.'

'Everything free!' she marvelled. 'Yesterday we spent five hundred *afghanis* on medicine. It's difficult to find money like that every day.'

I caught a hint of pride in her voice: her family valued her and paid out large sums for her recovery. She and Mariam went on to exchange news. There had been many visitors, so there was plenty to relate. When we announced that it was time for us to go, she got up with us and made her way slowly and painfully to the lavatory, leaning heavily upon her daughter's arm. The immense effort it took for her to cross the courtyard made me realise how very ill she had been.

It was a strange coincidence that the two women miscarried within the space of a few days, although I understood that pregnancies were often 'broken' during the hard months of winter. Work carried on as usual: women could not afford to rest or take special precautions against miscarriage. Losing babies was part of everyday life, sometimes a blessing if there were more than enough children already, although undoubtedly hazardous to women's health.

While talking to Mariam I discovered something very interesting about Tayereh's marriage. I had assumed that this had been her first pregnancy, but Mariam informed me otherwise.

'Not her first,' she said softly, after a moment's hesitation. 'She had a boy by her first husband. He's living at her mother's house; she looks after him just like one of her own children.'

I nodded, stunned at this new intelligence, grateful that Mariam had trusted me with the confidence. It seemed incredible that Tayereh had already been through the experience of pregnancy and childbirth, yet was inhibited from discussing those events in relation to her recent miscarriage. She had known motherhood and she saw her own child when she stayed with her mother, treating him like a younger brother. Through respect to Karim no one mentioned these facts, and I never spoke of them to Tayereh myself.

7

New Year

At last winter came to an end. Everyone began to talk about the coming New Year, which Persians and Afghans observe on 21 March, with the spring equinox. It was the beginning of the season of *meleh*s, outdoor picnics where men and women gathered separately for the day in parks and shrine gardens. The change in weather from freezing ice and snow to blistering heat occurred very suddenly and exerted a powerful impact upon everyday life. During winter people hibernated, snuggling around their *kursi*s for warmth, whiling away the dark evenings by telling stories. There were no weddings or big parties during those months. It was troublesome for guests to travel through ice and snow, hard to keep them warm and comfortable, and difficult for the women to cook feasts in their draughty kitchens. In summer people lived quite differently, migrating to cool north-facing rooms, seeking the shade wherever they walked or sat, and sleeping outside on their roofs or in their courtyards. Spring was a short season, an affirmation of life after the dead of winter: it uplifted people, and they responded to the sprouting greenery and bird-song with sighs of delight, just as if they were listening to fine poetry or music.

The women began talking eagerly about the big *meleh*s in the Women's Park which enclosed the mausoleum of the Timurid queen, Gohar Shad. For at least twenty days women and children gathered there during the daytime; it was a rare opportunity for them to assemble in a huge crowd and spend all day relaxing outdoors.

During our first year I had gone alone to see the women's *meleh*, but had been unable to stay long for I was mobbed by crowds. The soldiers who guarded the gate from male intruders barred my entry at first, but I pleaded with them for so long that they eventually let me through. They were worried about my camera, but I said I was taking official pictures for a university in England. A soldier accompanied me into the park and had to assert all his authority to stop naughty children from rushing at me, pulling at my clothes and exclaiming excitedly that a foreigner had come. It was impossible for me to stay there alone and unprotected.

Shortly before New Year, Mariam made an unexpected suggestion to me.

'Why don't you get yourself a "prayer veil"? It would look beautiful on you and it would be easier for you to walk in the bazaar.'

She meant an Iranian *chador*, as opposed to the face-covering *burqa*. Looking back, I realise that she was thinking about the problem of taking me with them to the women's *meleh*, where I would have attracted unwelcome attention had I once again gone unveiled.

It had never occurred to me to wear a veil, and at first I resisted the idea, feeling sure that I would be unable to keep it on my head. How could I ever stop such an unwieldy piece of cloth from slipping backwards or sideways, rendering me totally ridiculous? I disliked the idea of hiding myself, yet I could appreciate that it might be useful to become a little anonymous – if I could get away with it. I also knew that Mariam sometimes found it embarrassing walking with me in the bazaar, because everybody stared at our group.

Seeing my hesitation, Mariam doubtfully suggested that instead I could get myself a *burqa*, which was easier to wear, since the pleated veil was attached to a close-fitting cap that stayed firmly on the head. She added that they were very expensive – about 600 *afghani*s – and as I was so tall I would have to order one. I refused – I had once tried on the *burqa* whose latticework window provided very limited vision and felt stifling. We worked out how much material I would need for a prayer veil and calculated the cost. I felt I should follow Mariam's advice for I wanted the women to approve of me. I bought some black Iranian cotton with a tiny flower print of the type used for *chador*s, and took it to the house for Mother of Ghani to make up for me.

'Beautiful!' said Parwaneh enviously, fingering it with pleasure.

Mother of Ghani measured me, draping the cloth from my head to the ground, working along the selvage with the span of her hand, counting carefully. 'Fine! We'll make a Moslem of you yet!' she said.

'You'll have to give her twenty *afghanis* for making it up,' Mariam told me after she had gone. 'Don't give her more. That's the right price and she'll be content.'

A few days later the veil was ready. I tried it on, putting the straight edge of the semi-circular cloth on to my head and letting it fall around my shoulders and body. I tucked the material under against each cheek and held it together beneath my chin. The women smiled in approval, admiring my new elegance. I had thought I was buying something drab and shapeless, but they made me see that the prayer veil was a highly coveted item of fashion.

'Look, I've sewn this tiny coin into the top, right in the middle so you can easily find it when you put the veil on,' Mariam explained. 'Keep that in the centre and it will hang evenly on either side.'

I walked about the room, holding the veil closely around me, unused to the feeling of cloth dragging from my head. It pulled backwards and seemed constantly to need adjusting. Did I really dare wear it in the streets? I folded it up, not wanting to make an immediate transition. The men in the alley would surely laugh if they saw me appear in a veil.

I forced myself to wear it the following day on my quiet ten-minute walk through uncrowded residential suburbs to see Shirin, my singing teacher. I had recently begun going to the notorious Minstrels' quarter for lessons. Shirin, the subject of the third part of this book, belonged to the rival group of Sunni musicians working in Herat. Mariam did not openly disapprove of my relationship with Shirin, but it was definitely a matter of unspoken tension and divided allegiances. Walking along, I felt very strange and self-conscious, painfully aware of my shoulder bag bulging out on one side, making a lumpish shape under my veil. Gradually I began to gain confidence, relieved that I seemed to attract very little attention. I knew the awkward moment would come when I reached the bottom of Shirin's alley, where unruly children gathered. Surely I would be an object of ridicule, a foreigner dressed as an Iranian! As I approached, I steeled myself for the usual taunts and cries.

'Look! The foreigner's wearing a veil,' the call went up. 'Here she comes!'

I gave the boys a withering look which Heratis call 'a sour forehead' and uttered a curse, which shocked them into silence. My veil seemed to win me respect.

'*Wah wah!* Congratulations!' said Shirin. 'It looks good, and now you'll be freer. People won't bother you so much.'

The reaction among Herati women was unanimous: the veil looked beautiful and they were pleased that I had adopted their custom. They had not liked my Western clothes – the fur boots, thick jumpers and jeans that I had worn throughout the freezing winter. At last I was dressed in something they found attractive and fashionable. Now that it was warmer I was happy to wear loose Herati knee-length dresses over white, silky lace-bottomed trousers. I bought some sling-backed sandals from the bazaar and a long broad *qadifeh* scarf with which to cover my head in the house when necessary. Mariam had been absolutely right to suggest the veil.

Adopting the veil was a far bigger step than I ever imagined: it took me right inside Herati psychology and affected me deeply. Ironically this symbol of oppression had liberating aspects for me, since it minimised the differences between me and the Afghan people. I was freer, less bothered in crowds. If men stared I had only to pull the side of my veil around my face, indicating displeasure, and they had to respect my wish to be left alone. The veil also modified my behaviour in public for wearing it necessitated changing the angle of my head, lowering the face. I no longer stared about me as I walked, but kept my eyes down. Flashing eyes immediately destroyed my anonymity. In Afghanistan the 'white-eyed one' is self-assertive, overthrowing established hierarchies: it is a term of disfavour. Veiled, I became like a Moslem woman and accepted lower status: I walked more slowly and gently, slipping quietly along streets and alleyways and merging into my surroundings.

I do not approve of the veil, and I see it as a vehicle of oppression, through which men assert their power over women. I experienced the way in which the veil breeds a submissive attitude in women: the lowered head and downcast eyes, and the tendency to sink into the shadows. I also understand that the veil is very addictive; one quickly feels undressed and exposed without it. In my own culture I can walk the streets in colourful, outlandish clothes, thinking nothing of the attention I attract. There is no split between the public and private worlds: these are my clothes and I do not greatly care what people think. It was entirely different in Herat, where women did not express their personalities through dress. Very often they did not even choose the cloth they wore. People cared enormously about the public impression they made: it was selfish not to care, since one's reputation affected one's whole family.

It may seem strange that wearing the veil and becoming similar to Herati women actually resulted in my becoming committed to feminism. I became allied to women, and later thoughts and readings and the experience of motherhood opened my eyes to the ubiquitous dominance of men. The explicit purpose of the veil is to cover the sexual beauty of women from the eyes of men, but in practice it is a means of controlling women's sexuality. Dressed in a veil, one does sense its aura of sexual mystery and power, albeit a manipulative and subversive power. Ultimately, however, the veil curbs women from self-expression, by making them feel they have no place in the public world: it teaches them to be silent and self-effacing.

On New Year's Day John and I got up early to witness the raising of the *jendeh*, the sacred flag, at the shrine of Sultan Agha. Three sacred flags were raised at different shrines in Herat, and the most important flag of all Afghanistan was raised at Mazar-i Sherif, the shrine of Ali. The first day of the year had special significance and people believed that touching the flag-pole might cure their sickness, since it was imbued with blessings and healing power. Thousands of people made the pilgrimage to Mazar-i Sherif every New Year, many of them suffering from illnessess that no medicine or healer had been able to cure. The flag was up for forty days and people said that during that time 'Ali sat on his throne' and miracles took place. A continuous *meleh* called the Tulip Festival was held there.

Likewise people went to Sultan Agha in the hope of cures. The crowds were enormous, and there was a tremendous crush to touch the flag-pole and receive *barakat*, healing blessings. The throng was so thick that I could not see anything, but I later heard that four people had been cured, two men and two women. They had been blind and lame, and apparently people had torn off pieces of their clothes so as to have direct contact with the miracle. I tried to suspend my disbelief. I had seen nothing with my own eyes – only a crowd of people straining in the direction of the flag.

Like the two great religious festivals, New Year was a time of celebration. People visited one another's houses, where all kinds of sweets and biscuits were spread out on a large cloth. During the first three days men went visiting; women for the following ten. Everyone wore new clothes if they could afford them, so as to be fresh as the New Year, and some people dyed their feet and palms with henna. Shiah people cooked special biscuits and sometimes sprouted wheat in bowls

for symbolic greenery, as was the custom in Iran. Some Herati traditions reminded me of Iranian practices, and may have had their roots
in pre-Islamic fire-worship, the old Persian religion. Special significance was attached to Wednesdays, for instance: in Iran people jumped
over fires on the last Wednesday of the old year, and in Herat the most
important women's *meleh* was held on the first Wednesday of the new
year. Another big women's *meleh* took place on the thirteenth day,
which Iranians always spent picnicking outdoors, believing it was bad
luck to stay at home, and on that day they also cut the green sprouted
wheat and threw it out of their windows.

The long season of men's *meleh*s had already begun. They were like
huge outdoor fairs: every Friday for at least two months one was held at
a particular park or shrine garden. Tea-house owners took their
samovars, glasses and teapots and spread out carpets for their customers. Some even erected tents and hired musicians. There were stalls
selling different kinds of food, an arena for open-air wrestling, informal
bicycle competitions, and human-powered Ferris wheel rides for children. Groups of men sat cooking food, listening to music or playing
cards. Music blared from loudspeakers, and gypsies begged for money,
playing loudly on *sorna* and *dohol*, the double-reeded oboe and drum. I
had often visited these colourful open-air gatherings, but this year I
stayed away, shy of being among so many men.

Instead I went with Mariam and her sisters to the 'First Wednesday'
meleh in the Women's Park. The road was jammed with horse-carriages
and taxis, and large parties of women and children streamed through
the gate, carrying bundles of food, cooking equipment and carpets.
This year I held my veil tightly around me and slipped through the gate
past the soldiers guarding the entrance.

The park was an amazing sight. Thousands of women were gathered,
all wearing their finest clothes and laden with gold jewellery, a seething
mass of colour. The sun shone through the tall pines, casting a dappled
light over the whole scene. The crowds were thickest around the
mausoleum, a beautiful domed building covered with the remnants of
magnificent decorative tile-work, and around one of the massive old
minarets. The paths were thronged with people, and there were
hundreds of groups dotted around under the trees. Unlike the men's
*meleh*s there was little commercialism, no tea-houses and only a few
meagre stalls selling dried fruit and pumpkin seeds. Young boys sold
boiling water from samovars and women brought their own tea,
teapots, sweets and glasses. We sat near the samovars so we could easily
make tea, laying out our carpet in a space between parties of picnickers,
surrounded on all sides. In time all the women's carpets touched and the
space became communal.

Karim had not allowed Tayereh to come with us.

'I begged him to change his mind,' said Mariam. 'Our mother used to go to the *meleh*s every year, so why should he think it was a sin for Tayereh to go? He should trust me now I'm like the mother of the family. He wouldn't listen, and said the soldiers were there and it was sinful.'

The soldiers guarding the park were having a grand time. Sometimes they walked through the crowds, supposedly on patrol but feasting their eyes. Many women kept themselves a little covered with their veils. We took ours off for sitting, but put them around us for walking about. We sat watching the animated scene, dazzled and delighted, 'filling our eyes' with this unusual sight of crowds of women together. Several ropes had been slung from the high branches of trees, and girls took turns to swing on them. Some women worked hard pushing them, earning a coin for each girl's turn. I asked Parwaneh if she would swing, admiring the sight of the girls' hair and dresses billowing out above us. She looked longingly, but said she could not have a go as the soldiers were there. Certainly the girls were displaying their beauty: as they swung, their skirts flew up, showing their transparent silky trousers pressed against their legs. They caught their breath and gasped as they rose into the air.

At lunch-time Mariam served *pilau* rice which she had cooked at home. Some women were cooking in quieter corners of the park, but she preferred not to bring all the necessary equipment. A woman sitting near us looked after Mahmood while Mariam ate, and her own baby lay sleeping on a pillow Mariam had lent her. I could not help comparing their easy friendliness with our frosty English reserve. Eventually we grew bored with sitting and we went for a walk, leaving the children with Nassimeh. I was glad to stretch my legs, but I felt awkward at the prospect of meeting people from outside Mariam's circle. Heratis were possessive and I was afraid of embarrassing conflicts. As a foreigner I cheated by 'belonging' to several different families at once, each of whom liked to think of me as their special property. Before long some Minstrel girls, musicians from Shirin's group, saw me and rushed to greet me, inviting me to swing with them. Their faces were brightly painted with make-up. Mariam and Parwaneh recognised that they must be musicians and asked to meet the new bride who they heard had come from Kabul. I wanted to keep these two parts of my life separate, but found myself forced to walk over to them. When I saw Shirin's daughter with a train of siblings, she hissed at me, 'Who're they?', making faces in Mariam's direction. She explained that Shirin had not bothered to come to the *meleh*: she had seen enough of fine dresses and crowds at weddings. One of the other Minstrel girls tried to put lipstick on me, but I rebuffed her almost rudely. I was glad when we finally moved away. Through Mariam's eyes the Minstrels seemed brash and vulgar, while she appeared sedate and stuck-up through theirs. The confrontation of the rival families made me uncomfortable.

The afternoon passed slowly; it was tiring sitting cramped on the hard ground, and the dazzle of the fashions palled. I felt bored, but did not dare get up and walk around for fear of being noticed by other groups of friends. So this was what all the fuss was about! Herati women spent the whole year looking forward to this rare outing, but only after a long confinement could it possibly seem exciting. The women did nothing but sit and gaze at one another, occasionally taking a little walk together. Most of the time they sat in their own family groups. There was no singing or dancing because people were inhibited by the guards, and there was very little making of new acquaintances. It was simply a day to sit, enjoying the feeling of being together in a huge crowd, away from the house and under the trees. For women who spent their lives in domestic surroundings, there were very few opportunities to gather in large crowds; only at the *hamam*, unclothed and relaxed, at weddings, dressed to impress, and at these occasional spring gatherings.

As the sun dipped lower, people began to pack up and go. We parted at the gate and I joined the huge receding tide of women leaving the *meleh* carrying bundles of cooking pots and exhausted children. Although the day had been long, I found it had made a great impression upon me. After-images lingered in my mind: the waving branches of the dark green pines, young girls swinging above us with their hair and scarves flying behind them, and the lustre and sparkle of dresses and gold glinting in the dappled sunlight.

8

The Family Network

Now that the weather was warmer, Mariam took me on outings to visit members of her kinship circle, and I gradually pieced together their intricate genealogies and history. Latif Khan's family were originally ironmongers, and had only recently adopted music as a profession. Before he bought their present house, Latif Khan had lived with his brothers, and so Mother of Karim and Mother of Rahim had worked side by side as *ambejin*s, 'wives of brothers', a relationship for which we have no word in English. (There is a corresponding word for men too – *bajeh*, 'husbands of sisters'.) I also learned that Mother of Karim's mother was from Mashhad in Iran, and that at that time many Herati Shiahs had married Mashhadi women.

Mariam's social life revolved around the clan: there was a constant flow of visits and exchange of news among the women, and much discussion of the problem of finding a wife for Zahir. One of the women I liked very much was Mariam's cousin, Sima Gol, whom I sometimes called on myself. She was one of the most strikingly beautiful women I have ever met, and had a fine bone structure set off by a wide, sensual mouth and dark, almond-shaped eyes. I was also fond of her mother, a diminutive, stout little woman who was always cracking jokes and full of fun. Once, when we were alone together, Sima Gol told me how she had come to marry Ghulam Sarwar, a handsome and prosperous coppersmith.

'His family used to live near us, in the Iraq bazaar, but we didn't know them. They weren't kin. The first thing I knew was when Bibi' – her mother-in-law – 'came walking into our courtyard with several important-looking women. It was obvious that they had come with a marriage proposal, and since I was the only daughter in the house I was terrified!'

'How old were you?'

'About fourteen.'

'And where had they seen you?'

'I found that out later: Ghulam Sarwar had seen me himself,' she admitted shyly, explaining that the door of their house led into a dark tunnel, and that she could never see without raising the front panel of her veil. 'He had just been coming out of a neighbour's house, and he caught sight of me before I had time to cover my face.'

'So he saw your beauty. He fell in love with your face!' I exclaimed, delighted. Her story was just like the romantic verses of Herati love songs, which describe lovers smitten by a single glance.

Ghulam Sarwar had made his mother go and ask for her in marriage. The decision to accept or refuse the proposal lay with Mother of Sima Gol, whose husband had died years ago and who had brought up her children alone, earning money by taking in washing or baking bread. At first she refused their marriage offer, saying Sima Gol was too young, but they persisted in coming and said that Ghulam Sarwar was so desperately in love that he threatened to strangle himself if she did not relent soon. Gradually Mother of Sima began to soften. She saw that they were a highly reputable family who could offer her daughter a comfortable, secure life. Although Sima Gol was young, she wanted the best for her. While this was going on Sima Gol had felt very nervous. She had seen Ghulam Sarwar and thought he looked all right, and I guessed that she secretly welcomed the idea of him as a husband, while at the same time having mixed feelings at the prospect of leaving home. Eventually her mother accepted their offer, but the marriage was delayed by several months while they prepared her dowry. She recalled a particular incident when Ghulam Sarwar had seen her in the alley and called her to talk to him, but she had fled away in fright. She said he still sometimes asked why she had jumped away from him that day. Why had she, I asked? The marriage had not been arranged, she explained: he might have thought she was loose and then not wanted her.

Mariam commented that the marriage was happy and that Sima Gol had everything she wanted and a husband and family who loved her. Contrary to simplistic Western assumptions about 'arranged marriages', her touching story illustrated that romantic love could play a part, despite parents having the primary role in bringing about marriages.

One day Sima Gol came to Mariam's house in great distress.

'My uncle! He's determined to marry this horrible widow,' she moaned. (The term 'widow' applied to a woman who had been divorced as well as one whose husband had died.) 'I've just been to see her. It's a terrible mistake.'

Her half-sister had married into her uncle's household and Sima Gol was very close to all the women there. After his first wife died, she had helped them find her uncle a new one, but he had divorced this woman after a few months, complaining that she was ugly and constantly nagged him. Sima Gol told us that Massumeh, another uncle's wife, had now found him this widow, Parwin, much against the others' wishes.

'God! How will they stand having that Parwin as the head of their house?' said Sima Gol, pitying her half-sister and her fellows. 'What can Massumeh have told him?' she asked, gratefully taking the water-pipe Nassimeh had prepared for her. 'She's ugly, black-skinned, scrawny and dried-up!'

'What do you know about her?' asked Mariam.

'Her husband divorced her several months ago,' she replied, after a long smoke. 'He'd fallen in love with another woman and taken her as his second wife. Parwin can choose for herself whether to accept or refuse any offers. They say she refused to marry again at first. She's living at her mother's house with her two children, making a living by dress-making . . . Oh Mariam, she's not the type of woman we want in our family — so rude and vulgar!'

She said the 'needle and thread' was being sent on the following Tuesday, and invited us to meet at her mother's and together make our way to the party. We went as arranged, but to our surprise found the women busy washing clothes, not dressed and ready to go out. Sima Gol served us tea and told us triumphantly that the marriage had been called off. Her uncle had changed his mind. That morning he had gone to Parwin's house to make sure everything was ready for his guests, but her mother had been very rude to him. He had taken offence, and just at that moment happened to catch sight of Parwin, who had gone into the adjoining room to fetch something.

'She was free to show him her face. Did she think she was beautiful, or something?' laughed Sima Gol. 'He said to himself, "I don't want her", and stopped the whole thing there and then! What a close escape. The contract had been signed and he'd even sent her a watch . . .'

Sima Gol said her uncle should quieten down and stop thinking the thoughts of a young man. He wanted someone fat, she said, but he had not got the money for a plump young wife. Also he said he did not want children, but no man could order a young woman to take the pill. Most women would be afraid for their health. She doubted that he would ask for Massumeh's help again, seeing she had such poor taste. I realised how difficult it was for men, needing sex and companionship, yet having to marry without even seeing the woman. Men were reliant upon the goodwill and careful discrimination of their female relatives to find them wives. It seemed this uncle had got himself into a fix: who would be prepared to help him now?

Most of Mariam's clan lived in Herat city, many of them within walking distance, but she also had some relatives in one of the few Shiah villages in the valley. The kinship link was distant, but the connection was useful to both families. The head of the village family, Father of Now Ruz, a white-haired rustic, used to visit Latif Khan's house whenever he came to the city on market days to sell his crops. He would bring his old white donkey into the courtyard and tether it there, and he served the family in every way he could, chopping wood and performing any menial tasks. He also brought straw and certain village foods in return for their hospitality.

One day John drove us all out to Father of Now Ruz's village, as Latif Khan and Mariam had to pay their respects following a recent death in the family. There was a small exchange of gifts. Mariam brought the women some low-grade silver rings set with semi-precious stones, and some sticky *jelabi* – a syrupy sweet made of spirals of batter deep-fried in fat, bought from a confectioner's shop. Her presents were placed on a tray, which was returned with gifts from the family: some home-made bread and hand-embroidered handkerchiefs. Latif Khan and Mariam both made formal speeches of condolence on the family death. Then our hosts served us a village lunch of home-made bread, yoghurt and salad, and we drank whey flavoured with mint and dill.

We met Father of Now Ruz's old mother, Haji Bibi, so-called because several years ago she had been on the pilgrimage to Mecca. She told us how they had travelled in a party overland, taking all their food and provisions with them, and she described the rituals at Mecca. She had been surprised at some of the things she saw – Moslems of all races and colours, some with skin as black as night! All the people of Mecca seemed to waste so much food. She could not believe that they could throw bread away like dirt.

After lunch we were taken to visit several of the neighbours' houses, where everybody commented upon my age and childlessness. The villagers seemed very isolated, particularly the women, who regarded us as highly civilised and sophisticated. They constantly commented upon the style of our dress and demanded to know the price of everything in the city.

On another occasion I was invited to go with Mariam to visit her maternal cousins, Zahra and Azizeh, who lived in a prosperous suburb just outside the southern wall of the city. Mariam explained that Azizeh was getting married in the summer and her family wanted to get to know me before they invited me to the wedding. We dressed in our veils and Mariam hailed a *gadi* to take us to the house.

Both girls were engaged and receiving their fiancés for 'engagement play', which explained why they were so vivacious and excitable and kept pinching, kissing and even biting me. Azizeh was the younger (she was about fifteen and Zahra seventeen) and was going to be married first because her fiancé was soon to be called up for military service and his family wanted to bring her to their house before he went.

'This is my husband,' she said, showing us a small photograph, which she kissed and clutched to her chest. She said he was a carpet-weaver, and not from their clan.

'How often does he visit you?' I asked.

'About once a week or every ten days,' she replied, blushing at the mention of their 'engagement play'. 'They say it's not good for us to be together too frequently.'

'My fiancé's a teacher,' said Zahra. 'He's my first cousin.' She pulled out a photograph to show us, smiling happily.

They served us tea and played cassettes of music for solo dancing. Zahra made no protestations of modesty, but simply took to the floor. She was tall, rather bony and angular, but very tastefully dressed, and a wonderful dancer. At the musical breaks she would freeze, holding a pose – saluting, kneeling or framing her face with her hands. She did beautiful shivering movements, rolled her eyes, and moved her neck from side to side like a snake. We clapped in time, watching with admiration. We had an excellent lunch and afterwards the girls showed us their dowries, which they were both amassing for their imminent weddings. Their father must have gone to a great deal of expense. We examined identical sets of household goods with detailed interest, admiring two small carpets, silver-capped toiletries for their husbands to use in the *hamam*, china plates and teapots, alarm clocks and many other expensive and carefully chosen items. Then the girls requested a long photo session with my camera, with much changing of clothes and posing in different groups. Zahra insisted on painting my fingernails green and spraying scent all over me.

Of course they made me dance too, but not Mariam, which irked me.

'I'm senior to you. I've borne three children,' she explained later. 'Until you're a mother you're junior, and it's all right for you to dance. They couldn't ask me.'

In this way I took part in Mariam's social life and saw that it had considerable variety. Whereas Western friendships tend to be based upon similarity of interests, class and age, hers (and those of other Herati women) were drawn almost exclusively from the clan, and people were highly conscious of their kinship relationships and of interactions within the clan. Now that I was no longer a guest, but had become assimilated into the family, I saw less of the men. Latif Khan was friendly but more distant, and Zahir and Hossein used to joke and chat with me, but I rarely saw Hassan or Karim, and I regretted that now Karim never played his *rubab* for me, as he had done when I first started to visit the house.

9

Making a Marriage Proposal

Mariam had been keeping her eyes open for a bride for Zahir: she had to choose someone who would suit him and fit into the family. He said he would not like a girl who had Western clothes and emancipated ideas, and it was understandable that the family would not want an educated girl who would look down upon all of them as illiterate. Anyway, Mariam said girls who had been to school were poor workers and easily discontented. When seeking brides, women looked for traditional talents in cookery, sewing or embroidery, and the virtues of modesty and a willingness to work. The hierarchical structure of the family made it easier to choose girls from humbler backgrounds, such as Tayereh, since they naturally tended to be submissive in their new surroundings. There was an inherent conservatism in the system of women choosing brides, as it was safer to select a girl who would not outshine the others in knowledge or attainment. On the other hand, a bride could never be too beautiful, for she was to be shown off, glowing and dazzling, like a prized jewel.

Mother of Rahim (Latif Khan's brother's wife) hinted that Mariam should visit one of their relatives and take a look at their daughter, Aisheh. Her mother had been asking many questions about Zahir, and Mother of Rahim guessed that they were interested in having him as a son-in-law. Mariam told me that she liked the girl, although she was rather young and inexperienced, and that after consulting the family she had taken Mother of Rahim, her junior aunt Zainab, and Tayereh with her to Aisheh's house to make a formal proposal.

'And what was the answer?' I asked, excited that negotiations had begun.

'She refused us,' Mariam said calmly. 'But that means nothing. No one gives their daughter immediately. She said she'd ask Aisheh's father. You know, I think they might consent.'

She asked if I would like to accompany them on another proposal visit the following day. I accepted with alacrity, fully conscious of the honour she was doing me.

Dressed in our best clothes, Mariam, Tayereh and I set off, accompanied by Mariam's maternal aunt and her daughter-in-law. Parwaneh looked wistful at being left behind, but Mariam explained that it was unsuitable to take juniors on proposal parties, while on the other hand Tayereh had to accompany her every time since she would become Aisheh's senior *ambejin*. On the way we called at Mother of Rahim's house and she and Zainab joined us. When we arrived at Aisheh's home we paused at the front door and then entered in order of seniority, dipping our heads under the low doorway and walking straight in, first the maternal aunt, then Mother of Rahim, Zainab, the aunt's daughter-in-law, Mariam, Tayereh – and lastly myself, the most junior, a non-relative and childless.

'Is Mother of Sekhi at home?' asked Mariam, using Aisheh's mother's formal title.

'She's coming right now,' a young woman answered, rising to accompany us as though we had been expected.

She showed us into a low-ceilinged upper room where we could talk without interruption. We sat according to rank, with the maternal aunt and Mother of Rahim at the far end, next to the window. Nobody spoke until our hostess returned, bringing Mother of Sekhi, a tall shrewd-looking woman. The two women, who were *ambejin*s, sat together in the doorway greeting us formally in turn, whispering almost inaudibly as etiquette required. My heart fluttered when my turn came, but I managed to whisper replies and ask after their health. Mariam mentioned briefly that I was from Kabul and everyone kept up the pretence that I was a junior member of the family, not an interesting foreigner, although I guessed they knew my true identity. For some time the explicit purpose of our visit was studiously avoided, and Mother of Rahim and Zainab talked freely to our two hostesses while the rest of us maintained a dignified silence. Two water-pipes were brought in, and later a huge tray of tea was served with great formality. Mother of Rahim and Zainab were both outgoing and witty, and they enjoyed entertaining us with long animated anecdotes. The rest of us were more tense, preoccupied with our unspoken business. We listened as the four women sparred together, skilfully scoring points off one another through veiled references to the subject of marriage. Already a subtle process of bargaining for gold and bridewealth seemed to have begun, as Mother of Sekhi embarked upon a long account of a wedding she had recently attended, enumerating in detail the excellent cloths that had been presented to the bride.

'What's the point in buying second-quality cloth? It soon looks scruffy! You want something to last, don't you,' she said. The implication was clear: she would want the best for her daughter.

Mother of Rahim retaliated swiftly.

'When I was a bride I was jealous of my *ambejin*, Mother of Karim, God bless her! I could only think about how rich she was, with her gold and fine dresses, everything in the latest fashion. I looked at her bracelets and necklaces and thought about wearing ones like them. What a fool I was to think that way! Silk, satin, gold – such things pass away – they don't last! Do I pray to God to give me such things? Now all I ask is for Him to protect my children and grant me a safe passage to my grave. I've learned some wisdom with my years, for where is their mother now – for all the gold she wore? God rest her soul, she lies under the ground, where gold is good to no one. Death to gold!' she exclaimed, ending her speech with an emphatic curse.

Eventually she asked the question on all our minds.

'Has Aisheh's father given his answer?'

'He says he won't give her,' Mother of Sekhi replied firmly, looking over to Mariam.

I felt bitterly disappointed, and Mariam looked downcast, but then as Mother of Sekhi elaborated I saw a change in Mariam's expression.

'They'll give her,' whispered Tayereh at my side, having caught some nuance in Mother of Sekhi's speech.

What had happened? The refusal had apparently been definitive, yet somehow the bride's mother had given hope! I threw Mariam a questioning look and caught a slight nod of relief, and realised that negotiations were still continuing. Heratis were skilful and devious in their speech. After all, when offered tea one always refused politely. Things were never taken at their face value.

Mother of Sekhi was asking if Zahir was really keen to marry. Perhaps it was just his family who wanted to find him a bride. Mother of Rahim saw that she wanted reassurance and made a long speech swearing that Zahir's heart was completely set upon marriage and that he did nothing but visit all the holy shrines in Herat praying for his wish to be fulfilled. I laughed inwardly at her exaggerations. Mariam went on to say that he had mourned his mother for two years, but now had decided the time had come to take a wife. Their mother would not have wanted him to wait any longer. Had she been alive she would have been here with them pleading for Aisheh: her wishes were with them. She spoke persuasively, outlining the advantages of the marriage and the closeness of the two families. What could be better than a match between relations who already held one another dear? Then Zainab spoke, praising Zahir as a serious man, well respected in the community, disliked by no one, diligent in his prayers and fasts. God was pleased with his faith and his patience, she concluded. Aisheh's mother listened, but refused to give any firmer grounds for hope, unwilling to be wooed quickly by their flattery and assurances. She obviously enjoyed the power she held.

A tall, fair-haired girl came quietly to the door with a fresh box of matches for the water-pipe. Tayereh whispered to me that she was Aisheh herself. She crouched in the doorway, murmuring greetings to each of us in turn and then remained silent. To my relief, I found her beautiful. I had dreaded feigning enthusiasm for a bride who did not particularly please me, but her face was delicate and charming, and she carried herself with quiet dignity. She looked about fourteen; like Parwaneh, a working 'girl of the house' with kitchen grime on her clothes. But her beauty shone through.

The maternal aunt, who had sat in formal silence, eventually suggested that we should depart. On our way out we passed Aisheh in the semi-darkness. Mariam touched her hand and murmured a few soft words to her, a gesture which shocked and touched me. Somehow Aisheh had seemed inaccessible, like some rare prize, not a person whom one could simply address. Sitting in such long formal silence had deprived me of any power of expression! Was this how diplomats became cut off from the people whose fates they expended all their energy on negotiating?

Downstairs Mariam said goodbye to Mother of Sekhi. 'We'll call tomorrow. That'll make three visits,' she said, as though their acceptance was almost settled.

A week later the situation still seemed very uncertain. Aisheh's parents accepted the proposal, but sent a marriage contract with unreasonably high demands. This engagement document had to be signed by the bridegroom's family before the sending of the 'needle and thread', although in practice it did not seem to be legally binding.

'I don't see how we can possibly accept their terms,' Mariam said gloomily. 'They're asking for sixty thousand *afghanis* bridewealth, thirty sets of clothes, twenty pairs of shoes and thirty *mesqals*' weight in gold jewellery!'

I gasped. These demands were about twice or even three times what the family might have expected to give. However, they eventually signed the contract, and sent the bride a gold locket worth 3,000 *afghanis*, some flowers and cakes and sweets. At the same time they intimated that they could not really afford to bring everything they had promised, although Mariam privately conceded to me that they would have to give about half.

Zahir was showing signs of tension, and he was often moody.

'What's she like?' he would ask me repeatedly.

I assured him that Aisheh was beautiful, describing her fair hair, blue eyes and pretty face. Could he really believe what I said and what his sisters told him? A face like a moon and teeth like pearls? Lovely as a fairy? He nagged me for more details, but nothing could allay his anxiety. We both knew that even if I had not liked her, I would be obliged to praise her beauty, so there was an inevitable credibility gap.

'Is she like this?' he asked, showing me a postcard of a Pakistani film pin-up, a voluptuously curved sex goddess, lying languidly across a couch in a tight mini-dress and black fish-net stockings. Was this what he wanted, or thought he wanted? I said Aisheh was far more to my liking, trying to reassure him.

'She won't beat me, will she?' he asked, making a joke of it, cringing and flinching under mock blows, evidently wondering who would be 'master'.

Tension spread to other members of the family and a quarrel sprang up between Zahir and his father. Mariam said it was because Latif Khan was jealous of Zahir's lovely young bride, adding that he had been difficult when Karim married. She spoke to him herself. Did he want everyone to think he was a randy old man, jealous of his own son?

We received a smart invitation to the 'needle and thread' party. Although few, if any, of Zahir's guests could actually read the details of the time and place, the invitation card had become a necessary prestige item. It had an embossed design depicting two doves flying into a lilac sunset, with two golden rings threaded through a string caught in their beaks, although the exchange of rings was a Christian, not a Moslem, custom. Unlike Karim's 'needle and thread', this was purely a betrothal party. Zahir and Aisheh would not see each other until the engagement and *nekah*. About twenty close male relatives had been invited from either side of the family, and they were being entertained in a neighbour's house.

We, the bridegroom's women, made our way to Aisheh's house, carrying the *daireh*. In the villages women would have drummed all the way from their house to the bride's house, signalling to all the neighbours that they were on bridal business, but in the city women were shy to draw attention to themselves in the busy bazaar. Once in the alleys, Mariam took the *daireh* and drummed wedding rhythms until we were right inside Aisheh's courtyard. Then, with great dignity, we took our places as honoured guests in the family room.

'Where's Aisheh?' asked Mariam, after exchanging greetings with Mother of Sekhi and all the relatives and neighbours who had gathered to meet us.

Her mother said that she had been crying all day, and refused to come down. She was ashamed because they had not had time to go to the *hamam* in the morning.

Zainab came in alone, breathlessly, her pregnant stomach swelling in front of her. Mariam immediately asked why Mother of Rahim had not come with her as they lived in the same house. Zainab told her that Mother of Rahim was put out because Mariam had not called for her on the way. She advised her to send Nassimeh over to get her. Nassimeh pouted and flounced out of the room, saying she would not go, leaving Mariam very vexed and embarrassed that things were not going well. Mother of Rahim's non-attendance was an insult to Mother of Sekhi and the party.

Nassimeh came back to report that the men were having a music session. Some of the women wanted to listen, so we all put on our veils and walked to the neighbouring house where the men had gathered. We marched boldly across the courtyard in full view of the men, about twenty of us in a tight group. Although we were veiled, I felt uncomfortably conscious of their silent scrutiny. We arrived in a dark lumberroom. Trunks and boxes were stored on the ground and strings of dried vegetables hung from hooks in the ceiling. Girls jostled for turns to climb on to a wooden crate and peer at the men's party through a tiny

window that faced the courtyard, while the rest of us squatted in the
semi-darkness listening to and commenting upon the music. It seemed
ridiculous to me, but then I reminded myself that this was the closest
most women ever got to hearing the full professional sound of a male
city band.

Nassimeh returned, having apparently obeyed Mariam's request
after all, with the news that Mother of Rahim would not come. 'You
should have heard the way she cursed you, Mariam! "Obviously she
thinks she's got white hair already: just because she's arranging a
marriage, she's a senior, is she?"' Nassimeh was a good mimic. The
other women listened avidly, fascinated by this public rift between the
bridegroom's women. Mariam was very upset, and said she had not
meant to give offence. Her discomfort was relieved by the welcome
distraction of ice-cream, served out on little plates to all the guests. It
tasted delicious, flavoured with rosewater and cardamom and topped
with a green sprinkling of chopped pistachios. Afterwards Aisheh's
mother asked us to sing and dance for them, which was our duty as the
bridegroom's women. Mariam unwrapped the *daireh* and began to play.

'Tell Aisheh to come and sit with us!' she begged.

After a short piece, she handed the drum to Zainab, asking her to play
so that we could perform the circle dance – Mariam, Tayereh,
Nassimeh, Parwaneh and myself. Zainab played forcefully, shouting
encouragement as we danced, and just then Aisheh quietly entered the
room and sat unobtrusively by the door.

'Look – the bride!' whispered Parwaneh, breathless with delight.

They are bound to fight, I thought to myself, sensing that Parwaneh's
adoration of Aisheh was doomed to sour. I had seen rivalry between
sisters and wives: so often sisters became mean and jealous, and they
picked on brides when they finally came to live with them.

Mariam got up to dance, calmly taking her place in the middle of the
room. I had never seen her dance until this moment: the occasion had
never been fitting for her to do so. She moved with extraordinary grace
and expression, gesturing delicately, moving her hands in a flowing
series of perfect attitudes. Zainab drummed and we all clapped. It was a
timeless feeling, drinking in Mariam's beauty, enjoying this single rare
offering. What a waste of talent! Mariam never danced or sang at other
times: she was denied this means of self-expression for the sake of
honour and reputation.

Afterwards Zainab and I sang a slow lament together, a nomad song
about the bride leaving home. After each line the others joined in the
refrain:

> *Oh bride, don't cry because you're leaving*
> *We're taking you away like a flower to our own country.*

Aisheh's mother began to cry openly, and Aisheh sat stock-still behind her, tears shining in her eyes. Then Zainab broke the tension with a much faster song, calling on the girls to clap between the verses. Aisheh and the women laughed and enjoyed our music.

Two trays of gifts were brought back to the house and set down on the verandah, one covered with cakes and sweets, and the other bearing the 'needle and thread'. A golden needle and decorated thread were stuck into three fine squares of cloth, accompanied by a large sugar-cone dressed in a festive coat of red brocade. Mariam said that it would not be broken and eaten until the day of Zahir's 'sweet-eating'. On that day, God willing, he would have his first sight of Aisheh. The whole family gathered around and embraced one another, uttering formal congratulations and blessings. After weeks of tension and uncertainty it was a moment of happiness and triumph: Zahir's betrothal was sealed. Latif Khan praised their hosts' lavish hospitality, mentioning in particular the expensive ice-cream that had been served. All the men seemed in very good spirits after playing music together.

'What did they say about me?' Zahir asked Mariam anxiously.

'They were very pleased with you,' she assured him. 'Your mother-in-law said the men had all appreciated the way you went round to them each in turn kissing their hands the way I advised you. Everything went off well.'

He turned away from the gifts and stretched out on the string bed where he slept now that the nights were warm, spreading his *pattu* shawl over himself like a sheet. His still body spoke of exhaustion and relief now that the ordeal of the party was over.

10

Becoming Beautiful

The invitation arrived for the wedding of Azizeh, the younger of
Mariam's pinching, kissing cousins, and my name was included.
Mariam invited me to go with her to Zainab's the day before to have her
face 'smoothed', a treatment whereby facial hair was removed. Most
married women had this done before going to weddings, which were
important occasions for beautification and display. It might seem
strange to us, but women took great trouble to adorn themselves and
look attractive for the sake of their own sex. They never dressed up for
men. Even as brides they were washed, clothed, groomed and painted
by others. Fashion and beauty were a matter of status and aesthetics,
divorced from sex appeal, and at weddings and *meleh*s women enjoyed

showing themselves off to one another. Often they literally let down their hair, which at other times was kept plaited and covered with a scarf.

Zainab lived with Mother of Rahim in the old house where Mariam had been born. In contrast to Mother of Rahim, whose rooms were opulent with comfortable bolsters and a shining samovar, Zainab lived simply. Her room was stark and almost bare of possessions. Her husband got what work he could, shovelling rubble on building sites, or mining salt in the barren land near the Iranian border. Sometimes he was away for weeks, and Zainab had to manage as best she could, encumbered with two small children and a pregnancy, but she never complained and was always cheerful.

She told Mariam to sit by the window, in the light, and handed her a tin of white powder with which to rub her face. Nassimeh told me it was lime and that it softened the hairs. She began rubbing it on me. I had not fully decided to undergo the treatment, but I was curious, so I allowed her to continue. I watched as Mariam made sure her hair was all tied back into her scarf and then covered her forehead, cheeks and chin with the powder, avoiding her eyes. Zainab treated her first. She took some cotton thread and twisted it deftly into a kind of loop held in her teeth and one hand, so that as she moved backwards and forwards the cotton formed a scissor-like cutting edge along the face, plucking out the tiny hairs in a smooth movement. She worked methodically over Mariam's face, swaying backwards and forwards across her, like a bird performing some strange mating ritual, manipulating the threads in her teeth and hands. Every so often she wetted the threads with saliva to make them run more smoothly across the skin. Mariam sat still, bearing the tweaking pain bravely, while Zainab worked patiently for about half an hour. Then she took a penknife and plucked Mariam's eyebrows, gripping the hairs between her thumb and the blade. Finally she released her and handed her a mirror to examine the results.

It was my turn. I took Mariam's place and tucked my hair away from my face. Zainab surveyed me with a practised eye, pronouncing that she would not touch my hair-line, which was high enough already. She said she would start on my forehead, where there was least hair. She wet the thread and set to work. It hurt more than I expected, and felt like tiny pins pricking into the flesh. You try pulling out some of the hairs on your cheek and see how it feels! Tears sprang up in my eyes. I longed for her to finish, and kept still with great difficulty.

'This is nothing to the pain of your wedding night, is it? You remember that pain, don't you?' she joked, ridiculing my squeaks of discomfort. 'Wait until you're "on the bricks"!' – in the act of giving birth. (Herati women often raise themselves on bricks when they squat to give birth, hence the expression.) 'Mariam, if she cries at this pain, how will she be then? This is nothing!' she laughed, seeking to distract me. I sat squirming, tears running down my cheeks. Why was I doing this? When would it end?

'Azizeh must be having her face done ready for tomorrow,' said Mariam. 'You're like her, having your first treatment. It's as though you were a bride getting ready for your wedding,' she laughed, finding the idea ridiculous: a woman of my age!

At last Zainab finished. I breathed an enormous sigh of relief: my whole face tingled. She set to work on plucking my eyebrows, which did not hurt nearly so much, and then finally released me.

'Don't wash your face until tomorrow,' she advised. 'Leave the lime on your skin. Just rub in cream or Vaseline. Grease is beneficial.'

How could I go into the bazaar with a white face? Mariam could cover hers with her veil. I rubbed off some of the lime and put on a little of the grease she offered. My skin was itchy and swollen and I did not feel beautiful. I collapsed in tears when I got home. After we left, Nassimeh told me that I should have given Zainab a little money. Mariam had given her ten *afghanis*, as Zainab was very poor. I felt upset that I had not helped her, and also because my skin tingled painfully. My whole face had become a swollen itchy mass of tiny red bumps.

The following afternoon we arrived at Azizeh's house and were served sweets and scented drinks with great formality. Later the bridegroom's women arrived, drumming to announce themselves.

Parwaneh and I joined a party of about thirty women who went in a procession of cars to take the bride to the *hamam*. *Hamam*s were important meeting-places in the lives of Herati women; there were several of them dotted throughout the city. Usually women went in family parties, about every ten days, and there they would spend an hour or two washing and grooming themselves. Women also went to the *hamam* on the tenth, twentieth, thirtieth and fortieth days after giving birth, and performed various rituals for health and purification.

I regretted not being able to take part in the social life of the *hamam*, but an early experience when I went with Nassimeh and Parwaneh during my first year in Herat had put me off going again. There had immediately been a riot of excited girls curious to stare at me, so Parwaneh thought it prudent to use a private cubicle, rather than going to sit and wash in the public area. All the cubicles were occupied, so we begged admittance to one that was being used by another party of women. From outside there came a terrible pummelling and banging as people struggled to get in and see the interesting foreigner, and this persisted throughout the hour or so that we spent inside; it was like a siege.

The private cubicles had two areas: a dry vestibule where one changed and hung clothes, and a small room with a shower and tap where one sat and washed. To make matters worse, I found I did not know how to wash according to their criteria, and I did not possess the numerous accessories women brought with them to the *hamam*: crocheted flannels for rubbing the skin clean, a black pumice-stone for scraping dead skin from the feet and elbows, powders for rubbing on the face, eggs and henna for the hair, buckets for rinsing, velvet mats for sitting on while one dressed . . . I was washed in five minutes and did not know how to occupy myself, watching as they patiently rubbed the grime off their bodies.

I also became very self-conscious about my body. The notion of removing hair from the face for the sake of beauty was part of a general distaste for body hair. Moslem custom prescribes the removal of pubic hair, and the women in the *hamam* were amazed and disgusted that I had not done this. Out of modesty they kept their underpants on while they washed, but I had blithely removed mine, thinking it ridiculous to wash with clothes on, and not having brought a clean dry pair to wear afterwards. I sat on the wet floor, soaping my body and rinsing myself while the women stared and commented, clearly repelled by what they saw. I discovered that men and women used a depilatory powder to remove pubic hair; other women told me they preferred to pluck out the hair with chewing gum. They said they did not shave or use scissors – poor methods, in their eyes. One woman told me frankly that pubic hair was ugly and would get in the way during sex. I was struck by the ease with which women sat together, naked except for their pants, washing one another and chatting. They seemed completely relaxed and unself-conscious, and I envied this.

I never suggested another visit to the *hamam*, remembering those claustrophobic hours in that small cubicle, the stifling heat, and the drowning feeling when Nassimeh had unexpectedly dowsed my head with a bucket of water to rinse out some shampoo. However, I did not want to miss seeing what happened when a bride was taken to the *hamam* before her wedding. I told Parwaneh I would not wash this time, but would simply watch, and she did likewise. In any case, neither of us had brought our washing things.

As we filed down the steps into the *hamam* everyone murmured, '*Bismillah*'. We entered a large room with a concrete floor. Around the walls there was a continuous raised platform where people sat and dressed, and hooks were provided for hanging clothes. This large changing area had a very attractive old stucco plasterwork ceiling, and led on to another room where people actually washed.

The bridegroom's women placed a fine carpet on the platform and sat Azizeh down to undress her. She was limp and expressionless, allowing them to remove her clothes and dress her in a beautiful traditional *hamam* wrapper of red, gold and purple ikat woven silk. Then they undressed themselves, leaving only their underpants on. They led Azizeh into the adjoining room, which had a large cistern of hot water at the far end. We could see them through the doorway sitting in a semi-circle washing and shampooing Azizeh, scrubbing backs and rinsing one another with buckets of water.

I tried to imagine myself being washed by strange women who had become my mother-in-law, sisters-in-law and relatives. They were preparing their bride, knowing she would be in the arms of her husband that night. Azizeh submitted to their hands, showing no emotion. She was slim, barely mature, with fair skin and small round breasts. This bridal washing was a process of intimate familiarity with a new body, a new member of the family. I remembered once watching some other women considering a bride for their brother, opening her mouth and examining her teeth, calmly discussing her physical attributes, criticising her faults and praising her good points as though she were a young filly.

Eventually the women began to drift back into the changing room. They brought Azizeh with them, dried her and dressed her in new clothes.

'This is her finest dress now,' said Parwaneh as we watched. 'It was made by a male tailor. That's French velvet – they say it cost seven hundred *afghanis* a metre!'

I saw them tie a brocade bag around Azizeh's waist and something flat on to her upper arm, and asked Parwaneh about it. The bag contained cake 'so that she would never be hungry' and the Holy Koran was tied on to her arm. I had seen villagers tie bread on to the bride's stomach: cake was a city refinement!

It was early evening by the time our cortège reached the bridegroom's house. The music and dancing had already begun and the women looked dazzling in all their finery. Mariam had advised me to bring several dresses as it was customary to change in the evening and the following morning. At midnight Azizeh took her place on the bridal throne, joined by her husband, and they performed ritual ceremonies, feeding one another tastes of sweet food and drink, reading verses of the Koran, and viewing their combined images in a mirror. Azizeh looked transformed, immaculately painted with red lips and blue eye-shadow. The day we had visited her for lunch she had seemed girlish, but now she appeared almost voluptuous wearing make-up and a fashionable curly wig with a gauzy white veil like a Christian bride.

Her husband looked young, slim and serious. He wore a new Western suit and the astrakhan hat with which his father had crowned him during the men's evening rituals, which many of us had watched from the roof. Men were equally conscious of their dress and looks: it would be wrong to think that only women thought about expensive cloth or gold jewellery. Men spent large sums on good quality *chapan* coats, silk turbans, skin hats and watches. I was surprised when people insisted that men were more beautiful than women, but I think they meant that men were better turned out, their clothes always clean and pressed – at least those who were better off and did not do dirty menial work. They were highly conscious of the public impression they gave in the bazaar. Women, on the other hand, were usually dirty and unkempt from dealing with small children and housework, and only ever dressed up when they went out. It was understandable that they enjoyed weddings as rare occasions to make themselves beautiful for one another.

11

A Night at the House of Latif Khan

The day of our departure approached rapidly. John and I planned to leave Herat straight after the festival at the end of Ramadan. Mariam often used to invite me to stay the night at their house, but I would refuse, saying I needed time at home with John. Now that we were shortly to leave I suggested staying with them next time I visited, so that I could spend the evening and the following day in their company.

The fast had begun. From dawn to dusk nothing was ingested; no food, water or even medicine. Tempers often grew short and people were apathetic, needing to conserve their energy. Time passed very slowly without meals, tea or cooking to break up the day, but the nights were alive with feasting, merriment and music, and the streets were crowded with men sociably strolling along. Despite the rigours of fasting, people welcomed Ramadan since it was a holy month, during which they could gain religious merit through personal effort and self-discipline. They used to ask me if I was taking the fast, but I explained that I had so much to do before leaving that I could not afford the loss of energy. I also admitted that fasting was difficult and the thirst very uncomfortable.

I arrived at Mariam's house early in the morning so as to avoid walking in the heat, and found her sewing in the cool, north-facing summer family room. She was making some small trousers from an old garment, cutting out the cloth by eye and then sewing up the long seams with a running stitch. She needed plenty of trousers for Mahmood, as nowadays she put him in his swaddling only at night; otherwise he simply peed on the ground.

I took out my embroidery and set to work on a wall hanging of my own design. Mariam admired it and made me hold it up to see my progress.

'Who are you sewing for?' she asked, assuming I was working on a gift.

Women rarely sewed for themselves, but embroidered fine shirt fronts for their brothers or husbands, or they decorated wrapping cloths, alcove curtains or cushion covers for the house.

'I used to do embroidery too,' she went on, 'but now I only have time to sew or mend things like this.'

Tayereh, Parwaneh and Nassimeh came back from the *hamam*. Parwaneh flopped down on to a mattress, looking weak.

'The fast's killing me today, Mariam. I feel sick and I've got heartburn,' she said, closing her eyes.

'Then eat and forget the fast for today,' Mariam counselled. 'Anyway, if you bring something up your fast is broken, so there's no merit in it.'

Mariam was not taking the fast herself. She said it was too hard to breast-feed without drinking or eating. Women were expected to fast even if they were pregnant: the only valid reasons for not doing so were sickness, travelling or fighting a holy war. Women did not fast during their periods, because at such times they were ritually unclean, but normally they made up the days lost through menstruation later. Plenty of people broke the fast in secret, behind closed doors, but it was forbidden to eat or drink in the bazaar, and restaurants and tea-houses were closed.

At lunch Mariam persuaded Parwaneh to eat, but as a matter of pride she made us promise not to tell Tayereh that she had broken her fast.

Afterwards we drank tea and lay down, drowsy in the heat. I asked for news of Aisheh: they had recently visited her, taking limes as she had a fever. Mariam said that it was now her duty to bring Aisheh presents or medicines, for Aisheh belonged to them too. She complained that Mother of Sekhi would not let Aisheh visit them, as she maintained that it was not good for a bride to visit her husband's house before the wedding. Mariam seemed resigned to waiting until the spring for Zahir's 'sweet-eating' party.

Later Mariam killed a chicken for the evening meal. I watched her slit its throat, holding its beating wings against her knee. She tossed some water over the bricks to wash away the blood, then deftly pulled out the feathers and jointed the bird for stewing.

The men had been dozing in the shade, stretched out on their string beds. As the light began to melt into long shadows, they roused themselves for their ablutions. Soon it would be *iftar*, the time for ending the fast, 'when a black and white thread were no longer distinguishable'. Parwaneh spread out the cloth and set out the food ready for the sound of the cannon. Throughout the year it sounded at noon, and during Ramadan it also marked the beginning and end of the fast. The men performed their prayers and then gathered around the cloth, savouring the sight and smell of the food, awaiting the signal. At the boom of the cannon children shouted from houses all over the city, and people said their blessings and began to eat. Parwaneh brought two paraffin lamps from the alcove and set them down. We ate a delicious meal of rice, chicken, tomato salad and warm bread, taking occasional sips of iced *dugh*, a summer drink made of watered yoghurt, chopped cucumber and mint. Nassimeh noticed that the men had finished eating and quietly rose to pour water from the ewer for them to wash their hands, and then she resumed eating.

The men discussed where they would go for music that night, as during Ramadan professional bands came from Kabul to Herat, hired by enterprising tea-house owners: there was a choice of concerts every night. They left, planning to drink tea in the bazaar with their friends, meet at a concert and return home at one or two in the morning.

When they had gone we felt free. Tayereh came and joined us for tea and we sat overlooking the moonlit courtyard. I told them how sad I felt at the prospect of leaving them: it might be years before I came back this time, as I was planning to have children.

'But you will come. You came before,' said Mariam, reassuring me. 'By the time you come – who knows! Tayereh will have lots of children, God willing. Maybe Aisheh too: she'll be living here by then. We might have found a wife for Hossein. Parwaneh, you'll have gone,' she added lightly. 'You'll be living in some other house – married, and maybe with a baby!'

She looked calmly into the future, facing it with equanimity. Whereas I clung to them, dreading the disruption of our happy friendship, she comforted me, having faith that one day we would be reunited. I cannot help remembering her words and thinking of the very different and harsher fate that lay ahead.

I cocked my ear, hearing singing in the silence that had fallen among us. Nassimeh said it was their neighbours' *rowzeh*: they held it every Sunday night, just as the *sheikh* came on Thursdays in memory of their own mother. She suggested that we went up to the roof to listen, so she and I climbed the stairs with Parwaneh and Simin, and peered cautiously over the low wall so as not to be seen from below. Carpets had been spread out in the courtyard, and men and women sat listening to the melancholy singing. The two singers stood out of view, but powerful gas lamps cast their huge shadows on to the wall behind them: one of them held his hand to his ear as he sang. The message of the music was clear – the Shiah faith, a faith that overcomes death, martyrdom, persecution and suffering, teaching courage and resilience in the face of difficulty.

The sound of laughter, talking and music came from other courtyards as families sat enjoying the warm moonlit evening. Lights flickered from the Friday mosque, where the Holy Koran was being read chapter by chapter each night in the presence of the Governor and all the pious men of the city. From further away music blared indistinctly from the loudspeakers of the open-air concerts. The night was vibrant with life. We crouched together, absorbing all the sounds, staying so long under the starry sky that little Simin fell asleep at our side.

Downstairs I played and sang for them, but they refused to sing themselves. I knew Mariam had a lovely voice, having heard her sing lullabies to Mahmood, and I regretted the inhibitions that were placed upon her.

Our sleeping arrangements seemed complicated. We were all to sleep out in the courtyard until the men came home so that in Karim's absence Tayereh did not need to sleep alone. She explained that whenever Karim played at weddings she slept with Parwaneh and the others until he returned and called her upstairs. We unrolled the mattresses from their place in the alcove and laid them out side by side. Tayereh slept with Nassimeh on one and Parwaneh and I were put on another, but I moved on to a spare one, unable to settle down while so squashed. In the middle of the night we sleepily moved upstairs, the unmarried girls and I to the guest room and Tayereh to her own room with Karim. Latif Khan and his unmarried sons slept on string beds in various corners of the courtyard, and Hassan had a mattress next to Mariam. It was not exactly private for making love, but most Afghan women slept next to their children out in the open during summer.

Everyone woke late during Ramadan, having no incentive to get up and expend energy. Each night, just before dawn, Parwaneh woke up and warmed food for those who were fasting, and then returned to bed.

In the morning Mariam and I ground up some spices to make a medicinal cure for stomach ache.

'Hossein bought the ingredients from a Greek medicine shop yesterday,' she said, unwrapping the small packets to show me. 'This is "horse salt". It's better quality than cooking salt; you don't have to soak it to get rid of mud. And this is dried orange skin.'

Several packets contained small seeds similar to cardamom or fennel, but of different species. I also recognised *ajeghan*, tiny round seeds women gave to their babies for good digestion. Another packet contained a strange-looking object like a tiny elongated pine cone, which Mariam said was very hot, like chilli. I tasted the seeds and drew pictures in my notebook, fascinated by these remedies that were handed down from mother to daughter.

Mariam sent Nassimeh to borrow an enormous brass mortar and pestle from their neighbours, and we set to work grinding the spices with it. We sieved the powder and accumulated it in storage bottles, grinding the rest until it had all been reduced to a light brown dust. It tasted strange, but not unpleasant: 'salty, bitter and hot all at once', as Mariam put it.

She showed me some stones from bitter cherries and some dried rhubarb leaves, explaining that boiled together they made an effective remedy for infantile fevers. Ginger was much used, she added, particularly in medicines for babies and new mothers, but when you ground ginger you had to keep silent, otherwise it went stringy! She asked me if I could recognise a silk cocoon, and told me that if you put it against an aching tooth the swelling would go away. In this I detected an element of sympathetic magic, with the soft silk cocoon likened to the painful swelling in the jaw.

She gave me some samples to take back to England, and said that when Simin grew up she intended to teach her all about these remedies, including the use of spices in cooking. She also wanted to teach her how to sew and embroider, just as her mother had done with her. I wondered if she would send Simin to school, and suspected that she felt it would be enough to coach her at home.

During the afternoon Mother of Ghani called, but as she was fasting she did not have her customary water-pipe. She casually mentioned that her sons had found a large house on the other side of the city, and quite soon they would all be moving.

'How will you manage without her?' I asked Mariam after she had gone, surprised that they took the news with so little reaction: Mother of Ghani was like part of the family.

'There are plenty of women who need a little money,' she replied. 'I can always find help elsewhere. I give her money when she does things for us, you know. She's not at all well off. She has a lot of difficulties in her life. Her husband died years ago and her sons quarrel. Once they had a fight with knives.'

The shadows lengthened and I prepared to go.

'The time will pass quickly for you, now that you're leaving,' said Mariam. 'Already we're half-way through this month. One day we should go to Sultan Agha and visit my mother's grave. Next week, before you become too busy.'

12

Saying Goodbye

The visit to Mother of Karim's grave was my last outing with the sisters. Mariam said nothing, but I knew she meant it as a kind of leave-taking, a farewell to her mother's spirit. She told me that she had once had a dream in which I had been with them at Zahir's wedding, serving grapes to the guests. She said the dream had showed her that I had become like one of her sisters, honouring their guests and sharing in their happiness. She knew their mother was pleased with me and smiled upon me because I often visited their house and spent time with them.

We waited until the sun had lost its fiercest heat before setting off for the cemetery – Mariam, Fereshteh, Parwaneh and I. Mariam hailed a *gadi*, bargaining for the price before we climbed aboard, and we rattled through the busy bazaar, bells jingling, past the open shop fronts shaded with pines and out to the Kandahar Gate. Here there were no trees, just a huge dusty circle thronged with villagers selling their produce: mountains of melons piled high by the side of the road, donkeys laden with panniers, men shouting their wares, weighing goods and bargaining for prices. We took the bumpy road that skirted the south-eastern perimeter of the city, passing the ruined mud ramparts that had once defended Herat from sieges and invasions. To our left, flat fertile countryside stretched away towards the great river that watered the valley: it was a torrent in springtime but a mere trickling channel throughout the rest of the year. The harvest was being reaped during this golden season, and out in the fields cattle patiently separated the grain from the corn as they trod endless circles over the mud threshing floors. In the distance the jagged outline of the mountains that enclosed the valley was barely visible in the haze. How I would miss watching the mountains turn pink at sunset while the land below was already plunged in shadow, or catching a glimpse of their brilliant snowy peaks as I walked through the bazaar enjoying the yellow winter sun.

The massive white-washed shrine of Sultan Agha lay ahead, built in 1485 on high ground commanding panoramic views of the city and its ramparts. It was a landmark for miles, its characteristic outline surrounded by a halo of pigeons wheeling and circling in the sky. At that hot hour the shrine was deserted but for the resident mendicants waiting for alms at the gate, dressed in untidy turbans and tattered patchwork coats. They sat patiently with their prayer-beads, hands outstretched. We went inside and said prayers by the tomb, silently kissing it and leaving sweets as offerings. Then we crossed the court-yard and walked out into the cemetery, a vast open space dotted with crude stone markers. I wondered how we would find the grave: I could see no inscriptions and there was no apparent order in the arrangement of the irregular gravestones. I followed the three sisters, stepping over the rough stony ground, picking my way between graves. They found their mother's resting-place without difficulty – a rectangular stone slab set flat into the ground, its coat of green paint peeling and flaking from exposure to the sun. I could barely picture the scene when they had buried her, more than two years ago: Karim, his face scratched and disfigured with grief; Latif Khan, heart-broken but dignified; Zahir and Hossein, Hassan and other close male family members, their heads silently bowed. I did not know if the daughters had even witnessed the burial; perhaps they had come to the grave only afterwards to make their loud lamentations.

As we stood by the grave, a ragged man approached us carrying a bucket of water, like a vulture moving purposefully upon its prey. He muttered a few blessings and then tipped the water gently across the grave, transforming its surface to a bright translucent green. The stone dried before our eyes, and Mariam handed him a coin, sending him away satisfied.

'*Roshnayi*,' she whispered, explaining the water's significance. 'Light' – a spiritual light that cleansed and purified.

A humble prayer-chanter begged another coin, mumbling Koranic blessings over the grave. Then we were left in peace, kneeling together under the open sky, alone except for the wind and dust and the occasional cawing of crows. We knelt in silence around the grave for a long time, both hands in contact with the warm stone, like people at a seance, and then one by one we began to cry.

The day before we left Herat I visited Mariam's house for the last time, bringing various gifts. They modestly brought out mementoes they had prepared for me, apologising that this was all they had to give. Nassimeh had sewn a childish flower in coloured silks on a square of cloth, Tayereh had embroidered a delicate border on a white silky handkerchief, and Fereshteh shyly pushed some scented soap into my lap. Parwaneh proudly brought out a red woven head-scarf, saying it would keep me warm in winter. Mariam's gift was a 'needle and thread' with two fine kerchiefs. I caught my breath in delight, touched by her inspiration.

'You're interested in our customs, so I thought you would like this,' she said, smiling. 'I asked my father to order the needle from the goldsmith.'

I have the gift by me now. The golden cockerel at the top of the needle has a fan of feathers, like a peacock's tail, and a crest, called a *taj*, a king's crown. A small turquoise is set in his side and three small beads hang from his beak. The twisted green thread attached to the needle is barely visible, decorated with cardamoms and pearly beads and thick tassels of green, and silver, and puce. The kerchiefs that traditionally accompany the 'needle and thread' are of turquoise, orange and green hand-woven synthetic silk, and of silver and white brocade edged with a border of silver and net.

'This "needle and thread" is for you to remember us by,' she said on that last day. 'You can show it to people in England and say, "This is the custom of the people of Herat."'

It touches me to remember her words and feel that in writing this book I have fulfilled her wish. Once when I asked her the significance of the 'needle and thread' she said it meant that the bride and bridegroom would always be together and happy. Sadly, though we love and miss one another, Mariam and I have been forced apart through fate, but I recall a time when she once said, 'If the road is far, never mind: hearts are close.'

PART TWO

Mother of Nebi

1 Herat city from the citadel with the Friday mosque in the distance

2 (*Above*) the citadel from Pai Hesar

3 (*Below*) Timurid tilework on the dome of Queen Gohar Shad's mausoleum

4 The shrine of Seyed-i Mukhtar

5   A house and garden near the citadel

7   A nomad family in the Friday mosque

6   A young city girl

8   A bakery in the old city

9 (*Above left*) paddling in the canal before collecting water to take home

10 (*Above right*) a small girl wearing locally made gold and amethyst jewellery

11 (*Below*) a villager baking bread in her clay oven

12 A village wedding: women gather on the roof before making a procession to the bridegroom's house

13 (*Following page*) a procession arrives inside a village compound with gifts

14　A professional musician playing *tabla* drums in a women's band

15   A city bride and groom enthroned at their wedding: she is wearing a fashionable wig

16   A young professional musician dancing at a wedding

17 & 18   Portraits of a girl and woman at their nomad encampment outside Obeh,
sixty miles up the Herat river

20   A wedding procession moving through a covered alleyway

19   (*Preceding page*) the entrance of the Timurid shrine of Khwaja Abdullah
Ansari, three miles north of Herat city

21　Women in a procession playing the *daireh*

13

Lonely Woman

I first met Mother of Nebi in the summer of 1974. I already knew some of her family through an American nurse who worked in Herat and employed her brother, Farouq, as a cook. They were a clan of villagers who had migrated to the city during the 1960s in search of better work and improved living conditions. I was particularly fond of Mother of Farouq, who encouraged me to visit her sometimes. It was typical of Mother of Nebi's isolation that she was one of the last I came to know from among her large extended family: she observed strict seclusion and rarely left her compound for weeks on end, living apart from the others, with her husband, Shemsaddin, and their five children.

Although she was often depressed and lonely, she could be high-spirited, especially when surrounded by people. She loved being the centre of attention and enjoyed visitors, but rarely went out herself. Her troubled nature was explained by a serious mental illness, apparently caused by spirit possession, during the early years of her marriage. She told me that for a whole year she had been severely disoriented and subject to states of panic and hysteria, and the experience had obviously left permanent scars. Her self-confidence was not strengthened by the strict purdah imposed on her by her conventionally pious husband, whose public quarrels and grudges had the effect of isolating her, just as Mohammad Omar's had done with Fereshteh. Unlike Fereshteh, she did not complain or hate her husband, but usually took his part and withdrew into her own stronghold.

She was very different from Mariam. While Mariam was a mediator and an ambassador of her family's interests, Mother of Nebi was an uncompromising individualist. She could be generous and helped people when they came to her, but she lacked Mariam's unselfishness and tact. Mariam was calm and cautious by nature; Mother of Nebi was passionate, temperamental and uncontrolled. What particularly drew me to her was her exuberance in performance, her creativity and her delight in music.

However, first impressions stick in one's mind, and on the day I met her she was preoccupied and troubled. I had encountered Mother of Farouq by chance in the street outside my house. She said she was going to visit her daughter and invited me to join her. In those days Mother of Nebi and I lived in the same area where later we became next-door neighbours. It was a spacious suburb in the north of the city, a quarter of an hour's walk from the new city tourist bazaar and further from the Friday mosque and the old city. The streets were straight, laid out like a grid, bordered with irrigation channels and trees. On either side rich Heratis lived in comfortable, fairly new houses set in pleasant gardens – 'comfortable' in that they were far from the flies and smells of the old city, yet often without basic amenities, such as a tap, and equipped only with outside latrines. Behind these new houses there were older, more cramped living complexes with narrow alleys.

We walked straight through a heavy wooden door at the end of a cul-de-sac, and entered a walled garden. Mother of Farouq whispered that the opulent, modern house with ugly mosaic brickwork belonged to the rich landowner for whom Shemsaddin worked as a gardener and caretaker. We skirted along a mud path and entered a gloomy outhouse at the side of the garden, where Mother of Nebi and her family then lived.

She was sewing by the window, a small, stocky woman of about thirty. She uttered a listless greeting and then, scanning my face and clothes without a smile, pulled over a cushion for me to rest my back against. Her face looked weary and joyless.

'Firuzeh, put the kettle on!' she called out sharply, and then resumed her work.

She bore a striking resemblance to Farouq, her brother, having the same hooded eyes, but whereas Farouq's expression was obsequious, her mouth wore a discontented pout. Sullenly she dragged her needle through the cloth, keeping up a fast torrent of stories and complaints. Although she was addressing her mother, she kept her eyes fixed upon the child's garment she was mending. Then she ended her speech and needlework abruptly and simultaneously by breaking off the thread with her teeth. The sun streamed in through the open doorway, illuminating the aimless play of buzzing flies against the worn striped matting. The room was shabby and simply furnished with thin mattresses and a pile of rolled bedding in one corner. The noise of children playing outside cut through the silence.

A young girl served us tea, smiling shyly. Mother of Nebi talked on, making no effort to include me. Her mother listened intently and whispered back, huddled close, a thin, gentle woman with weak, squinting eyes whose former beauty was barely discernible. It was clear that the two women had pressing matters to communicate.

That day I perceived Mother of Nebi as worn-out, depressed and preoccupied with problems. I later realised that she was a creature of moods, and that I had caught her unawares and on an off-day. This heavy, care-worn self was only one persona: other aspects of her character remained to be explored. I had in fact met her in the middle of a family crisis. In defiance of her stepfather, Sadiq, and Farouq, she was sheltering her runaway sister, Firuzeh, from an unhappy marriage.

Over the months I got to know Mother of Nebi and her family better. Her eldest son, Nebi, was thirteen and the apple of her eye. He had a soft, gentle face, grey eyes and a slender build. He was smartly dressed and rode a bicycle to school, where he was doing well in his studies. When his father was not at home, he used to boss his mother, as was expected of a growing son. Mah Gol and Meri Gol, the two daughters, aged ten and eight, had recently been withdrawn from school so that they could help their mother. I remember seeing them walk into the city together, dressed in their black uniforms and white scarves. Shemsaddin's employer had urged him to educate his girls, but now that they were approaching puberty they were kept at home. Finally there were two younger boys, Abdullah and Nadir, aged about six and three. Nadir was spoilt and out of control, always clinging to his mother and whining. She was impatient with them and dealt out smacks, sweets and threats as rough discipline.

Shemsaddin was a sturdy man, already in his fifties, with a turban and speckled grey hair and beard; a well-meaning, simple villager struggling to make his way in the city. He clung to prescribed modes of conduct and was rigorous in his observation of fasts and prayers. Although he was suspicious of the freedom Western women enjoyed, he did not interfere with my friendship with his wife, which gradually blossomed.

I wanted to learn Herati music, and Mother of Nebi was willing to teach me, so I became a frequent visitor. By this time they had moved into a house in one of the alleys behind the new suburbs, as Shemsaddin had saved enough to make a down-payment on its purchase. They had a small courtyard, a well, a grapevine, a shed where they could keep a sheep, a bread oven, a tiny half-enclosed kitchen, and four rooms. By village standards they were distinctly comfortable. Mother of Nebi enjoyed singing rural songs from her childhood and Mah Gol and Meri Gol liked to join in the choruses, clapping in time. All too often Mother of Nebi became carried away during performances, lacking the patience to practise drum strokes, or unable to slow the pace of a song so that I could extricate a melody or rhythm. She was not an ideal teacher because her versions of songs varied from day to day, but she excelled as a performer and was especially skilled in the art of improvising poetry, particularly the slow, highly ornamented style known as *charbeiti*.

I recorded her music: she had a good repertoire of village songs and dance rhythms, and a strong, expressive voice. When I later tried to record other women singing I appreciated her openness and generosity all the more. She was always eager to display her talents, whereas so many women were shy, self-conscious and frightened of being over-heard by disapproving neighbours. To me the most evocative of all our recordings is a long lullaby she improvised one hot afternoon when Nadir was restless; even at that age she sometimes rocked him in the big swinging cradle, and the rhythmic creaking of its hinges is clearly audible on the recording. She rocked him vigorously, interspersing her singing with the chant '*Allah Hu!*' – 'He is God!' – one of the invocations used by Sufis in their *zikr*, or ritual gathering. She sang out strongly, silencing the whole room with her long dreamy improvisation, invoking Ali riding Doldol, his holy white horse, and describing Nadir's heart being swept off to sleep by a river. She sang of her hopes for her boy – that he would grow tall and study the Koran like a *mullah* – and of her devotion as a mother: dawn had broken and still the mother was tied to the cradle, tending her child. Verses poured out of her, a perfect example of her skill in drawing upon a rich fund of folk poetry and making it her own.

Unfortunately our friendship was later marred by jealousy. I am afraid she felt hurt and disappointed when I began going to Shirin to learn music, although I had long since abandoned the idea of formal lessons with Mother of Nebi. I still maintained a close association with her, but she saw my singing improve and could not keep pace with all my new songs. She must have felt painfully aware of her own cultural backwater, since she had little access to new music herself, and she was probably mystified that I spent so much time with the Minstrels who held such a low status. Sometimes at her house I was asked to sing and unwillingly I upstaged her for a while. It was as though she had taught me to use wings and then found I could fly far beyond her reach.

I puzzled over her isolation. She went out rarely, yet had a wide circle of women she could have visited regularly – close relatives or fellow migrants who lived in her own alley or a few minutes' walk away. As her next-door neighbour and frequent visitor, I could see that she was resigned to family feuds and did nothing to smooth relationships when Shemsaddin quarrelled. Shemsaddin's own sister Anar Gol lived next door, but Mother of Nebi never visited her, partly because Shemsaddin had fallen out with her husband, but also because she was jealous of Anar Gol's freedom as a childless woman. She was cold to several other women in her family, and I realised that the ill-feeling caused by Shemsaddin hindered her from fostering close relationships. Yet I knew that she was strong-willed enough to overcome these obstacles, and that part of her resignation to all this bitterness was an indulgence of her own feelings of agoraphobia.

Other women made the best of any opportunity or reason to get out of the house, but she chose to stay in. She never went to the *hamam*, but washed at home. She did not make vows which necessitated regular visits to local shrines. She had almost no contact with the city, and after more than ten years she still could not have found her way from the Friday mosque to the citadel. She went out so little that the outside world was unfamiliar and she felt lost in it. Once, when she took me to visit some people in our alley, she hesitated outside, unsure if it was the right house, even though they lived just three doors away.

Shemsaddin kept her at home. She did not have permission to go shopping: he bought everything she needed, including dress material and embroidery silks. She had never been to the old clothes' market near the Friday mosque or to visit a goldsmith's shop to look at the jewellery she coveted on other women. She had no occasion to talk to male strangers, either bargaining in shops, buying a ticket to board a bus, or haggling to settle the fare for a *gadi*.

She was also closely veiled. Once I asked her to enumerate the men to whom she showed her face. She paused to think: her brothers, Farouq and Timor; her stepfather, Sadiq; her brothers' fathers-in-law; a first cousin (now that he was married); and finally, Agha Seyed Osman, her spiritual healer, as holy men were above considerations of purdah. She said that she hid from her sisters' husbands as Shemsaddin disliked them. I asked who decided whether she should hide. Shemsaddin, of course! When he brought visitors and shouted 'out of sight!' she knew she had to hide. It was up to him.

Her mother thought Shemsaddin was too strict. She confided that had she known how he would keep her daughter she would not have supported the marriage. All she could do was to visit her and keep in close touch herself. But no one had the right to criticise a man for keeping his wife too secluded, and Mother of Nebi actually took pride in hiding herself. Although the explicit purpose of purdah was to avoid the flaunting of sexually attractive, mature women in front of strangers, thus protecting family honour, it could be used as an expression of antagonism or mistrust between men. In practice men had the power to withdraw their wives from view and to sever relationships with their kinsmen. Much of what Westerners criticise in Islamic patriarchy springs from men's ability to distort and transform given cultural patterns to the detriment of women's rights.

Shemsaddin was a simple man who loved the fire-and-brimstone aspect of religion and relished accounts of the horrors of hell that awaited sinners. He believed in suffering, and agreed when Mother of Nebi once stated that women had harder lives than men, but he saw no need to try to relieve her burdens. I sensed that he was threatened by the power of women and needed to assert his own authority. Maybe his status as an orphan or the fact that he had married into his wife's family made him feel vulnerable. Compared to Mother of Nebi, who was bright and creative, he was somewhat slow-witted, which may have increased his need to control her. Yet she rarely showed resentment. Sometimes she argued with him, sometimes she ignored him, but she was not cold towards him.

Once, when we were alone together and she was irritated over something, she launched into a rare outburst against the strictures of purdah.

'What isn't sinful, tell me that? Walking bare-headed, talking so the neighbours can hear you over the wall, listening to the radio, going to the cinema . . . ? Just tell me what isn't a sin!'

I had never heard her speak like that before and it shocked me. Normally the hard rules of her life were kept internalised and never questioned.

The drama of Firuzeh, the runaway sister, showed me the strong side of Mother of Nebi's character, and demonstrated that she was someone who could act forcefully and take personal responsibilities. Firuzeh, Sadiq's daughter, was the timid girl who had served tea the day I met Mother of Nebi. She had been engaged to her first cousin since childhood and the bridewealth had been paid over the years, but her fiancé grew up to be a bad character and she did not want to marry him. Her father had felt unable to extricate himself from the agreement, and had given her away, but the marriage proved to be a nightmare for her. Her husband was often out at night. She guessed he must be in a gang, stealing or visiting prostitutes, and she was fearful of spirits and hated sleeping alone. When he came home he was cruel to her and sometimes beat her. One day, after several months of misery, she slipped out of the house and escaped, leaving all her clothes and costly dowry possessions behind. Sadiq and Farouq were furious and refused to take her in, so she went to Mother of Nebi, who gave her shelter.

Sadiq was really a mild and easy-going man, and he did not force her back to the marriage. He probably realised that her husband was unsuitable and a dubious character, and Mother of Farouq undoubtedly spoke for Firuzeh. He was therefore obliged to repay the bridewealth and put up the fees for Firuzeh's divorce. All this, including the wasted dowry, meant considerable financial loss. Firuzeh stayed with Mother of Nebi for three months, the statutory period of purification before remarriage, during which the paternity of a pregnancy could be established, and the divorce went through. (Divorce was not uncommon, and could be obtained quickly through well-established channels. I heard they pleaded that Firuzeh's husband had inflicted anal intercourse upon her, but possibly this was a ploy which guaranteed a successful outcome.)

There were family disagreements about Firuzeh's remarriage. Her younger sister, Habibeh, was married to a wealthy engineer, Resul, an outsider and an orphan who had come into their family. He offered to put up the bridewealth on behalf of his younger brother, but Sadiq's other son, Timor, disliked Resul and did not want his brother to come into the house. The two men almost came to blows, and Timor talked about leaving the household, but in the end remained. Firuzeh could not stay indefinitely with Mother of Nebi and, as no other solution presented itself, Resul won the power struggle and brought his brother into the family. There was a brusque exchange of formalities and

Firuzeh settled quietly into her second marriage, now accepted back into her paternal home as a new bride.

When I discovered what had happened I warmed to Mother of Nebi, the sister who had provided sanctuary. Her support had been vital. Without her protection at that crucial time Firuzeh might have been forced back into an unhappy marriage, or thrown to the mercy of more distant and perhaps less scrupulous relatives.

14

Possessed by Spirits

I pieced together Mother of Nebi's history, in particular the circumstances of her mental breakdown, although the clan had recently
become so riven with quarrels that it was hard for me to imagine them
all living together in their village compound, as they had once done.

Their village, Bagh-i Ali, 'Ali's Garden', was about ten miles from the
city, an hour's journey by mini-bus on a dirt-track road. It had a
mosque, a school, a shrine and a tree-lined stream running through it,

and was surrounded by walled gardens of grapes, apricots and pomegranates. Mother of Nebi had a happy childhood in an extended family that included grandparents, aunts, uncles and cousins, all in the same compound. She never knew her father, who died in tragic circumstances when she was a baby, but Sadiq was a mild and tolerant stepfather. He was also her uncle, having married Mother of Farouq in accordance with the custom of 'inheritance' of brothers' wives, and as he was several years younger than Mother of Farouq, she was a strong partner in the marriage. They had several children whom Mother of Nebi helped to raise.

Mother of Nebi's love of music flourished during childhood and she became a well-known performer. Village women loved music-making: it was their chief form of entertainment. At celebrations they did not hire professional musicians, but performed themselves, vying to excel one another. She told me that as a girl she was often called on to sing and dance at weddings. Even on ordinary days she and a group of young girls used to sit outside and play the *daireh*, singing together for hours. Whenever she had a chance to sing or perform, an extrovert quality came to the fore, and I saw that she thrived upon the attention of an audience. She loved the village dances, which were more energetic than those performed in the city. She would spin and clap until she became hot and dizzy.

She was about fourteen when she married Shemsaddin, her first cousin. He came from the neighbouring village of Du Chenar, 'Two Plane Trees'. His father had died when he was quite young and his mother had remarried. Quite suddenly she too had died, when Shemsaddin was in his thirties, and her death precipitated his marriage into the family: as an orphan, he came to live in Sadiq's house. For the bride there were no tears and no trauma of leaving home, no struggle to develop new relationships with in-laws, and no need to adapt to a new environment. Her surroundings were the same, but her freedom was curtailed and she could no longer leave the compound without permission. The walls closed in on her, and often she had to sit apart from the rest of the family so that she was not seen by unmarried male relatives. Her breakdown occurred a few years later. She described its onset, which she remembered with intense clarity.

'It was night, and there was a full moon shining like a lamp in the sky. I was sitting alone in our room, waiting in the moonlight for Shemsaddin to return home. He had gone to buy paraffin, some distance away. Suddenly I started talking to myself, but without understanding what I was saying. I didn't know what was happening, but I was beating and scratching myself. When they found me I had pulled out great handfuls of hair . . .'

She was deranged and periodically hysterical or lethargic. Her condition was instantly recognisable to those around her as *maraz*, 'the illness', or possession by spirits. It was a state which aroused intense anxiety and which people believed could be successfully treated only through exorcism. Her illness may have had something to do with postnatal depression, or the death of her first baby, but perhaps it was caused by her rigid seclusion. No one offered these practical explanations, although it was tacitly acknowledged that people suffered from *maraz* when their circumstances were unhappy. Once at a wedding, when a bride became possessed, I heard someone whisper that it was because she was being married as a junior wife, implying that her *maraz* was an expression of unconscious dissatisfaction and impotence. It is significant that *maraz* plagued women more than men, perhaps because they had less control over their lives.

Mother of Nebi was taken to various healers, but without success. Then Sadiq and Shemsaddin took her to Agha Mohammad Ali, a famous holy man who lived in a distant village. She told me that she sat in front of him and he struck her hard on the head and shoulders. It did not hurt, but she felt the force of his blows and from that day she slowly began to recover. She visited him once a week for about a year.

'Agha' simply means 'father', a title of respect. Her Agha was a direct descendant of the Holy Prophet, and a hereditary healer. I never met him: he died in 1976, in his late forties, after a long illness of tuberculosis. He carried on working until his death, singing prayers over his patients and curing them with his holy breath. (He did not worry about infecting others, Mother of Nebi commented, having picked up some Western concepts of germs from Holly, the American nurse.) Thousands mourned him and came to pay their last respects. His son, Seyed Osman, carried on his work.

People believed that certain holy men could cure sickness by communicating life-force through touch, breath, spittle, chanting or written prayers. These healers specialised in treating intractable and chronic conditions, particularly sickness associated with psychological disturbance.

Mother of Nebi described to me a dramatic cure she had once witnessed.

'A whole crowd of us were waiting for blessings in the Agha's room when they brought a woman before him. She had been struck dumb and become paralysed in her right arm. First he whispered in her ear, urging her over and over again to speak, and then he took her paralysed hand and fixed it in a wooden vice.' She described a contraption like an instrument of torture, with wooden blocks between the fingers and a string that crushed the bones together. 'If her hand had been normal she would have screamed with pain – but she didn't even flinch! Then the Agha questioned her: "When were you struck dumb?" and she found she could speak again! She told him that a man had come to her father asking for her in marriage, but he had refused him. That was when she became dumb and paralysed.'

After more hours of chanting prayers the Agha had apparently proceeded to cure the woman's paralysis. I was fascinated: her story sounded like a Freudian case history of hysteria and sexual repression. It seemed that the Agha used force and shock as a technique to unblock trauma.

There could be no doubt that faith played an important part in these healing sessions, particularly if it was reinforced in such a dramatic manner. People attributed miracles to holy men such as the Agha. I heard stories of Aghas travelling long distances in an instant, making roses bloom in winter, or escaping confinement by shrinking to the size of a mouse. They were held in awe, and only they had the power to exorcise spirits.

Belief in spirits such as *jinn*s, fairies and angels was widespread. We know of *jinn*s as 'genies' springing from Aladdin's lamp, ready to obey commands, but they were not necessarily servile and could be mischievous and malevolent. They belonged to the Islamic and pre-Islamic cosmology, half-way in the hierarchy between humans and angels. They were often frightening in aspect and people were afraid of the places where they were supposed to gather, as they could contact the human soul and cause mental derangement or death. It was said that they loved water and flowers and frequented *hamam*s, gardens, orchards and streams. They were active at night and haunted shrines. Some people were afraid to sleep alone at night, nervous of prowling *jinn*s. Nightmares and sleepwalking were symptoms of *jinn* interference, and if children slept poorly they were taken for exorcism.

After recovering from her breakdown, Mother of Nebi developed an unusual skill for divination through voluntary spirit possession, and before the Agha died she became his disciple and received his formal permission to prophesy for people. Apparently female shamanistic cults existed in the north of Afghanistan, undoubtedly related to the widespread Middle Eastern *zar* possession ceremony, but female diviners such as Mother of Nebi were rare in the Herat area. The Agha also gave her a book from which her son Nebi could copy healing prayers to be worn as amulets known as *tawiz*es, a common form of cure or protection against evil forces. She showed me its pages, which were inscribed with esoteric formulae derived from the arrangement of letters and numbers.

She built up a small circle of women who came to her for divinations. They wanted to know how loved ones were faring on distant journeys,

or sought to discover the cause of a mysterious illness or the whereabouts of lost objects. Her work brought her prestige and a degree of
financial independence, although half her earnings went to the Agha. It
also gave her a means of slipping through the net of Shemsaddin's
control, for he could not stop her from visiting her Agha, or quarrel
with her work as a diviner.

There was a definite link between the activities of Agha Mohammad Ali
and Sufism, the esoteric, mystical expression of Islam. Sufism has
flourished in that wide area of central Asia for centuries. Although
during the 1970s it was in evident decline, there were still some active
brotherhoods in the countryside. (The Soviet invasion has apparently
precipitated a resurgence in Sufism, and some traditional religious
leaders have become commanders in the 'holy war' against the invaders.) Like Agha Mohammad Ali, Sufi leaders are charismatic, and
trace their spiritual authority through dynastic chains. They are normally based at particular shines or Sufi gathering-places known as
*khaneqah*s, and part of their work consists of healing people through
personal contact and blessings. Agha Mohammad Ali did not lead an
active brotherhood or hold weekly gatherings for *zikr*, the 'remembr-
ance of God', although he did attend the *zikr* which was held in the main
mosque after the Friday midday prayer.

I was particularly interested to learn that Mother of Nebi's father and
grandfather had both been Sufis, and it was clear that she was attracted
to this world of transcendence and spiritual power. She told me that her
father's brotherhood had a practice known as *chilleh*, 'forty days', a
period of spiritual retreat during which they fasted and kept silence.
They ate only one date in the evening and a piece of bread in the
morning, and spent their time meditating and saying their prayers.
These retreats were part of the initiation into the brotherhoods, during
which devotees were said to experience terrifying encounters with *jinns*.
If they could 'tame' the *jinns*, they gained personal power, just as
Mother of Nebi claimed to have 'tamed' the *jinns* that possessed her so
as to use them in divinations.

The focus of the Sufi brotherhoods lies in the performance of the *zikr*,
the ritual repetition of the holy names of God, aimed at achieving
ecstatic union with the divinity. It can take many forms, according to
the various Sufi orders: one of the most famous is that of the Turkish
Mevlevi 'whirling dervishes', a dancing *zikr* with musical accompaniment. The Chishtis also use music, though the Naqshbandis have a
silent, inner *zikr*. Mother of Nebi's father belonged to the Qaderi order,
and he regularly sang religious poetry as an accompaniment to their
spoken *zikr*. I have seen this performed: the Sufis stand in a circle

rolling their heads back and forth, breathing rhythmically as they chant '*Allah Hu*' or some such religious formula. The singers move slowly around them singing in a highly ornamented style, evoking the intoxication of divine love and sometimes sobbing with emotion. *Zikr* usually lasts many hours, a very powerful and sustained performance that induces an altered state of consciousness through hyperventilation and the constant rolling of the head. I later witnessed Mother of Nebi working herself up in a similar manner in the presence of her Agha.

Although she never knew her father, Mother of Nebi seemed to have inherited his spiritual intensity and love of poetry and singing. Her grandfather, who lived to be quite old, was also steeped in mystical poetry and adept at improvisation. She was clearly following in their path and becoming as close as she could to being a Sufi herself. While the literature of the Sufi movement does mention female Sufis, the brotherhoods in Afghanistan were dominated by men and it was only possible for women to have a marginal and subsidiary role. I have not heard of any instance where women actively participated in the *zikr*, and in any case Mother of Nebi's Agha did not lead one. None the less, it is clear that she was attracted to this ecstatic, devotional way of worship.

15

Villagers

In autumn 1976 we took a house in Mother of Nebi's alley: our front doors were opposite one another. She encouraged me to visit her and often used to send her children to summon me. I wanted to learn embroidery and she taught me various stitches and patterns such as floral arabesques or decorative borders. She also demonstrated the way to draw designs on to cloth, and showed me how to sit holding my work taut between my knees. We enjoyed sewing together and talking.

She and Shemsaddin maintained many of their old village habits. She baked bread in their clay oven rather than buying it from the bakery, and they hung sliced aubergines on strings and spread tomatoes out on the roof to dry in the sun, laying in food for the winter as people did through necessity in the villages. She used to prepare a rural dish called *qolur torush*, a tasty powder which could be reconstituted to thicken soups, made from flour, garlic, yoghurt, tomatoes and ten different spices all fermented together for several days before being dried out for storage. City people enjoyed it but derided it as rustic. They also kept a sheep in their compound, which they milked twice a day in order to make yoghurt. Before winter they killed the animal to prepare stocks of dried meat known as *land*, which could be stewed when fresh meat became scarce and expensive. Herati people liked its taste very much and often dried some meat for *land*, though it was usually bought ready-jointed from the butcher.

I witnessed the sacrifice of the sheep, performed by Shemsaddin. He began by untying the animal and giving it a dish of water, stroking its wool gently and saying it would be sinful to kill an animal which was thirsty. Then Mother of Nebi tied its feet together to prevent it from struggling and they laid it sideways on a slab of stone, with its neck stretched out. Shemsaddin took his knife and uttered a loud blessing before slitting its throat so the head was almost severed from the body. Blood spurted and gurgled on to the stone and the sheep twitched violently. When all the blood had drained out, he made an incision into one leg and began blowing into it, inflating the skin so that it separated from the carcass. The children worked at pulling out the wool, and later Shemsaddin extracted the insides and disposed of them, keeping the liver as a delicacy. Nebi cut it into small pieces, rubbed it with a little salt and began to barbecue it immediately, fanning some embers and distributing titbits to the eager children. Afterwards I saw Mother of Nebi roasting the sheep's head and feet over an open fire, scraping charred areas away with a knife and forcing off the hooves when they had become soft. The children helped to rub rock salt and chilli powder all over the jointed meat, which was then threaded on to a pole and hung up to dry in the sun. It took at least ten days for the meat to dry, during which time it attracted a great many wasps. That evening I watched Mother of Nebi melt down the sheep's tail – Afghan sheep have big tails which yield a large amount of cooking fat.

Her kitchen was a tiny shelter without a doorway, barely providing room for the two of us to squat together on the floor. The walls were black with soot. A small shelf sculpted from mud held matches, a tin of spices and salt, and a protruding hole had been moulded through which she could put the handle of her cooking spoon when it was not in use. Wood for fuel and dry thorn for kindling were kept in an out-house.

The tail was chopped into small pieces, rubbed with salt and placed in a big cooking pot, which was then put on the fire.

'We did this every year in the village,' she said, wiping sweat from her face. 'This tail fat is very good – far better than that tinned vegetable fat from Russia we have to use in the city. That's so full of water that it splatters in your eyes and melts to nothing. Only "yellow fat", the butter we get from churned yoghurt, is better than this tail fat.'

'Won't you miss the sheep?'

'Its feed was getting more expensive now the season's ending, and its milk had dwindled. It was time to kill it for meat – that's what we had it for,' she replied unsentimentally.

The fat melted very slowly. She had called me to keep her company while she waited. Our faces were lit by the fire burning brightly under the pot. Every so often she poked another log underneath to keep it going well.

'Does it remind you of the village?'

'In a way, yes. I've always done this, like all other villagers. But here our standard of living is better. There's no work for Nebi's father in the village – only being a peasant and share-cropper. No one can get on and help themselves if they live in the village.'

At last the fat had all melted. Chunks of it swam in a clear, frothing liquid, sizzling with heat. She carefully removed the pot from the fire and took out a similar pot into which she began to ladle the clear fat, avoiding the chunks from which it had been rendered. I admired the skill with which she ladled the scorching oil, not a drop of which was spilt. Afterwards, when it had cooled a little, she ladled the fat into two large storage tins. Only the chunks of fat remained, swimming in a little of their own hot oil. Then she threw in about half a kilo of chopped meat and a large quantity of sliced onions, setting them on the fire and stirring briskly as they cooked. When they were done she served them on small plates and sent them as tasty offerings to some of her neighbours and close relatives, each accompanied by a loaf of her own home-made bread. In this way they shared in the celebration of sacrificing the sheep, rather as guests shared wedding blessings through eating sugared nuts. I noticed that she did not send any to certain relatives: through these small gestures of goodwill, links were maintained or left broken.

Despite Mother of Nebi's rural ways, she did not seem to miss her village, and she never made any attempt to return on visits. Even when duty pressed her to attend funerals, she stayed behind and Shemsaddin went alone. She appeared aloof, but I think she was unwilling to expose herself to people's scrutiny and jealousy, or perhaps to the flood of feelings and memories that such an outing might engender. She existed in limbo, no longer actively part of her village, yet an outsider within the city.

Nevertheless, her small circle of clients for divinations and *tawiz*es was drawn from her clan, from Bagh-i Ali or Shemsaddin's neighbouring village, Du Chenar. One day I had my first opportunity to see her give a consultation. We were sewing together in her sunny courtyard when a woman from Bagh-i Ali came through the front door. Nebi immediately went to usher her male escorts into the guest room, ordering his mother and sisters to go indoors out of sight.

'She's come for a divination,' whispered Mah Gol, as we scurried indoors.

Our visitor was small, thin and poorly dressed, with the unmistakable hooked nose and dark skin of a villager. She sat down and nervously adjusted her veil as she mumbled greetings, barely looking at me or showing any interest in her surroundings.

'Mother of Nebi, you must help me. I've got three grown-up sons and I've been trying to find a bride for my eldest, but whatever I do no one will have him,' she said urgently, fixing Mother of Nebi with pleading, passionate eyes. She said her body ached all over with the tension and worry of it.

At first Mother of Nebi was reticent.

'I don't do this kind of work for people outside the family,' she began unwillingly. 'It's not worth my while. People come and drink my tea and then leave the house without giving me anything. I have to give half my money to the Agha Sahib, you know. He gave me his permission to prophesy and half the money is due to him.'

We all knew that she would perform a divination, but that she was establishing her terms. Her guest did not look discouraged, but carried on talking about her problems, begging for pity. Mother of Nebi looked unmoved, but went to her cupboard to fetch her prayer-beads, which had been blessed by Agha Mohammad Ali, and which she used to go into a trance. She told the villager to sit directly opposite her and then started handling the beads, muttering softly, eyes half-closed. Her children, the visitor and I watched intently as her lips began to move and her upper body swayed. Strange sounds emitted from her mouth, soft at first but gradually becoming louder; harsh incomprehensible noises that issued from the back of her throat. She was supposedly tapping into the spirit world, and this was the sound of the *jinn*s speaking through her. Her client watched keenly, her eyes full of tears.

After several minutes Mother of Nebi subsided into silence, shuddering a little. She kept her eyes closed and moved her lips fractionally. Then she seemed to recover consciousness, and straightened up and opened her eyes.

'Your son has been bewitched,' she pronounced.

'Who did it?' asked the woman, not doubting Mother of Nebi's verdict.

'A man neither near nor far.'

'It could have been his father's brother,' suggested the client, apparently satisfied with that vague explanation. Witchcraft, curses or spells could 'close' a person's luck or good fortune, so that no good could befall him. The work of a diviner often lay in pronouncing who had done this, so that appropriate steps could be taken.

'Your son used to have a friend,' Mother of Nebi went on, watching the woman intently to see if she took up this lead. 'He was a very close friend, but not now.'

'Not really. He's never been that close to anyone,' the woman answered, looking a little puzzled.

Mother of Nebi let her remark go and waited for her to speak again.

'What about my other son?' she asked. 'He's gone to Iran. I'm so worried about him. Give me news!'

Mother of Nebi started to count her beads again. This time she seemed almost eager to lapse into a state of possession. Her eyes rolled upwards and she began to babble as before. Then she came to and made her pronouncement.

'He's well. He's with a friend and they've saved lots of money. They wanted to return for the New Year, but then they decided to stay. His only sadness is missing his mother. But he's working hard and earning plenty of money.'

The woman was delighted, and uttered grateful thanks.

'That's a very strong spell they put on your boy,' Mother of Nebi went on seriously. 'I'll ask Nebi to write a *tawiz* for you to give him. And I advise you to go to our village shrine – it's very old and powerful. You're right to be worried about your son. I can see he's in trouble.'

Gravely she told her that he 'had the dust of fairies on him'. Fairies were supernatural spirits that could be mischievous and malevolent like *jinn*s but were very attractive in appearance. I knew that she was exercising latitude in prescribing this *tawiz*, since her Agha had permitted her to give them only to promote work, to help personal relationships and to provide protection on journeys: she was not really authorised to protect against evil spirits.

'You're right, he does have fits,' the villager whispered. 'Sometimes it happens when he hears *sazdohol* music or when he does the stick dance.'

As she left, the woman obsequiously kissed Mother of Nebi's hand, uttering servile phrases of gratitude, and when they walked to the doorway I saw her secretively press money upon her. Mother of Nebi felt the note in her hand and began sending elaborate goodwill messages back to the village, brightening visibly. After the client had gone, however, she complained angrily that she had paid her only twenty *afghanis*. Villagers had no idea of the cost of living in the city, she said, hoping her client would at least bring money the following week when she came to collect the *tawiz*. Copying them out meant a lot of work for Nebi. She consoled herself with the thought that the villager must realise that the blessings would have no effect if she did not pay for them.

I was curious to find out about witchcraft, and asked how the unlucky young man's enemies had put the spell upon him. She replied guardedly, saying wicked people did such things, though she knew nothing of their methods. Perhaps they took seven threads of different colours and tied knots in them while singing certain words, she hazarded, but closed the subject firmly.

Mother of Nebi's work as a diviner was very important to her as a matter of prestige and financial independence, although it was extremely sporadic and brought in very little actual money. The fact remained that she was failing to attract clients from the city. She thought a jealous enemy must have 'closed' her luck, and did not seem to realise that her customers might be dwindling because she had offended people in Bagh-i Ali and Du Chenar. Villagers were sensitive and felt inferior towards city-dwellers, whom they regarded as stand-offish, and no doubt they were hurt by her aloofness.

Her alienation from Bagh-i Ali was quite clear. Years passed between visits, and her old home must have become increasingly strange and distant. Yet the village was so much part of her: the stories, dances and songs that she still performed came from her girlhood there. It was also the place of her marriage and breakdown, and therefore dangerously potent with memories.

16

The Betrothal

Relations with Shemsaddin's village, Du Chenar, had become strained
through a misfired marriage settlement for Nebi. Originally he
had been engaged to the eldest daughter of Ghulam Mohammad,
Shemsaddin's first cousin, but unfortunately the girl had died, so a
younger daughter, Sherifeh, was given instead. No bridewealth was
paid. Shemsaddin thought his cousin was simply happy to secure a

stronger link with his prosperous city kin, but this proved to be a grave mistake.

I remember attending the betrothal party for Sherifeh and Nebi, which took place during the summer of 1974, shortly after I first met Mother of Nebi. Sherifeh was only about five, and was dumpy, unattractive and graceless, looking unnaturally stiff in a dress of metallic brocade. Her cheeks were flushed crimson and she cried continually unless placated with sweets. Her mother cried too, dabbing her eyes with a pink scarf. She wore typical village clothes: a full-skirted, mid-calf-length dress, patterned with huge luminous orange and lime-green flowers, over loose Punjabi-style trousers which had long since gone out of fashion in the city.

The *nekah* was performed and the two children became future man and wife. Nebi showed no interest in the festivities, intent only on fighting pitched battles with his small cousins. I found the party depressing. I wondered why many close relatives were absent, ignorant of the feuds that split the family. The atmosphere was humid with sweat and the skin of the *daireh* was slack and made a dead sound. Mother of Nebi kept screaming at the children to be quiet while she led the singing, and older women flapped their scarves to keep flies from settling on sleeping babies, cursing children who almost trampled them. The rooms were stiflingly hot and overcrowded with rowdy children, who constantly disrupted the music-making. I left with relief, carrying away a festive bag of sugared nuts, my head aching from the din.

Problems with the marriage alliance arose later, when Shemsaddin needed to raise money for the mortgage on his new house. He went to the village to sell some land but, to his dismay, Ghulam Mohammad laid claim to it as bridewealth for Sherifeh. The other villagers supported him, so at great expense Shemsaddin took the matter to court. The judge ruled that the land now belonged to Sherifeh, but that when she married it would become her husband's property. Consequently Nebi's parents were anxious to finalise the marriage, afraid that Sherifeh might die and the land would be irretrievably lost. They were also conscious of their expensive obligation to honour Sherifeh with fine presents at every festival. The problem – and it was a major one – was that Sherifeh was still very young and her parents were not morally obliged to let her leave their home before puberty.

Mother of Nebi and Shemsaddin were outraged at the misfortune that had befallen them. He was sorely wounded by the rift with his village kinsmen, but took pains to rebuild relations. In this case he could not afford to bear grudges for too long, since the village, the land and his kinsmen represented the deepest form of security.

Nebi was growing up. His voice had already begun to break and a light down grew on his upper lip. He was intelligent and studious, with a quiet, serious demeanour. According to duty, he continued to visit Du Chenar, taking small gifts, and he managed to form a good relationship with Sherifeh's family. She was shy, but they played childish games alone together and he gradually won her confidence. At home he ignored his sisters' taunts about 'engagement play' and kept silent when his parents cursed Ghulam Mohammad. I was impressed with the equanimity with which he weathered his difficulties.

Occasionally Sherifeh and her mother, Mother of Nassar, visited Mother of Nebi for a few days. The girls teased Sherifeh mercilessly when Nebi was not there, and they pulled her hair and mocked her clothes. Mother of Nebi did not stop them. It was clear that she had no affection for her prospective daughter-in-law. I was shocked when she publicly shamed Mother of Nassar in front of neighbours, relating the story of the stolen land and vilifying Ghulam Mohammad.

'At least if Sherifeh came to our house she might learn a few things,' she said, putting forward her case for an immediate marriage. 'Already my girls can do most woman's work. Mah Gol can cook and work a sewing machine and they can both do embroidery. What will the girl ever learn in that ugly village? As it is she can't even serve tea!'

Sherifeh clung to her mother, half hiding under the *kursi* quilt, but Mother of Nassar was neither brave nor articulate, and said nothing in their defence, although her eyes pleaded piteously for sympathy and support. Mother of Farouq spoke out against her daughter and said it was a sin to send a girl away from home too early. She was not going to let her youngest, Bassireh, go too young: she wanted to keep her in school. I remembered that Mother of Farouq had told me that she herself had been sent to her husband's house at seven, and I guessed that it had been a very painful experience.

The custom of child betrothal died hard in the villages because of their preference for paying bridewealth in instalments. Although the marriage of girls before puberty was relatively uncommon, there were some cases; for example Peri, Timor's wife, who was also from Du Chenar. I remember her starting her periods. Mother of Farouq whispered that she hoped she would not now become pregnant as it was harmful for girls to give birth before they were really mature, and because Timor had to go away on his military service. I did not know whether to conclude that they were already having full sexual intercourse or not. Certainly they slept together, but they may have been told to hold back until she began menstruating. In the event Peri did become pregnant and produced a pathetically small baby the following year.

I felt sorry for little Sherifeh, who was only about seven or eight by this time and seemed very helpless and unprotected, and I certainly did not think her parents should give in to Mother of Nebi's pressure to proceed with the wedding. When Sherifeh came to stay, Mother of Nebi gave the couple a bed together so that they would become used to one another, but she complained that Sherifeh cried, and assumed that Mother of Nassar had frightened her from becoming too intimate with Nebi. She assured me that Nebi would not try and 'do anything'. I gathered that sexual counselling was a matter for women and wondered what she told him, but I felt sure that she put her son's, not her daughter-in law's, interests first.

Koranic law specifically rules against marriage and sex before puberty, but in practice there seemed to be little protection for girls such as Peri or Sherifeh. Some people defended child betrothal, and said the bride and bridegroom became used to one another from an early age. No doubt many happy and stable marriages emerged, but I am sure that the custom caused suffering. It was noticeable that the stance older women adopted depended very much upon whether they were mothers or mothers-in-law. Mother of Farouq may have been firm in protecting her own daughter, yet she had accepted the marriage of her son, Timor, a lusty young man of twenty, to the little flat-chested child, Peri.

Before the Festival of the Sacrifice, which marked the yearly pilgrimage to Mecca, Shemsaddin went to the bazaar to buy cloth for Sherifeh. It was customary to wear new clothes on this great festival, and it was his duty to provide them for her. He proudly displayed his purchases – three metres of fine fashionable cloth for a dress, two metres of crêpe for a scarf and two metres of white nylon for trousers.

'Why did you have to spend so much?' Mother of Nebi burst out angrily. 'None of us can afford to wear this!'

'I had to get something decent,' he answered defensively. 'The villagers will see this cloth and think how well I'm doing in my job.'

'They only have to visit this house and look at the state of our boys' clothes!' she cut in angrily. 'What did you get for them?'

'They'll have to wait. We can't all have new clothes for every festival,' he said firmly.

She turned her back on him and refused to serve him tea, furious that he had given Sherifeh priority. She was more concerned about her own neighbours' opinion than that of people in Du Chenar. Meri Gol burst into tears when she saw the cloth and Mah Gol flounced away, stung with jealousy.

Three days before the festival, we took the gifts to the village. John drove us, taking all the family except Nebi, who had to attend school, and his mother, who resolutely refused to cross Ghulam Mohammad's threshold. We left early and drove south through the bazaars towards open country, crossing the wide river bed by the ancient bridge, Pul-i Malan. Then we headed west on a dirt-track, bouncing and jolting over pot-holes. The children giggled and squeaked with excitement. We followed a small tree-lined canal for some miles, passing through several peaceful villages, and then Shemsaddin directed John to turn off on to flat desert scrubland dotted with dry thorn bushes. It was hot and dusty away from the greenery of the canal, and we left a pluming trail behind us, like a plane drawing a white line across the sky. Eventually, after an hour's driving, Shemsaddin pointed out Du Chenar, barely distinguishable in the distant haze.

Mother of Nebi had been right, it was not a beautiful village. The land lacked water and much of it was barren salt marsh. The two plane trees that gave the village its name offered shade for some villagers waiting for the mini-bus that was their only means of public transport to the city.

'Call Father of Peri and say he has guests,' ordered Shemsaddin, sending a boy ahead with news of our arrival.

We made our way along a walled lane to Timor's father-in-law's house, where we were to assemble for the procession to Sherifeh's house. The men went to the guest room, and the children and I climbed some rough clay steps to the family room, which led on to the flat roof. This was connected to that of the neighbouring house, where some women were sitting in the sun spinning wool on rustic spinning wheels. Mother of Peri, small and ruddy-cheeked like her daughter, welcomed us. Mah Gol and the children suddenly seemed overawed and self-conscious in their best city clothes and they blushed awkwardly as they mumbled their greetings.

I went over to watch the women spin, and they immediately asked after Mother of Nebi. Why had she not come? Mah Gol fumbled and muttered an unconvincing excuse, pink with embarrassment, and I hastily explained that she had been obliged to stay because Nebi was at school. It would have looked bad only to have come for one day, I added. Throughout the day everyone asked the same question and I became increasingly skilled at making her excuses, but I knew the village women felt slighted. Mother of Peri defended Mother of Nebi too, but everyone knew that the real reason for staying away was because she was still sore at Ghulam Mohammad.

Shemsaddin brought the gifts upstairs, tactfully averting his eyes from the spinners, who scurried out of sight. Everything was arranged on three round trays, each of which was covered with a bright scarf and knotted underneath – the cloth for the dress and scarf on the first, a big packet of sugared nuts and the trouser cloth on the second, a smaller packet of sugared nuts (of better quality and for the men), some henna and perfume on the third.

Before setting off to Sherifeh's house with the gifts we had a simple lunch of bread and *qorut* (a reconstituted dried milk product bartered from nomads), and downstairs the men were served fried eggs and bread. When we told her about it, Mother of Nebi complained indignantly – *qorut*! It was mean of her to despise their village food, especially since Mother of Peri was taking her place and acting as female leader of the bridegroom's party.

About twenty women and children assembled on the roof for the procession. No doubt they were happy to leave their work and come to a party, but they also knew that non-attendance would be interpreted as a hostile gesture. Most of them wore the traditional village veil, a homespun cloth worn on the head and knotted loosely in front, leaving the face exposed. Three children led the procession, carrying the trays on their heads. The men followed, then a crowd of boys, and finally the women and children. One of us played a *daireh* and we clapped in time as we walked along the narrow lane. Once, Father of Peri stopped us, raising his hand and crying 'Ho!' for silence while he shouted out a couplet of poetry. The crowd called loudly in response, raising their hands and clapping. Mother of Nebi commented later that men said verses in the lanes, but women recited them inside the front door. Had she been there she would have chanted out two verses at the top of Ghulam Mohammad's steps, she added, demonstrating her fine sense of performance.

It was not far to Ghulam Mohammad's house. He was a bent old man with a long wispy beard, and looked affable and benign, not at all the devious trickster I had been led to imagine. While he escorted the men into the guest room, Mother of Nassar led us into another, extremely dingy, room. She gave each of the tray-bearers a small coin (again Mother of Nebi was critical, saying they should each have received two coins wrapped in a coloured handkerchief). The compound was very poor. There were two meagre rooms above a storage space for animal fodder and fuel. I remembered that Mother of Nebi had said they did not even have a latrine, but squatted in their courtyard like animals. The rough uneven steps must have been treacherous when icy. Conditions in villages were certainly harsh compared to the city.

We settled ourselves: the older women sat against the far wall, scrutinising our urban fashions with interest, commenting upon details of the girls' cloth and jewellery and ridiculing their platform shoes from the second-hand bazaar. A woman opened our packet of sugared nuts and spread them on a tray, and someone else took out the gifts and passed them round for inspection. Sherifeh was nowhere to be seen. Mother of Nassar had gone to make tea for the men. One of the visitors asked how much Mah Gol's ear-rings had cost, touching them and exclaiming with distaste that they were only plastic. Another turned to Mother of Peri and enquired whether Mah Gol was engaged yet. They smoked a water-pipe and discussed village boys who might be suitable.

In another corner a group of newly married teenage mothers huddled together, pulling out their breasts and thrusting them into the mouths of their babies, who all seemed to need comforting. Near the door some little girls gathered around the *daireh*, taking their turn to sing before the women. Mother of Peri tried to whip up a party atmosphere by calling on the young mothers to dance. They passed over their babies and stood up unselfconsciously, unlike city girls who always acted shy and needed coaxing.

It seemed no time at all before word came that John was preparing to leave. The women were just about to begin singing, and they were shocked that we wanted to go so early. They uttered the usual polite phrases for keeping guests longer, afraid that someone had taken offence. My husband wanted to go, I explained, soothing their anxious protests and appealing to their sense of male authority. Mother of Peri urged us to stay the night, otherwise everyone would say she had not had room for us.

I was disappointed to miss the music-making, but relieved to escape the thinly veiled atmosphere of hostility towards Mother of Nebi. I found the villagers oppressively concerned with what everyone said and how things looked from the outside.

However Shemsaddin seemed elated and confident that he had made a good impression: the visit had been a success.

We arrived home to find Mother of Nebi listless and irritable. Probably she had been bored and was annoyed to have missed all the fun. Having refused to compromise herself by taking part in the outing, she had had no alternative entertainment. She pounced upon Nadir, seeing car grease on his best clothes, and there were tears and recriminations. Her hatred of Ghulam Mohammad and distrust of the Du Chenar villagers had only been strengthened by her miserable, lonely day.

17

The House of the Healer

Mother of Nebi promised to take me to meet Agha Seyed Osman, the son of Agha Mohammad Ali. We went there on Friday morning, taking all the children to be blessed, apart from Nebi who stayed to guard the house while his father was at the midday prayer. Walking outside, veiled, Mother of Nebi appeared flustered, as she was unable to shout to control her children. She took an alleyway in order to avoid going through the tourist bazaar, but was shocked and discomforted at the way children called out and taunted me (I had not yet begun wearing a veil). When we finally arrived, she seemed breathless and relieved to have crossed the no-man's-land between the twin sanctuaries of home and the Agha's large compound.

We were given preferential treatment and told to sit in the house of Agha Mohammad Ali's junior widow, rather than in the place where other clients gathered. The room was modest but pleasant and adorned with many photographs. Mother of Nebi pointed out Agha Mohammad Ali, a white-haired man looking down benignly from his gilded frame, and his father, whose image had been hand-tinted from an enlargement of an old black and white print. A stout woman wearing a heavy white cotton veil, the junior widow, brought us tea and settled down to exchange news. Mother of Nebi complained that her customers had dwindled and that she had very little money to bring to the Agha. She said she had come specifically to ask him to bless Nadir, who was having nightmares. Nebi was coming to join us later: she particularly wanted blessings on him so that he would do well in his exams.

'You're having another baby, I see,' said the junior widow, looking significantly at her belly.

I looked sharply at Mother of Nebi. Weeks ago she had dismissed the idea that she might be pregnant, not wanting it to be true. I now realised that her pregnancy had become quite obvious. She explained to the junior widow that she had had severe stomach pains and the doctor had made her stop taking the pill. Since then she had not had a period. She admitted that she was probably in her fifth month, calculating by the moon.

We were joined by Peri and Bassireh, who came in response to a message, and the junior widow served us all lunch. Afterwards we went to visit the Agha. We crossed the courtyard and entered his small dark prayer-room, which was filled with women waiting for blessings. The Agha himself sat cross-legged in a low alcove, emitting a soft, droning chant over a woman directly before him. He rocked gently to and fro as he sang and then he leaned forward and blew out through pursed lips to conclude the blessing. The woman bowed and shuffled backwards. Mother of Nebi did not wait to take her turn, but settled immediately in front of him. I sat a little behind her, scrutinising the Agha, but keeping my head respectfully lowered. He looked about twenty and was stout and ruddy, simply dressed in white cotton clothes, a white turban tied tightly around a plain skull-cap in the manner of a *mullah*, and a grey overcoat from the second-hand bazaar to keep out the cold. It was hard for me to see him as saintly, yet he had the confidence and dignity of a doctor or business man. Shelves in the alcove behind him were piled with papers which had been rubber-stamped for *tawiz* prayers.

Mother of Nebi put some money at his feet and I also passed some forward, as I had decided to ask for blessings. First she requested him to sing prayers over Peri's baby, who had been very weak since her birth, so Peri nervously moved forward and he chanted a short prayer over them. Then she asked for prayers for Nadir and the other children. Once her business was over, she suddenly went into a frenzy, shaking violently where she sat. She pulled her scarf over her face and began waving her head up and down, swaying her upper body from side to side more and more violently as she grunted '*Allah Hu!*' like a Sufi. This type of ecstatic behaviour is widespread in the Moslem world. The heavy rhythmic exhaltations and impassioned sweeping movements of the head (which induce dizziness and trance) are like a dance of spirit possession.

The Agha impassively watched her rasp and convulse at his feet, quite unperturbed by her performance, waiting for the fit to take its course. The other patients stirred and looked on with interest. Mah Gol and the children squirmed with embarrassment at the spectacle their mother was making. Finally the Agha began to soothe her, gently ordering her repeatedly to be quiet and calm. Gradually she ceased her shaking and writhing. Her scarf half covered her face at an odd angle, and occasional spasms still passed through her slumped figure.

When her fit had completely abated he asked her why she had delayed so long in coming to him. Her reply was hoarse, but passionate and dramatic – she had had very few clients. Five long months had passed but she had little to bring him.

'Never mind,' he replied. 'Listen, I want to ask you a question. Something has been taken from me. Who took it and will it be returned or not?'

She went into a short trance and then loudly announced that a man had taken it. She could not tell who he was, but the thing had been taken far away. The Agha would not see it again. He accepted her word, and then turned towards me, asking what I wanted. She explained that I had been missing my homeland and called me forward to be blessed. I bowed my head and he sang over me. Afterwards he wrote out a prayer, and asked for my mother's and my own name, scribbling confidently on the paper. He added this to two other stamped *tawiz*es and folded them deftly into a thick, neat triangle, instructing me to wear it around my neck. Before we left he handed more written prayers to Mother of Nebi, like a doctor briskly handing out prescriptions. I would have been interested to watch him cure other patients, but Mother of Nebi led us all out, having no desire to linger.

We went to the visitors' room in the senior widow's house, joining a group of women sitting companionably around the *kursi*. Some were visitors and others belonged to the Agha's household. Mother of Nebi boldly demanded some scraps of cloth from the senior widow, who rummaged and found some and gave her a needle and thread so that she could cover the *tawiz*es immediately. After her encounter with the Agha she seemed full of energy and buoyancy.

She introduced me to a beautiful young girl with delicate blue tattoos on her forehead, the present Agha's wife, a nomad from Badghis, some distance towards the border with the Soviet Union. I asked her how she had come to marry the Agha. Apparently her mother had been very ill and everyone thought she would die, but she had vowed that if Agha Mohammad Ali cured her, she would give the baby she was carrying to his son – if it was a girl. The young wife was that baby. Her family had long been followers of the Agha and she had come to the house as a bride when she was about ten. Every spring her father came to Herat to sell things in the market and he stayed with them. When he had finished his business and bought provisions, he took her back to visit her mother for twenty days. The senior widow told me that the girl had had no children, but that the Agha said it was God's will and refused to take another wife. I asked who would carry on his work after him, and they said that in time he would choose from among his brothers.

An old woman sat listening to our talk, and a small girl huddled at her side. They had made a long journey from a distant village. I asked what had brought them.

'I came for my eyes. They're dim,' she replied, 'and I also brought my little granddaughter. Her chest is bad – and she's got this misshapen hand.' She held up the girl's hand which had only three fingers, and two of those were joined by a web of skin. 'It's been like that from birth,' she added.

Another visitor commented that she could have had an operation to separate the two fingers, but the girl stoutly said that it was sinful.

'I wouldn't take her to visit those doctors' (she meant Western-trained physicians), 'they make you show your body, and touch your cheeks and look in your mouth,' said the grandmother.

The other women demurred, not liking to contradict. The girl had not even reached puberty, yet the notion of sin was being applied. Judging from their clothes, the family had very little money and I doubted that they would have given high priority to such an operation. Girls became brides, they would reason. What was the sense in spending money? The poor girl hid her hand under the quilt, obviously hoping the painful subject had now been closed. Then the senior widow asked Mother of Nebi to perform some divinations for her. She complied, but refused to divine for the others, saying her head had begun to ache.

It was past three o'clock by the time we left. Nebi had joined us, eaten some lunch saved for him by his mother, and seen the Agha. She suddenly seemed anxious to get home, fearing it had become late: Shemsaddin might complain that she had stayed too long.

I commented to her that the Agha had a hard life, continually healing the sick. I thought of the long hours he spent in that cold, gloomy room, and wondered how he managed without a partner to share the work. He saw men too, she told me: there was another room by the front door which was always full of patients. Sometimes crazy people were brought to him in the middle of the night, or he was called out. She said he worked day and night singing prayers over people. The Agha's women worked indefatigably too. There were always guests and they had to make tea for each newcomer and serve meals for whoever happened to be there. In return visitors brought whatever gifts or money they could afford.

I pitied wives of healers. Inevitably such women were kept in particularly close seclusion, and they were put to service for the community at large. Bent over their cooking pots day and night, continually surrounded by sick people, they rarely left their courtyards – especially the women of Aghas in rural areas. The wife of a Sufi Agha I met told me that during five years of marriage she had only once been back to visit her family.

I saw that Mother of Nebi derived considerable comfort and refreshment from visiting her Agha's women – perhaps more than from seeing the Agha himself – and when she went to the house she spent much longer with them. Her meetings with the Agha were brief and intense, but it was the women who gave practical sympathy and advice, who served meals, and who listened to problems. I felt their work was valuable, yet given little recognition.

Faith healing was very important to the Afghan people. They went to a local *sheikh* or *mullah* for prayers to cure minor sicknesses, but men such as the Agha could help in serious or chronic cases. Personal faith in such a man could effect dramatic changes: renewed hope made complete remission of symptoms possible. People were often suspicious of Western-trained doctors, nervous about unwanted side-effects from strong drugs and frightened by unfamiliar procedures such as X-rays, giving blood and urine samples, or being physically examined. Often women or even girls, like the one with the webbed hand, were excluded from medical treatment on the grounds of purdah. With the Agha they at least had hope.

18

The Lost Children

As I returned home one evening in mid-December, I caught sight of
Mother of Nebi's sister, Habibeh, and Farouq's wife, Zuleikha,
hurriedly leaving her house. They barely greeted me before rushing off
down the alley, obviously distraught, so I went to discover what had
happened. I guessed it was something serious, since Zuleikha never
normally visited Mother of Nebi on account of an old quarrel between
their husbands. Meri Gol blurted out that their sons, Jalil and Ahmad,
both aged four, had gone missing.

In the family room the paraffin lamp on the *kursi* threw huge shadows on to the walls, and the children seemed unnaturally quiet, as though they had just witnessed a dramatic event. Mother of Nebi appeared in the doorway, carrying in another lamp from the kitchen, and told me that the two women had come to ask her to divine their sons' where-abouts.

The two families had recently moved to newly built adjoining houses on an open piece of land about fifteen minutes' walk from where we lived, but Mother of Nebi had never been there, which impeded her from 'seeing' where the boys were. One house belonged to Sadiq, Farouq and their dependants, and the other to Resul, the wealthy engineer whose brother had married Firuzeh. The two houses were surrounded by fields divided by narrow irrigation ditches and slippery paths; a place fraught with danger at night. Mother of Nebi explained that Habibeh had been at home, minding her new baby, and assuming that Jalil was all right playing with Ahmed in Zuleikha's yard. Zuleikha's brother had been sent to the bazaar, and the boys had followed him out of the front door. Zuleikha thought he had taken them with him, but in fact he told them to go back and went without them. They wandered off and no one knew they were missing until over an hour later, when the boy came back with the shopping.

I asked what she had seen in her divination. She spoke heavily, straining to capture the sense of a few Persian words that had come out while she had been possessed. I had noticed from her previous divi-nations that a word or phrase often gave the key to her interpretation of a problem, but this time she seemed unsure of her message: 'North, east, west: in the town . . . Don't say the water-channel.' She puzzled over the words as if trying to understand an obscure dream.

'Habibeh was so upset,' said Meri Gol softly. '"I haven't the strength to bear it," she said. She's already lost two babies, and she's afraid this new one will die. It's so weak and she has so little milk . . .'

'And only last week she went to the hospital to get contraceptive pills,' added Mah Gol, setting down a tray of tea. Now Jalil would die out there in the cold, leaving her childless, was the unspoken thought.

'They'll be found,' their mother contradicted them firmly. 'I remem-ber when you went missing, Mah Gol. It was the mulberry season. We searched everywhere: you were missing for about three hours! In the end we found you sitting beneath a mulberry tree eating the fruit that had fallen.' She laughed as if to seek reassurance from the memory. 'And once Nadir got lost; he was only about three. We looked and looked until we were sick with worry, but in the end there he was playing in a neighbour's house – quite happy!'

'But there's no moon tonight, and the weather's freezing,' I said, sipping my tea in silence, disturbed by a vivid image of the little boys crying and shivering in the cold; barefoot and frightened.

The front door banged and Shemsaddin appeared in the doorway. His anxious face made it clear that he too was involved in the search. The children kept a meek silence as he took his place around the *kursi* and informed us that he had just come from Sadiq's house, where the women were out of their minds with worry. Their husbands had still not come home; the women were afraid they would beat them when they heard the boys were missing. He took a sip of hot tea and sighed deeply, invoking God's mercy, saying the children were sure to be found, but meanwhile we all had to suffer.

He recalled a time when a small boy had gone missing in Bagh-i Ali. The village men had all searched for three days, and they had even dived into the canals and probed for the body with long poles. Mother of Nebi remembered that the women had been crazed with grief, scratching their faces, tearing their hair and ripping their clothes: the whole house had been filled with lamentation. They had asked her to divine the boy's fate.

'I went into a trance, and I saw his corpse,' she said, dramatically, her children listening wide-eyed. 'I didn't tell them he was dead. I kept the knowledge to myself, letting them hope. On the fourth day they brought his body to the house.'

Shemsaddin shook his head sadly – the boy was found drowned in a weir. The present circumstances gave his story a chilling reality. As they conjured an increasingly frightening atmosphere in the shadowy room, I felt as though they wanted to frighten their own children from straying.

'Canals are very dangerous,' Shemsaddin went on. 'Mother of Nebi's own father died from swimming across a freezing stream, you know. She had just been born, and he wanted to take a short cut home to his wife. He had been at a *meleh* with friends. They tried to stop him, but he insisted. The water was icy with melted snow and he caught a chill.' He remembered how that evening a doctor had examined the sick man and checked his harsh breathing, but then left the room without a word. 'Haven't you got any medicine, doctor?' they had asked.

'If he lasts until midnight, he might survive,' the doctor replied.

'That was all he said,' recounted Shemsaddin. 'The doctor was right: he died at eleven o'clock that night.'

'This is the coldest time of the year, the forty days of deepest winter!' said Mother of Nebi, sensing the fear and excitement of her audience. 'Now is the time when wolves are driven down to the villages in search of food, when thick snow falls and bitter cold makes them crazy with hunger. They come close, even during the daytime.'

Had she really seen wolves, I asked? She described two occasions when she had seen them in Bagh-i Ali and had run for her life. Everyone fell quiet as she went on to tell a story.

'Once upon a time there was a family travelling back home from Pul-i Malan – a husband, wife and their small baby. They were riding on their horse in the middle of the day. It was deep winter and there was thick snow. They were returning to Ziyaratja, their village, when suddenly they saw four or five wolves prowling near their path, so they quickly turned off and rode up to the shrine of Mullah Kalan – the Big Mullah – where they could take cover.'

I could picture the scene. Ziyaratja, 'The Place of Shrines', was a large village nestling against a dramatic backdrop of craggy mountains. In the past it had been an important religious centre and I had visited a small underground chamber where Sufis went on forty-day retreats. The ruins of the majestic shrine of the Big Mullah dominated the village from the mountainside, its majestic arch recently collapsed through neglect.

'They left their horse tethered inside the walls of the shrine and climbed on to the roof, crouching down and keeping very still as they watched the black shapes of the wolves against the white snow . . . Suddenly they saw a young man riding out of the village. He had a gun slung across his saddle and a belt of cartridges over his shoulder. They thought he must be crazy riding out like that. Maybe he hadn't seen the wolves. The husband called out to him, although in doing so he drew attention upon them.

"O brother!" he shouted. "Can't you see your blood is in danger? There are wolves on your path!"

"I'm not afraid," the man replied. "I've got my gun!" – and he rode on. Only a minute later they saw the wolves pounce. They tore the man and his horse to pieces. There was no time for him to load his gun or fire a single shot before the animals were at his throat.'

There was a strangely exhilarated silence in the room. It was as though the children were invited to picture their cousins like lost lambs in the dark wilderness, bloody and torn, ravaged by wolves. I was struck by the contrast between this head-on encounter with fear and my own protected English childhood, where such emotions had been tightly suppressed. Mother of Nebi's children participated fully in the drama: they were expected to feel for Jalil and Ahmad and to be cautioned by their example.

Impatiently Mother of Nebi ordered Shemsaddin to go out for news, and then took her prayer beads and allowed herself to become possessed, trying again for some clue to the boys' whereabouts. She rolled her eyes upwards and shuddered and shook, spitting out strange sounds, harsh and panicky. Then she fell silent, fingering her beads and letting her thoughts run on.

'I can't tell where they should look,' she said at last, sounding immensely tired. 'But I know they'll be found.'

She ordered Mah Gol to fetch some bread for Nadir, who had begun to whimper, and announced that she was not cooking supper. How could she have the heart to eat, thinking of the little ones out there in the darkness? They would all go to bed on empty stomachs.

I called for news the following day. Meri told me that the boys had been found and were safely at home.

'They were found this morning,' said Mother of Nebi, who looked worn out. 'Last night I knew they would be missing until daylight, but I kept that knowledge from the mothers, feeling sure they'd be demented. A woman saw the boys wandering about just as it was getting dark, and she took them in. One of them had wet clothes on – Ahmad, I think – as he'd fallen into the irrigation ditch. She dried his clothes, gave the boys soup and put them to bed. They weren't frightened. They told their mothers they'd been to a party! Last night I was confused. I went to sleep thinking I might discover their whereabouts through my dreams. When I woke up I said to Shemsaddin, "They're well and they're together. They'll be home today."'

I had wondered how sincere and effective she was in her divinations, and whether she was simply skilled in putting on a convincing performance. How much did she bluff and guess? I wanted to believe that she had special powers and could tap into another dimension, but I was not sure. It was understandable that it had been particularly difficult for her to divine the whereabouts of her lost nephews, just as doctors cannot make an objective diagnosis when their loved ones are sick. I had sympathised with her frustration at being unable to 'see' clearly, but noted that she now claimed to have had a firmer idea of the situation than had been apparent the previous night. I also sensed it was important that her gift of divination be vindicated.

Stories about the lost boys circulated for weeks, gradually becoming more far-fetched and extravagant. If anything her reputation as a diviner was enhanced. People emphasised that she had said the boys would be found, and that she had predicted Ahmad's fall into the water channel, but were her divinations simply based upon common sense? It had seemed obvious to me that she had been unable to make any significant predictions, and she had admitted as much herself. She knew from her own experience that children who wandered were usually all right. I suspected that had the boys been drowned or killed she would have turned things around and claimed to have kept the truth to herself, as in the case of the boy who had been drowned in the weir. She might even have referred to the stories she had told, saying that they hinted at her foreknowledge of disaster. No one questioned her powers: trust in her was implicit. She certainly performed a valuable service for women in need of counsel, but I noticed that she usually made prophecies which confirmed their existing beliefs or were wide open to interpretation.

It was striking that all blame for the loss of the children had been assigned to the mothers, and that Jalil and Ahmad were not punished or admonished in any way. Children were not deemed responsible for their actions until the age of seven, which was taken as a milestone in maturity. However, Mother of Nebi had taken the opportunity deliberately to scare her own children and had even sent them to bed hungry so as to emphasise their cousins' plight. I felt that the incident was intended to serve as a lesson to them. Drama was not remote or fictionalised: it came from real accidents, deaths or calamities. What I had seen was the raw material for stories told around the *kursi*. Although everyone had been genuinely anxious and upset, the spine-chilling atmosphere and frightening tone had had an element of unashamed excitement and ghoulish entertainment.

19

A New Baby

Mother of Nebi's pregnancy advanced, but she was unwilling to make preparations, resentful of the new life growing inside her. She had little patience with her five children: what did she want with another? They were naughty, they tired her, and they simply generated work. I gave her some material to make baby clothes, but she put it aside without interest or gratitude, admitting that she felt disinclined to care for the child she was carrying. Eventually she asked me for some plastic sheeting to use on the floor for the delivery. Like almost all women in Herat she planned to give birth at home. People went to the hospital only if there were complications. She also asked me for money so that she could send Shemsaddin to get 'yellow fat' and certain spices from the bazaar, which she and the baby would need for a special diet during the forty days following the birth. She predicted that the birth would occur soon, during the dark phase of the moon, and that she would have a girl.

Early one morning I was woken by loud knocking. It was Nebi at the door.

'The baby's born. It's a girl!' he announced excitedly.

I followed him to the house, bitterly disappointed that I had not been called to witness the birth. We passed Shemsaddin sitting on a wooden bed in the courtyard, looking tired and bored after his long banishment from the delivery, as men were strictly excluded. The baby had been born only ten minutes before. Mother of Nebi was still squatting on the ground, supported by Mother of Gol Shah, a neighbour, who faced her and held her arms, and Mother of Farouq, who held her from behind. She was fully dressed, except that she wore no trousers, and her body was completely covered. Her head was bare and her hair was wet with sweat. She looked exhausted. She welcomed me weakly, her voice completely hoarse.

'We're waiting for the afterbirth,' said Mother of Gol Shah, who was acting as midwife. She had no medical training but was experienced in helping women in labour. 'We sent over to Anar Gol's for a water-pipe. Smoking can sometimes help it come.'

I leapt up, suggesting that I fetched my own, which I kept in case visitors needed to smoke. I ran back with it, filled the bowl and lit it. Mother of Nebi took a puff and immediately coughed, unused to the harsh tobacco; at the same time she had a contraction and expelled the afterbirth. They wiped the blood from her legs and gave her a pad to staunch the flow, and then led her over to the bed. She walked slowly, leaning on her mother's arm and fussing for someone to fetch her scarf.

In all the rush I had not even looked at the baby, who lay wrapped in a cloth on the floor, quiet but apparently healthy. The midwife asked Mother of Nebi's permission before severing the umbilical cord. Then she ordered Mother of Farouq to clear away the afterbirth and bury it.

In came Anar Gol, wide-eyed with excitement. She took hold of the baby and cleared its nose with a downward movement of her thumb and forefinger, seeming amazingly confident for a woman who had never had a child of her own. Afghan babies were not precious china dolls people were afraid to handle; in fact, Mother of Gol Shah had to prevent Meri Gol from trying to pick the baby up. She took the baby herself and stuck her finger into her tiny mouth, explaining that she was 'freeing her tongue'. Then she dressed her in a rag nappy, dress, jacket, swaddling and a head-scarf and bonnet, and laid her next to her mother.

Mother of Nebi said she had considered calling me for drugs, but had been dissuaded by the others. She had started in labour during the night, but had not informed anyone, otherwise they would have been obliged to stay up and lose their sleep. This secrecy at the onset of labour was typical of Herati women. Mariam told me she had got up early in the morning, already in labour, and had boiled water for her own medicinal brew. It seemed a matter of duty to cope alone for as long as possible. At about two o'clock Mother of Nebi had sent for Mother of Gol Shah and her own mother. By that time she had already fainted twice during the contractions. She said she walked about while she could, waiting for the time when she would have to push. She was still having contractions and pressed my hand inside her dress for me to feel. Her skin was hot and sweaty.

I went home to get painkillers. It had become light and the birds were singing. Shemsaddin lay dozing on the bed outside. When I returned, Mother of Farouq was serving tea. Shemsaddin followed me into the room, but did not even glance in the direction of the baby. He seemed displeased and irritable at all the disruption, but silently accepted a glass of tea. Mother of Nebi propped herself up on one elbow and drank, but refused any food: later they would cook her a dish of *changali*, a special food for newly delivered mothers, made from fat, bread and sugar, all of which were 'hot' and nourishing.

'This birth was much easier than Nebi's!' said Mother of Nebi, becoming more lively. 'I was in labour for two days with him. In the end they sent for a *gadi* from the city to take me to hospital, but by the time it arrived the baby had been safely born. We gave the driver sweets and money and sent him away. It's very difficult in the villages where there are no doctors or nurses to call in an emergency. You just have to pray everything will go well. It's especially dangerous in winter, when there's no chance of getting through the snow.'

Mother of Farouq searched in a trunk and found a little purse of eye-kohl and its blunt application stick. It was passed around and we each blackened our eyes, finishing with the new baby, whose eyebrows and eyes were thickly painted. I asked why this was done and was told that as we were all sleepy this would ensure that the baby slept well. There was an atmosphere of relief and celebration. Nebi returned from a local shop with a special herb which they put in a glass and infused in tea before straining it through Mah Gol's grubby scarf and spoon-feeding it to the baby. I winced at their tender ministrations, but said nothing.

That afternoon John and I took Mother of Farouq and the baby to the Friday mosque, accompanied by all the children except Mah Gol. Mother of Farouq carried the baby around the inner courtyard; this was supposed to give her a long life. We continued on our way to the dyers' quarter and walked down a narrow alley past long skeins of wool dripping with dye. An acrid smell came from the cauldrons inside. Mother of Farouq stepped boldly into a workshop and asked the dyer to perform the protective ritual. Expertly he inscribed a large circle over his cauldron with the baby's body and then dipped in his finger and made black marks on her cheeks and forehead, receiving a small coin in return.

Many babies died within days of being born, so there were numerous rituals and prohibitions designed to give good luck and protection. In some families no visitors apart from those who had been present at the birth were allowed to enter the house for ten days, but Mother of Nebi did not enforce this rule. She had five children and could afford to take risks.

I described to her a recent experience when I had been excluded from a friend's house, where a baby had just been born. I had begged admission, tired from my long walk, and they had finally let me in on condition that I did not speak. Later they softened and brought the baby to show me. I smiled but kept silent throughout the visit, terrified that I might inadvertently cause offence. Mother of Nebi asked if it was their first baby. I explained that their first had died and that the mother had taken another two years to conceive again. The first baby had been too weak to suck and I remember seeing the mother express milk to feed her with a spoon. I had never before seen a woman express milk – she sat in the courtyard squeezing it into an enamel bowl – and I thought it looked painful. In that family all three daughters-in-law had lost babies and had experienced a great deal of grief and anxiety.

'Like any Afghan family,' said Mother of Nebi. 'What woman doesn't know the pain of losing a baby? My mother – how many has she lost? Habibeh – she's not yet twenty and she's already lost two. Your friends were frightened of the evil eye or of *jinns*, that's why they would not let strangers into the house. I didn't go and visit my own sisters after they had had their babies. I waited until ten days had passed. If any harm had come, the blame might have fallen on me. People might have said I brought in *jinns*.'

During the first weeks, a baby was never left unattended. He or she usually wore an array of charms pinned to the bonnet or swaddling band, and a bead glazed with turquoise and pricked with two dots like eyes, which was intended to ward off the evil eye.

The next day I found Anar Gol at Mother of Nebi's house, busy

making bread for the family. She was squatting in the passage, rhythmically kneading dough in a bowl which she held between her knees.
She was a stout, smiling woman, not unlike Shemsaddin in looks, but
without his grim expression. Previously she had always seemed like a
visitor, but now she was working as a member of the household. She
wistfully told me that she wanted a baby of her own, but had still borne
no child after several years of marriage. Her co-wife next door had eight
children, so it was clear that her own fertility was at fault. I had to
apologise and say that I had no medicine that could help her.

'I've visited shrines, but my wishes haven't been granted,' she said.
'Once Mother of Nebi did a divination for me. She said my co-wife had
put something in my tea,' she whispered, narrowing her eyes.

Predictably, the two wives were on bad terms and did not speak to
one another. Anar Gol believed her co-wife had 'closed' her luck so that
their husband would love her less and the senior wife more. What about
adopting a child, I asked? She laughed, saying her husband would not
want that: he already had so many by his co-wife. He would be happy to
raise her child, but not the child of another man.

Anar Gol lived virtually alone. She took the opportunity of the baby's
birth to enter into the life of the family. She and Mother of Farouq
stayed for several days and together with Mah Gol they did all the
washing and cooking, and looked after Mother of Nebi and the baby. I
found another visitor in the family room, an old blind neighbour, who
also seemed to be taking refuge from an unhappy family situation at
home. She was patiently churning yoghurt to make 'yellow fat' by
rolling it back and forth against a cushion.

'Yellow fat's good for the baby,' said Mother of Nebi, who sat
propped against the wall. She told me Mother of Gol Shah had been to
visit her, and that she was coming in daily for ten days. The midwife's
legs were really aching from supporting Mother of Nebi in labour.
'When I delivered for Firuzeh and Habibeh my legs hurt for days!' she
went on. She had hardly had time to recover from one labour when they
called her for the next. The sisters and Zuleikha had all given birth
within days of one another. I had heard of other similar cases of
simultaneous births: the phenomenon was reminiscent of the way nuns
or girls living in dormitories find they menstruate at the same time.

'Would you ever act as a midwife?' I asked Mother of Farouq.

'No! But my own mother was very experienced,' she told me. 'She
knew how to make the pains come more quickly by breaking the bag of
waters.'

I shuddered, thinking of the risk of infection.

Mother of Nebi was in an expansive mood. She recalled Habibeh
swearing during labour, and told us how a woman in Bagh-i Ali had

completely forgotten herself and shouted out to her husband, 'Niko! Come and get this thing you put into me out.' Everyone laughed. Mother of Nebi explained to me that it was shameful to swear or use foul words in labour: one should call on God, praying for Him to take the pain away. Even in the act of birth it seemed necessary to maintain self-control. It was a public event and women had to take care to keep their bodies covered, for babies were born in full view of the women and children. Sometimes relatives were invited over, and they would drink tea, tell stories and make music to pass the time before the birth.

On the third day Nebi announced the birth and took sugared nuts to all their relatives. Babies were given a name on this day. It was not usual for the parents themselves to choose the name, leaving it instead to a senior member of the family, or to a *mullah*, who selected it by opening a holy book at random. Anar Gol chose this baby's name: she was called Zia Gol. Heratis liked similar names in families – Mahmood, Massood and Mahboob for three brothers, or Halimeh, Habibeh and Khadijeh for three sisters. Now there were three girls, each ending with 'Gol', meaning 'flower': Mah Gol, Meri Gol and Zia Gol.

I brought Mother of Nebi money and presents for Zia Gol's 'face-seeing', in accordance with the custom of bringing gifts the first time one saw a baby or a new bride. She looked feverish, and told me that she had had a high temperature in the night, known as the 'third day fever'. Her milk had come in and her breasts were very painful. She had been expressing milk to send for Habibeh's baby, as Habibeh's milk was not plentiful. She was worried by lumps under her arms, but declared that whatever happened she would carry on feeding: she could not afford to lose her milk.

Out in the courtyard her mother and Anar Gol were draping clothes on the washing line. Mother of Farouq was going home that day, for Timor was back on leave from military service and it was his last evening. I asked why he had not come to visit the new baby. Mother of Farouq said he was tired and it was as well to be careful: he did not want his fatigue to harm the baby. People bided their time before visiting, waiting for Zia Gol to muster her strength.

On the seventh night after the birth we assembled at the house to play the *daireh*, an old custom designed to scare away *jinn*s. Luckily Shemsaddin had to go out, so he was not there to dampen our spirits. Anar Gol brought her stepchildren, some of whom were keen singers, and Mother of Farouq came with Bassireh. We took turns to sing, and even Nebi joined in the fun.

At first Mother of Nebi sat quietly against the wall, playing the role of the convalescent, but soon the party atmosphere got the better of her and she could not resist playing the *daireh* herself.

'Let's have "Fatimeh Khanum"!' requested Meri Gol.

It was a comic dance about an ugly bride. Nebi got up and danced the part of the bride and Mother of Nebi sang. At the end of each verse something terrible happened to the bride – she was blinded, lamed, became dumb and so on, and became uglier and uglier. Nebi limped around the floor while we clapped in time, rocking with laughter at his performance. The joke was on the poor unsuspecting bridegroom.

Anar Gol's stepdaughters took turns to sing popular songs they had learned from the radio. Mother of Nebi sang older village songs from her girlhood and Mother of Farouq and Anar Gol sang traditional village-style quatrains, improvising their selection of verses.

We sat together until almost midnight, unwilling to break up the gathering. Eventually Anar Gol decided to take the children, who were dropping with fatigue, home to bed. Outside, to our surprise, we found everything was glistening with rain. There had been a spectacular thunderstorm, but in all our revelry we had not heard a thing.

Baby Zia Gol grew and thrived. Her cheeks became dimpled and she delighted us with smiles and chuckles. Mother of Nebi fed and tended her lovingly, her heart won over.

Afghan babies are kept swaddled for their first months. Women said that if they were left loose, their legs and arms would not grow straight. The custom is widespread, and although new-born babies derive comfort from the feeling of being wrapped, used to the secure, closed environment of the womb, it cannot be necessary to constrain them for so long. Swaddling seems symbolic of the hierarchical, conformist society.

Nappies were made of old rags stitched together, similar to the pads worn by menstruating women. They had to be washed and dried over and over again. They were not placed between the legs, but around the hips. Mother of Nebi used to lay the swaddling band and the triangular swaddling cloth on the floor, followed by several layers of stitched-rag pads. Then she would place Zia Gol's shoulders level with the top edge of the cloth and wrap her up, tucking in either arm and folding the bottom of the triangle up over her legs. After that she would cross the band in front and behind and tie the baby into a firm parcel. Finally she used to touch Zia Gol's stomach and the ground alternately three times, as Herati women did 'to take away the pain', presumably from the stomach to the ground.

The hallowed forty days following the birth passed by safely and Mother of Nebi gradually regained her strength.

20

The Evil Eye

One evening I noticed a persistent after-image of blurred colour in my left eye. It blotted out the words of the book I was trying to read, like some maddening piece of fluff on a camera lens. I wondered if I had been dazzled by the glare of the setting sun on a long homeward journey from a distant village, but the problem persisted. My Herati friends all told me that I had been struck by the evil eye, and they advised me to have a divination performed to discover who had 'put the glance' on me.

Belief in the evil eye was very widespread. It was thought that destruction could be caused inadvertently by someone admiring a person or object without uttering the protective formula, '*Mashallah*'. Once, in the Minstrel quarter, I saw a clear example of the work of the evil eye. One of the musicians had brought out a brand-new harmonium and was showing it off to us. As he went to put it away, the glass cover that fitted over the reeds slipped from his hand and broke: he had been praising it and now it had been blighted. Another victim of the evil eye was a girl they called the Burnt One. Someone had admired her, and she had had an accident with hot fat, severely disfiguring her face and neck. She had been very beautiful, but now she was hideous.

I heard about various methods of divination for the evil eye, all of which involved reciting names of possible instigators while eggs (or seeds) were pressed, knocked or cracked. When the egg broke, the name that was simultaneously uttered revealed the identity of the person who had 'put the glance' on someone. People assured me that my eye would not heal until I knew, and so I went to Mother of Nebi for a divination, putting myself into a positive frame of mind and hoping this would speed my recovery.

She carried some embers from the kitchen and rested the shovel on two bricks on the floor, and then fetched her prayer-beads and sat opposite me, placing an egg upright on top of the embers and slowly waving a fan to revive the fire. The room was quiet: Zia Gol lay asleep in her cradle and Nebi was concentrating upon his school books in a corner. The other children were all outside and we were undisturbed. She stared at the egg and began softly chanting in a descending sequence, every so often blowing with pursed lips, and passing her beads through her fingers all the while.

'That fire's not very hot,' remarked Nebi, looking up. 'The egg will never burst at that rate!'

'*Black eye, jealous eye, green eye, evil eye,*' she intoned, fanning and watching the egg blacken in the heat.

Then she ordered me to say the names of the people I visited, starting with the women in Shirin's house. I began reciting names, but felt uncomfortable and ashamed, disliking the idea of accusing anyone. I passed over their names with relief, and then went on to identify all the members of Latif Khan's family. She fanned the embers, but nothing happened. I mentioned other people, musicians who called regularly at our house, and people I knew in the bazaar. It was a distasteful process. When I had run out of names, I hesitated, watching the egg intently, and seconds passed by in silence. I could think only of naming people in Mother of Nebi's own clan, but I felt awkward and embarrassed about doing so.

'What about Latif Khan's house?' she prompted, not having recognised the names I had called.

'I just said those,' I replied.

Suddenly there was a loud bang. Sparks flew all over the room as the egg burst. She clapped loudly and shouted with triumph and excitement, 'Dust on Latif Khan's eyes! The egg has burst.'

Mah Gol ran in, alarmed at the explosion, and immediately began stamping out the live sparks which had scattered all over the room.

There were tiny burn holes everywhere, on my dress, on Mother of Nebi's dress, and on the mattresses where we had been sitting. She seemed quite unconcerned by the damage, brushing sparks off her dress, laughing and exclaiming excitedly, 'Damn Latif Khan!'

Half the shell of the egg had been blown off. The white was cooked and part of the yolk protruded from under the edge of the shell.

'Look! A face!' she said, touching the exposed part of the egg. 'Here are the eyebrows and here is the tongue.' She pointed to the flap of the yolk, but to my mind the features she saw were somewhat fanciful.

Now that the cause of my illness had supposedly been identified, I should have felt relieved, but I had no sense of catharsis. I was not convinced. Why hadn't the egg burst when I first pronounced Latif Khan's name? Yet I had to admit that his glance could be admiring, and he did have an eye for female beauty . . . I recognised that my case was unusual: normally a divination for the evil eye would be performed by a circle of women who all knew the people that the 'victim' encountered daily, and so the naming of suspects was straightforward.

Mother of Nebi began to calm down after the excitement. She predicted that my eyes would take a long time to heal, because it had taken a good while for the egg to burst. She recalled Timor's illness the previous summer, when her mother had also asked her to divine, and said the egg had been slow to burst then too. He had indeed been weak for many months. I asked who had put the evil eye on him, but she refused to tell me. Although I had understood that the evil eye was involuntary and there could be no blame or recrimination, I felt her secrecy belied this. Why had she damned Latif Khan's eyes if there was no blame or reproach?

I asked if anyone could cast the evil eye, or only certain people? She said anyone could, except children: they were innocent. It even sometimes happened that harm could be done by admiring someone's work. Once her eyes had become infected after a neighbour had praised her embroidery.

She sent for Abdullah and Meri Gol to take the egg away, and wrapped it carefully in a piece of bread. 'Put this egg at the roadside at the bottom of our alley,' she commanded the children. 'Don't eat any of it yourselves. A dog'll eat it and, God willing, Veronica's eyes will heal.'

I went to consult the best eye doctor in Herat, who had been trained in London and also happened to be a music-lover and an acquaintance. His first-floor surgery was in the new city. I climbed some rough brick stairs that stank of urine to the waiting-room, where men, women and children squatted resignedly in every available corner. Some had eyes that were bandaged and others were visibly diseased. Women held babies with suppurating eyes, and fanned their faces to keep the flies from crawling on the pus that oozed out. My feeling of panic and horror mounted, in direct contrast to the calm passivity of the other patients. But I did not have to wait long. No one protested when I was shown in to see the doctor next, for they accepted my special status as a foreigner and guest. After a careful examination the doctor pronounced that I had conjunctivitis and perhaps trachoma. He told me not to worry: he treated trachoma all the time, and my infection was in an early stage. He magnanimously refused to accept a fee and gave me a prescription for antibiotic pills, ointment and vitamins.

The infection took months to heal, a confirmed case of trachoma. I applied the ointment day and night and prayed that the treatment would work. I also avoided 'hot' and 'spicy' foods, which my friends told me were irritating and unsuitable for my eyes. 'Cold' and 'sour' foods, such as cucumber, lime juice, or yoghurt, would be soothing. The eye doctor laughed when I asked him about diet. He said it was pointless avoiding certain foods, and that people only did this because it gave them a sense of satisfaction to be doing something. But among Heratis it was by no means unusual to apply more than one system of healing, as I did. Agha Mohammad Ali, a traditional healer, had consulted a Western-trained doctor for his tuberculosis, and had even moved from his village to the city in order to be near him. This was not viewed as absurd or contradictory: Heratis were pragmatic and expedient in their solution to sickness.

The threat to my eyes emphasised the issue of health in a very personal way, and made me appreciate the deep anxiety women experienced over illness. As mothers and nurturers of the family they had a vital responsibility, and yet they and their children were especially vulnerable since they depended upon their husbands for money for cures. It was iniquitous but true that men could deny women and children recourse to medical help, and it was no wonder that women placed importance upon methods such as divination or diet, which were at least accessible and within their control. Gratefully I applied my ointment, pitying the majority of people who went untreated. Mother of Nebi's blind neighbour had never consulted a doctor for her eyes. People went blind for lack of treatment for diseases such as trachoma, which were easily transmitted through polluted water and through the dust which blew into one's eyes during the high winds of the summer months.

'Slowly, my eyes became dim,' the old woman told me. 'No, I didn't go to a doctor. How could I go without money? I can still see a little light even now.'

She was not yet quite blind.

21

Leave-taking

During our final weeks I saw less of Mother of Nebi. I was deeply involved in playing music with my teacher Shirin and had very little spare time. Mother of Nebi resented this and was less friendly.

Two engagements took place quite suddenly. I was visiting Mother of Nebi's aunt, Mother of Yunis, when to my astonishment I heard that Mah Gol had become engaged. I was hurt that Mother of Nebi had not told me the news herself, and asked who Mah Gol's fiancé was.

'Hafiz, my sister's son,' answered Mother of Yunis. 'You've seen my sister, Mother of Faizeh, haven't you? Her son. He's away now, working in Iran. He's very young, seventeen maybe . . . I can't understand why they kept it secret from you. No one else seemed to know either. It's very strange. We'd have known nothing ourselves if it hadn't been for hearing the sound of the *daireh* going past our door: Meri Gol and the boys were out taking the "needle and thread" for Hafiz!'

When I visited, Mother of Nebi was evasive and avoided my gaze. She said they had only sent over the 'needle and thread'; I had not missed a formal party. When I asked directly about the bridewealth, she said nothing had yet been decided, and added that in any case half the money would have to be spent on Mah Gol's dowry. I could not understand the reason for the secrecy and atmosphere of shame. Mah Gol looked embarrassed, but showed no repulsion at her future prospects. At least she was not marrying into a village and going into exile.

Mother of Yunis had an unmarried daughter, Sadiqeh, who one day blurted out some news about the bridewealth for Mah Gol.

'Did you hear? They're giving a hundred thousand *afghanis* for Mah Gol, and they've already paid twenty thousand!'

This huge sum explained all the elusive behaviour. Mother of Yunis hushed Sadiqeh, annoyed at her indiscretion. Although bad feeling existed between herself and Mother of Nebi, she respected her niece's right to secrecy from outsiders such as myself. Sadiqeh blushed and put her hand to her mouth.

Two weeks later Sadiqeh suddenly became engaged herself, to a prosperous young man from the old city. Mother of Yunis worked as a cleaner in a girl's school and his mother had seen Sadiqeh there and liked the look of her. Mother of Nebi was furious with jealousy. Sadiqeh had received fine presents and Mah Gol had had nothing. It was better to marry outside one's clan, she said: they treated new brides with more respect.

'Mother of Yunis held a party for the bridegroom's women to meet our clan, but she didn't invite us,' she added crossly.

She was preparing to bake, sprinkling flour over her big board and then shaping the dough into individual balls. She took her anger out on the dough, handling it roughly. I walked with her to the side of the house, where the clay oven had already been lit with dry thorn. It was unreasonable of her to expect to be included in Sadiqeh's festivities when she behaved sourly towards them, especially as she had been so secretive over Mah Gol's engagement.

She took up the first ball of dough, patted it into a flat oval on a small pad and then slapped it vigorously against the hot inside wall of the oven. When each loaf was cooked, she forked it out, splashed it with a little water and set it on its side to cool. Her lips worked silently and her face had an expression of concentrated fury as she brooded over Sadiqeh's new-found riches. Baking was a penance: the smoke and heat stung her eyes. When they had first bought their house she had worked for months raising money by baking, charging a small commission from neighbours for each loaf. She had deliberately not taught her daughters to bake, so that they did not suffer her own discomforts.

When I visited two weeks later, she was very upset because Shemsaddin had forced her to sell a gold necklace that she had only recently bought, the hard-earned reward for tailoring and embroidery she had done for me. He had insisted that he needed the money to pay their uncle for wheat, and when she had suggested selling their sheep to raise the money, he had refused. She complained that he had sold the necklace at a loss of 300 *afghanis*, and despaired that everyone would make fun of her and ask what had become of it.

It was Ramadan. She fasted piously every day, even on the days when she menstruated although they brought no merit. Every evening she washed herself scrupulously and performed her prayers before the breaking of the fast. She suffered the pangs of thirst and hunger without complaint, enjoying the test of her will. Fasting suited her secluded way of life. Very little changed, since she did not have to forgo any outings in order to conserve her energy. Her days were more fulfilled than usual.

I spent a last evening with the family. When the cannon sounded we had our meal and then Shemsaddin went to the Koran-reading at the local mosque. We sang songs and played games with the children, and Mother of Nebi posed riddles for us. Later she entertained us with some strange stories, which seemed to possess an inner kernel of meaning. The children settled quietly, used to the familiar pattern of their mother's tales, the soothing darkness and the gentle flicker of the lamp.

I paid farewell visits to the various houses of the clan. I brought a 'face-seeing' gift for Sadiqeh, who had become a new bride. Her appearance shocked me. In two weeks she had lost her plump, girlish looks and taken on the glazed air of an insomniac. She was besotted with her husband. It was clear that his nocturnal visits had robbed her of sleep and dulled her appetite for food. He had ordered her to fast every day and she looked thin and nervous.

It was sad visiting Mother of Farouq for the last time. Bassireh, the youngest daughter, sat apart, rocking to and fro as she read a chapter of the Koran. She was doing a complete reading for the month, reciting a chapter a day. They had no recent news of Timor, still away on military service and a constant source of worry.

'We will miss you when you go,' said Mother of Farouq softly. 'Mother of Nebi will be lonelier than ever now.'

Mother of Nebi took me to say goodbye to her Agha. As before, she threw herself into an ecstatic fit, swaying from side to side, chanting and grunting. He watched patiently from his alcove and then calmed her. Later we visited him in his private room, which was nicely decorated and carpeted. He took my camera and examined it and then asked for it as a gift, but Mother of Nebi quickly said it belonged to the university. He handed it back without offence but I disliked him for asking.

I was sad at the prospect of parting from Mother of Nebi. Looking back on our friendship, I knew that our best moments had been when her spirit was fired and she had been lost in the present moment, becoming so completely immersed in dancing or singing that she forgot her bitterness. I remember one occasion when we had gathered around the *kursi* at dusk, singing by the light of a single paraffin lamp – Mother of Nebi, her mother, Bassireh and the children. She had begun improvising verses about Timor, a soldier far away, and our eyes had filled with tears as we each felt the pain of separation. She rocked to and fro as she sang, and her eyes were closed as though nothing else mattered.

That evening Shemsaddin was away and we felt free. Suddenly Nebi sensed that he should take control, for it was late and the children had become unruly. He ordered his mother to get up and cook supper, but she retorted that her heart was full, and defiantly struck up another song. When she was inspired she glowed. The world could go to the devil: she did not want to lose touch with these deep feelings. She would dance until she got dizzy, drum so her ears rang, and tell magical, awesome stories that held a circle of listeners wide-eyed and spell-bound. Most mysterious and unusual of all was her gift of divination and communicating with spirits. In all this she fascinated me.

I took my leave of her on the very morning of our departure. The Land Rover was packed and we faced a long, precarious journey overland. I felt jittery and nervous as I crossed the alley and walked straight into her compound, my veil on my head, all ready to go. She jumped up as she saw me, letting out a wail of panic and grief. I found I had no tears, although my stomach lurched sickeningly. My mind was still filled with the last trailing threads of packing and with the numb sadness of leaving Herat. I tried to comfort her, and then left her sitting in a crumpled heap, her eyes streaming with tears.

There was sadness, but also relief in parting. I felt a weight roll off me, as if I had been wrenched away from her pain. For me she symbolised the imprisonment of purdah; an intelligent, strong-willed and highly creative woman chained and smothered by an ignorant, bigoted husband. Had she been a man, would she have suffered *maraz*?

Would she have been jealous, resentful and malicious, poisoned by her own frustration? I could imagine her life as a man: free, out of the house, hard-working, responsible, pursuing her own interests. As a woman she bowed submissively, confined to domesticity and the labours of serving her family, her creativity stifled. She was not simply the product of that particular culture – frustrated women like her exist in many societies. Her inferior role, her struggle for her own voice and her submission to great outside forces haunt so many of us.

PART THREE

Shirin

22

Becoming a Pupil

Although I knew Shirin for less than a year, we became very close through music. We met by chance at a wedding, to which John and I were invited by a friend who was performing in an expert village dance group. Other occasions for their dancing had been modest, so I was surprised when we arrived at a particularly lavish and prestigious wedding.

I was soon taken to see Shirin's band at the women's party in a neighbouring house. Two large rooms were lined with women and children laughing, chatting and enjoying the music, and I was put in a place of honour between the young daughters of the provincial Governor. Senior women smiled and exchanged greetings with me and continued smoking contentedly on their water-pipes, their prayer veils spread comfortably over their laps. Shirin, a lively, buxom woman in her mid-thirties, was playing on the far side of the room, surrounded by an excited crowd of girls. She led the singing, accompanying herself on the harmonium, and other young, glamorously made-up girls played two *daireh*s and a pair of *tabla* drums. She began each vocal line, which would be completed by her accompanists in order to save their voices from undue strain. This gave their music a distinctive leader/chorus quality.

The Minstrels were of great interest to me; they performed in professional all-women bands which were unique in Afghanistan and, as women's musical culture was more compartmentalised than men's, they were important disseminators of new popular music. They copied the repertoire of male urban bands and imitated their sound with the use of harmonium and *tabla*. Unfortunately, because they did not use male chaperones and sometimes played within view of strange men, they had acquired a bad name. Some people thought, wrongly, that they were loose women. They flouted the conservative Afghan expectation that women should not earn money in public, an idea which was being eroded by the secularisation process (particularly with regard to high-status work such as school-teaching), and they also aroused traditionalist Islamic prejudice against music. But their image as exotic and daring outsiders made them especially fascinating and attractive to me.

I had heard that Shirin was the best of the Minstrel singers but I had not actively pursued contact with her. I assumed that I should have to pay to record her, yet did not have the funds to collect music like a professional ethnomusicologist, so I was delighted that I now had the opportunity to meet her and enjoy her music in its natural context. When the musicians took a break, I went over and spoke to her. She welcomed me, said she had heard about John's music research, and introduced me to her girls.

'This is my eldest daughter, Gol Dasteh,' she began, indicating the dark, curly-haired seventeen-year-old who had been playing fast, driving *tabla* rhythms, 'and these are my other daughters: Ferideh,' a vivacious, wicked-eyed ten-year-old, 'and Zahra's the one sucking milk!' She laughed loudly, pointing to the small child at her fat breast. 'This is Nadieh, my uncle's wife, and Jamileh, my brother's wife,' she concluded, waving a hand at the *daireh* players.

I took an instant liking to Shirin, who was open, friendly, smiling and relaxed. We sat chatting about people and music, undeterred by the curious crowd of listeners who inevitably gathered round us. When she questioned me about John's work or about my view of Herat, it was as though she was interviewing me on behalf of the others, who listened and openly commented. Lunch was served, and she invited me to eat from her tray. It was ironic that I should have forsaken the elevated company of the Governor's daughters, whom I hoped would not take offence, in order to consort humbly with musicians.

After lunch, Shirin drew her harmonium towards her and asked what I would like her to play. I did not request any particular songs, but I asked permission to record her; she gave it freely and even supervised the placement of the microphone. There was an expectant hush before she began.

She sang in the *charbeiti* style that had made her famous, a nostalgic, highly ornamented solo performance. She had a rippling, clear, light voice with a sweet sound that suited her own name, which itself means 'sweet'. Her face was warm and expressive, bare of make-up except for a thin line of kohl encircling her lively brown eyes; her smooth forehead was marked by a single criss-cross tattoo of faded blue, and she wore her hair with an old-fashioned kiss-curl in front of each ear. Her lament silenced the room and the women sighed in appreciation. She sometimes looked upwards calling on God to reunite lovers, and her verses evoked the tormenting pain of love and separation.

After two long, sad songs, she changed the mood, and called on her younger daughter to dance and sing. Ferideh stood coyly in the middle of the room, giggling and self-conscious. Her voice was a little raw, and occasionally she needed prompting by her mother. Although she was still flat-chested, she had made up her eyes boldly with black and green, and as she sang she made childish gestures imitating the singers in the public theatre. At the end of each verse she broke into a fast dance, spinning around and flashing her eyes coquettishly. Already she was an assured performer, enjoying our attention, her coyness half-affected.

When her song had ended, Shirin decided it was time for me to dance. Ignoring my howls of protest, she struck up a tune on her harmonium: the 'tourist dance'. She shamed me into standing up, saying the Governor's wife had requested me to dance. I should stop fussing and acting shy. I danced as best I could, but felt hot in my woollen jumper and wished that I had been warned to dress up for the occasion. Gradually the clapping, drumming and excited shouts of appreciation and encouragement helped me to relax and enjoy dancing, until I eventually sank to the ground, laughing and out of breath.

When I had recovered, Shirin made me sing. I told her I had learned a little from my neighbour, Mother of Nebi, and she asked me which songs I knew. The wedding guests were eager to see what I could do and I knew I would have to give in. Shirin wisely told me that if I wanted to

become a singer I would have to conquer shyness and get used to singing
for people – words that I have never forgotten. She encouraged me by
saying that she would sing with me and play the harmonium: with the
band behind me it would sound really professional.

We moved the instruments and settled opposite the Governor's wife
and the senior women, who wanted to hear me. I chose a village song
with easy words:

> *We've brought the horses to the door of the house*
> *We're taking away our bride – she's going to her house*
> *Mother of the bride – are you listening or not?*
> *We're taking away our bride – will you allow it or not?*

A different member of the family is addressed in each verse: 'father of
the bride', 'sister of the bride', and so on.

'You sing and then I'll play,' said Shirin slyly, not wanting to admit
that she did not know the song. She picked up the tune easily and the
others joined in on drums. I sang nervously, driven on by the band
backing me, encouraged by the clapping and eager looks from the
audience.

'She sings well,' said the women tolerantly.

'She sounds like us; she's learned our language!'

They were delighted, laughing when I forgot the words or made a
mistake, quite captivated by my efforts. Shirin played up to the
situation, raising her arm and threatening to clout me if I went wrong.
Here we were at a wedding and I had been turned into the main
attraction! We were a comedy act, with Shirin as the strict and angry
teacher and myself as the incompetent pupil. I enjoyed it, apart from
being painfully conscious of my shortcomings as a singer. The other
musicians were smiling and supportive, and covered for my false
entries. There was a burst of warm applause as we finished my third
song; I put my hand on my heart, bowing and apologising.

'I'll have to come to you for lessons,' I said to Shirin. 'I want to learn
to do better than that!'

'Don't worry, I'll teach you, she said. 'You've already become
my pupil today! Just come to the Minstrels' alley and find me. Any
of the children will show you where I live. Come whenever you
want.'

We parted on the best of terms, promising to meet again soon. I could
not believe my luck in having met Shirin in such ideal circumstances,
and having got on so well. I was thrilled and delighted at the prospect of
having lessons from the most famous of Herat's female vocalists, and
longed to get to know her better.

I did not know how much to believe of the Minstrels' scandalous reputation. I heard that they practised free love and incest, that the women were prostitutes, and that the boys danced at illicit parties and sold their favours to men. In Herat there was a strong connection between dancing and prostitution: the Baluch people known as Chelu, who lived in white-tented encampments on the edge of the city, were musicians (playing their own special instruments), dancers, pimps and prostitutes, and some of the women who sang, danced and acted in the government theatre were also courtesans. These facts led people to assume that the Minstrel women must also be available, though this proved not to be true.

People said the Minstrels were like Jats, the barber-musicians with whom they did in fact have secret genealogical links. The Jats had a low social standing and rarely married outside their own clan. They were despised and feared, and no outsider would have countenanced adopting their traditional professions of barbering, carrying out circumcisions, acting in the folk drama, or performing on their musical instruments, the *sorna* and *dohol* (known collectively as *sazdohol*). They lived in enclaves in the city and inhabited certain villages, and they even had their own secret language – sets of phrases they could use if they did not wish to be understood by outsiders. As public entertainers, the Minstrels were likened to Jat actors who daubed themselves with flour make-up, cracked lewd jokes and dressed up as women or animals in their satirical farces. Jats were notoriously grasping, loud and insistent in their begging. I had often seen *sazdohol* musicians playing from house to house at festival times, according to tradition. In the villages they had a customary right to collect alms in grain at harvest time. When they were given money or presents they shouted praise to generous patrons but insulted those who were mean. Likewise if the Minstrel women felt they had not received adequate payment, they indulged in loud, shaming protests at the end of weddings.

The stereotype of the uncouth, greedy Jat clung to all professional musicians in Afghanistan, even to dignified men such as Latif Khan. No matter how well-mannered or finely dressed they might be, musicians were liable to be insulted and called Jats at the slightest disagreement with people. There had been efforts by the government to raise the low status of musicians, and people sometimes gave them the honourable title of 'artist', but underlying prejudices persisted. It was hard for me to tell whether the stories of the Minstrels' immorality were slander or based upon fact.

A few days after my encounter with Shirin, I screwed up my courage and visited the Minstrels' quarter, wondering if I was walking into a den of iniquity. They lived quite near the tourist bazaar, about ten minutes' walk from my house. As I approached the alley I recognised one of Shirin's young sons, who immediately left his gang of friends and escorted me to the house, followed by a trail of rowdy boys. About twelve compounds had been built along a narrow twisting lane, some of them connected by their roofs. The last house belonged to Salim Jan, the Minstrel patriarch and lead-singer of the male family band. The path did not lead anywhere, so the only people who came into the alley were its inhabitants or outsiders seeking to engage one of the women's bands. It was the only area in Herat where women sometimes sat outside chatting in a Mediterranean manner, since the Minstrels did not seclude their women from their own clan. Their quarter was elevated and from some windows you could see right across the city, overlooking caravanserais and the ruined north wall: the whole plot of land had been bought in the 1930s by the original patriarch, Minstrel Amin, for the tiny sum of 300 *afghanis*.

I followed the boy into Shirin's courtyard, which was small, white-washed and unpaved, but brightened in one corner by a green vine. Gol Dasteh, the eldest daughter, greeted me from a balcony that connected the back and front rooms of the house. Shirin seemed pleased to see me and, as the guest room was too cold, she took me into her tiny upstairs family room at the back. We sat by a window overlooking the court-yard, and Gol Dasteh brought a fresh shovelful of embers to warm the *kursi* brazier. The walls were dirty, covered with fingermarks and scratches etched in the plaster, and the furnishings were scruffy and threadbare. I was surprised the family was so poor. Their smart wedding clothes had led me to think they must be affluent, but this was clearly not the case.

Shirin began telling me about her recordings at Radio Afghanistan, obviously seeking to impress me. Three years ago she had been paid 1,000 *afghanis* for singing five songs with the radio orchestra, and she proudly reeled off their titles, one of which was the *charbeiti* she had sung for me at the wedding. She said they had offered her a permanent job for 8,000 *afghanis* a month, but she had refused. Her husband had been against it, she was not fond of Kabul, and she had too many children to take on such a professional commitment. On another occasion a German radio team had offered her 20,000 to make some recordings, but she had not wanted to make the long journey to Kabul during the late stages of a pregnancy. I was impressed: schoolteachers earned only about 2,000 a month, and her singing obviously commanded high sums. I commented that it would have been hard for her to have gone to Kabul: wouldn't she have missed all her relatives?

'God, no. I don't care a damn about them!' she countered sharply. 'They're all jealous of my success, and they want to steal my patrons.

They'd be glad if I went. No, I wouldn't want to leave Herat. Kabul's so dirty and crowded. Herat's green and the air's good here.'

She had five sons and three daughters. I wrote down their names in my notebook. Yaqub, her eldest, was about twenty, still studying in school, and the youngest was Zahra, the baby I had seen suckling at the wedding. Shirin's sister, Golnar, lived in the two front rooms of the house, but they were not on good terms. As soon as she could afford to repay Golnar's mortgage, Shirin intended to get her out. The other member of the household was Hakim, her husband's orphaned nephew, a musician we already knew.

Gol Dasteh brought tea and, as news of my arrival got round, the room gradually began to fill with visitors. Jamileh and Nadieh, the other girls from the band, joined us. I reminded Jamileh that I had first met her at Karim's 'sweet-eating', and handed her a photograph of the occasion which the others all fought to see. She looked considerably less glamorous now, wearing no make-up, her hair matted, and with a scruffy veil around her shoulders. Did she wear a veil outside, I asked, having wrongly assumed that these independent women went unveiled? She said they had to cover their faces, otherwise people stared, but declared that she envied my freedom. I remembered that at the wedding I had been surprised to see the musicians cover themselves as they made their way down the alley to the bridegroom's house, where there had been some dancing after the male guests had left. The Minstrel women lived on the border of seclusion: although they wore veils in the street, they bared their faces to strangers within compound walls, and they argued and negotiated about their payment with men. When they were making their way through the bazaar in their *burqa* veils, they were nevertheless conspicuous with their instruments.

Jamileh left, carrying a huge bundle of spinach she had just fetched from a local shop. It was significant that she had been to get it herself, for normally shopping for groceries was done by men or children, so that women did not have to go out. I was not surprised that she had this freedom of movement, but her spinach reminded me that these women were hard-working and practical. They cooked meals and washed clothes just like ordinary housewives. At weddings, dressed in their finery, they gave a misleading impression of ease and affluence, yet they had a heavy workload earning a living and caring for their families.

I was introduced to Salim Jan's second wife, Faizeh, who was young and pretty, with fresh, rosy cheeks. Shirin jokingly commented that Salim had gone off both his wives and was always going to see his girlfriend, who was married herself, although her husband was unaware of the affair. Faizeh seemed unconcerned at her husband's public infidelity. I was very surprised to hear the women talking openly about adultery. Perhaps it was true that the Minstrels were freer than most people. Certainly they seemed quite casual about a matter of honour that others took very seriously. Faizeh added that Salim wanted to make the girlfriend his third wife, and we went on to discuss polygyny. Did English men take more than one wife, Faizeh asked? I told her that it was against our religion and law, but that sometimes people played around outside marriage. I asked if it wasn't hard having a co-wife: I didn't think I could share a man. Didn't she feel jealous when he was sleeping with his other wife? She said they took turns, and pointed out that it was an advantage to have another woman's help and companionship. Shirin said that Faizeh and her co-wife got on well. Some women didn't mind, but others quarrelled bitterly. Shirin had had a co-wife herself, but she said she had forced her husband to end this second marriage.

Polygyny was customary among the Minstrels. Since their wives brought money into the household, there was an economic incentive to marry several times. Islamic law allows a man to take up to four wives, but only rich or important Herati men had as many as four; for instance Aghas, who needed women to service their numerous guests. Men liked talking about taking a second wife, but few actually had two, and it was generally admitted that two wives meant trouble, jealousy and fighting.

A small, plump, beaming man entered the room – Shirin's husband, Khalifeh Sultan. She immediately made room for him around the *kursi* and introduced me as her new pupil. He greeted me warmly and made a long speech, telling me to make myself at home and come whenever I wanted. Shirin decided to show me off, so she told Gol Dasteh to fetch the *daireh*, and then warmed its skin over the brazier to make it taut. When she ordered me to sing, Khalifeh Sultan smiled and nodded encouragingly, saying I must not feel shy.

The visitors all watched with interest as I played, but Shirin listened critically and ordered me to drum harder: the sound was too weak. Away from the tolerant and joking atmosphere of the wedding, this was suddenly like an audition, and I felt very uncomfortable and exposed singing all alone.

'Her drumming's poor, but her voice isn't bad,' she said to the others, when at last she had told me I could stop. 'It sounded much better with the band.'

She explained that they should make allowances for my age and the fact that their language and culture were foreign to me. Then she turned to me, saying she would teach me a new song.

'This one's very popular at weddings at the moment. What shall we do? Do you want to write down the words first?'

Laboriously I copied the lyrics, struggling to distinguish the beginning and end of each poetic line, sometimes unsure of the actual words. With so many people watching, it was a painful ordeal. Shirin commented that of course they used their memories when learning something new; for none of them could write. We tried to sing the melody together. She sang the lines over and over, but my progress was disappointingly slow, and to make matters more confusing, the verse and chorus had a very similar melodic pattern. I found it hard to concentrate in front of such a large crowd, and after a while Shirin took the *daireh* and gave the beat herself, enabling me to focus more upon the singing. Eventually I suggested trying another song, which I already partially knew, and she dictated the words for me. The result was more successful. She turned triumphantly to the others and boasted at how quickly I had learned.

By now it was late and I was feeling tired. Both of us had been put off by all the onlookers. I closed my notebook and announced that I would have to leave, and some of the guests started drifting away, seeing that the spectacle was over. Awkwardly, I pulled out some small presents for Shirin – some hairslides and lipsticks from England – and I gave her some money in an envelope. Khalifeh Sultan looked offended, and told me to keep my money: I was their guest. He tried to push the envelope back, but I insisted Shirin kept it.

'After all, I've become your pupil,' I said, pressing the gifts into her hand. 'That's right, isn't it, for me to bring something for my *ustad*? Let these be "pupil-gifts".'

'It'd be remiss for me not to take her offerings,' she told Sultan, smoothing over his discomfort.

He and Gol Dasteh insisted on walking me down the alley, and they would have escorted me all the way home had I not made them turn back.

23

The Rival Bands

The history of the female bands went back to Salim Jan's father, Minstrel Amin, the founder of the clan. During the late 1930s he married women who were talented musicians and formed them into a group playing the Indian instruments, harmonium and *tabla*, which were currently being adopted by male Herati bands. He created a new phenomenon, a band of female singers and instrumentalists who sang and danced to entertain women, and it was highly successful. He proceeded to find more wives for his brothers and sons, thus expanding the number of musicians, until over the years his original band proliferated into the five main groupings that existed while I lived in Herat.

Neither Shirin nor Sultan were direct descendants of Minstrel Amin, although Shirin could claim a distant link with his mother, who belonged to a village Jat family. Shirin was drawn into the clan through the marriage of her sister, Golnar. Their family was not well off and at that time lived on the outskirts of town, by the Kandahar Gate, where their father had a musical instrument workshop.

'When Golnar was about fourteen, Minstrel Amin came to my father and made him a proposal,' Shirin told me. 'He wanted Golnar as a wife for his nephew, on the understanding that she would join his wives' band. In return he invited my father to move house and go and live in his quarter.'

'Did Golnar know about music?'

'Not especially. He didn't select her for her voice or anything. He just needed girls who could play the *daireh*. My father was from Kandahar and had no family here, so he agreed. We gave Golnar in marriage and Minstrel Amin gave us a couple of rooms in his house. It was better for us all to live in the new city.'

Among the Minstrels marriage revolved around considerations relating to the female bands, which were recruited on the basis of kinship. Their success lay in attracting new musicians such as Golnar from certain urban and village Jat families with whom they had marriage links. No one outside the Jat group would have dreamed of giving a daughter in marriage to a Minstrel as this would be viewed as tantamount to selling her into infamy. If a Minstrel daughter had proved herself a good musician, efforts were made to secure her a husband from within the clan who would allow her to continue working. Minstrel marriages were totally atypical. Because the girls were a continual source of income, little importance was attached to the bridewealth and there was no preference for marriage between cousins. Indeed, Minstrel women sought unusual qualities in a daughter-in-law: she needed to be bold, unafraid of performing in public, and confident at defending herself against leers and general disdain. The maidenly virtues of docility, modesty and shyness were a positive disadvantage, since girls needed to show independence and spirit if they were to be successful musicians.

Shirin's marriage was more complicated than Golnar's, for she had already become established as a valuable musician. When Golnar began playing at weddings with Shahzadeh, Minstrel Amin's fourth wife (who died young, a few years before I came to Herat), Shirin accompanied them. She quickly picked up the music; Shahzadeh encouraged her to sing and corrected her mistakes. Shirin was a wonderful singer; a nightingale, as Shahzadeh called her. She was bold, mischievous and a natural performer, so obviously talented that there was soon interest in her marriage, which would secure her a place in a band. Various women wanted her in their bands and made offers for her to marry their sons or brothers, but naturally Shahzadeh did not want to lose her. Shirin's father had died, and her mother was content to let Shahzadeh organise Shirin's future, and grateful for the money she brought in.

Shirin herself liked Shahzadeh's nephew, Sultan, an orphan who had come from his village on a protracted visit. Although Shahzadeh had originally planned to find someone else for Sultan, thus bringing another member into her band, she decided to arrange for him to marry Shirin. No one seemed deterred by the fact that as a girl Shirin had been engaged to her first cousin. Shahzadeh simply paid him 2,000 *afghanis* compensation and it was broken off. She bought new clothes for Shirin, paid the wedding expenses, and gave the bridewealth to Shirin's mother on Sultan's behalf. It was a love match. How different Shirin was from other Herati brides! She knew the men who were her possible husbands, could speak out and express her own preference, and succeeded in getting her own way. Sultan told me himself that they used to cuddle a little under the *kursi* quilt, and he sometimes kissed her when no one was looking. Shirin used to bring him sweets when she came back from weddings. They had some freedom to flirt together.

Shahzadeh made one important condition: Sultan had to sign a letter promising that he would never withdraw Shirin from her band. He told me that on her death-bed his aunt had given him back the letter and freed him of his promise, but in any case there had been no question of Shirin retiring. She was highly successful and they depended upon her income.

By the time I came to know Shirin, about twenty-five Minstrel women were working as professional musicians, some performing only occasionally. They were loosely grouped into five bands comprising four or five players. A minimum of three was necessary (on harmonium, *tabla* and *daireh*), but extra girls allowed some to sit out and breast-feed their babies, or instruments to be swapped around. Younger girls usually accompanied their mothers and helped mind the small children, and as a result they too gradually learned to perform. Normally Shirin led her own band, but if a wedding was not very grand Gol Dasteh deputised for her. Nadieh and Jamileh took it in turns to play *daireh* or *tabla*, but neither could play the harmonium. Although only about ten, Shirin's younger daughter, Ferideh, was already becoming an integral member of the band and could play the *daireh*, join in the singing and perform a few song-and-dance acts.

Band members were recruited on the basis of kinship, not friendship or musical talent. Band-leaders took their unmarried daughters, daughters-in-law and brothers' wives to play with them. Once a musician married, she automatically became a member of her mother-in-law's band. The leaders were almost like husbands: they controlled their musicians and their special permission was needed for a player to go out occasionally with a rival band. Having assumed that the Minstrel women enjoyed some sort of solidarity as outcasts, I was surprised to discover that feuds were rife among them. This enmity was based not upon quarrels between their men, as might have been expected, but upon commercial competition between the bands.

Although Shirin was acknowledged as the best individual singer, her band was not ranked highest – it was more or less on a par with two others. Clients not only wanted entertainers who played well and knew the latest songs, but also sought beautiful, finely dressed musicians who would add lustre to their gathering. One of the most popular bands belonged to three hugely fat unmarried sisters, Soraya, Amaneh and Najibeh; people admired their brash beauty, slick manners and expensive clothes. Shirin's other main competitor was Salim Jan's young sister, Leila (Shahzadeh's only daughter) who led a large band of very attractive girls. She was unmarried, rich and pampered, the queen bee of the whole clan – a full-lipped, heavy-lidded beauty, who was always immaculately dressed in extravagant clothes and jewellery. I had seen her at a wedding the previous year, but noticed that she had now lost weight and developed a discontented pout. Shirin said she was pining for a husband, but Salim did not want to let her marry while he could continue to profit from her earnings.

The three bands led by Shirin, Soraya and Leila vied with one another for the best bookings, boasted about their fees, and lied and exaggerated to make one another jealous. The two lesser bands were led by a woman called Sara and Shirin's sister, Golnar.

One evening I was preparing to leave Shirin's house when one of her rivals, who had come to view me, began insisting that I should visit her. Her name was Negar, and I remembered her playing *tabla* in Leila's band the previous year. She reproached me for not having come to her house as promised. I agreed to go, politely but non-committally, but could see Gol Dasteh making faces behind her and shaking her head. Negar stood up and left the room at my side, urging me to go right then so that next time I knew my way. Although Gol Dasteh's signals were unequivocal, I was rather fascinated with Negar's faded beauty and could see no harm in accompanying her home, so I allowed her to lead me down some muddy lanes amid the barking of many dogs. Dusk was falling and the call to prayer sounded from a nearby mosque. I intended to stay only a few minutes. Her hallway was plunged in darkness; when she opened the door on to a spacious room, two oil lamps, which had been set down on a highly polished metal tray, threw a soft light on to the faces of a number of people gathered around a large *kursi*. I particularly remember her husband, Yusof, a thin, unsympathetic-looking old man; her mother, a flabby, pock-marked creature who fixed me with lifeless, bloodshot eyes; and her dazzlingly beautiful daughter, Rokhshaneh, who had long black curls, eyes like deep pools, an ample bosom and a profusion of gold jewellery.

Once I had arrived, there was no question of leaving without drinking tea, which took some time to appear. Negar apologised that the power had failed, but added slyly that 'poor Shirin' did not even have electricity. She tried to please me by bringing out their harmonium and dictating the words of a new song, but the light was poor and I was tired. When she attempted to invite John and me to supper another night I was evasive. All this was more than I had bargained for.

When I next saw Shirin, I immediately underwent an inquisition by her and Sultan about my visit to Negar's house. I told them I had simply drunk some tea and left as soon as I could, but I was alarmed that they both seemed to take the matter so seriously. Shirin said there were three dogs in Negar's compound and they had been worried that I might get bitten, but then the real cause of concern emerged. They were not on good terms with that household. I apologised and said I had not realised this; after all, Negar had come to visit Shirin that day. Shirin brushed this aside. Everyone came to look at me; she could hardly turn people away. She told me to listen carefully. This was a notorious area, and people were inclined to gossip and slander one another. She didn't want me to go to other houses in the alley, but just to come to her. She had many enemies, who were all out to do her down, and it was best for me to stay away from them. Sultan reinforced her request, and told me to come straight to their house, where I was safe, and not to set foot in any other. I promised to do as they asked, although I was eager to meet other musicians and visit their houses. However, I was visiting the alley under Shirin's protection and knew that as her pupil I had an obligation to respect her friendships and enmities, so I resolutely refused all other invitations.

I discovered that Shirin's quarrel with Negar went back to the time of her marriage. Yusof, the thin old man who eventually married Negar, had originally laid claim to Shirin and had even taken her to court. I guess that Shahzadeh, his sister, had promised that he could marry Shirin if she stayed in her band, but then it seemed expedient to marry her to Sultan. Shirin told me she went to court in her veil and had to show the judge her hand to prove that she was immature, thus invalidating Yusof's claim.

Shirin was wary of too much contact with her rivals, but she took me to visit Leila and Salim's house, where she had lived for many years as Shahzadeh's daughter-in-law. She felt it correct that I should pay my respects to Salim, the head of the clan, and she was also very fond of Leila, whom she had looked after as a baby when she first joined her mother's band. Faithful to Shahzadeh's memory, she cultivated a good relationship with Leila.

Although I was tempted to make other friendships among the Minstrel women, my steadfast loyalty to Shirin earned me respect and saved me from being caught in jealous cross-currents. None of her competitors could boast of a pupil, so I gave Shirin prestige, which she rated as more valuable than money. Unlike my teacher of miniature-painting, she did not fix a monthly fee; in fact she made no demands for payment and accepted whatever gifts I could bring.

'It doesn't matter about money or presents. Just come whenever you can – and don't leave it too long!' she said. 'When they ask, I tell my enemies that you pay me five hundred *afghani*s a lesson,' she joked. 'It shuts them up and makes them mad with jealousy!'

24

A Woman of the World

Shirin was fond of telling people how she had obtained a divorce for Gol Dasteh. I heard the story on the first day I met them, when she was still fresh with the triumph of success. The women at the wedding listened with interest, casting curious looks at Gol Dasteh, who remained silent while her mother talked. It was understandable that most Herati women found the public world frightening and intimidating, and they were clearly impressed that Shirin, a poor illiterate woman, had made her own plea in a court of law and succeeded in winning her case. An important effect of the segregation of women was that it kept channels of power – religion, law and government – in the hands of men, but Shirin's contact with the outside world and her wider experience armed her and enabled her to battle successfully for the divorce.

Sultan had arranged for Gol Dasteh to marry a relative, Aziz, in exchange for his two sisters, one of whom became a wife for Yaqub, Sultan's son, and the other a second wife for Sultan himself. Shirin stipulated a condition similar to Shahzadeh's, and made Aziz promise that he would not withdraw Gol Dasteh from the band: he was to come and live with them. They went to a shrine, where he swore an oath on the Holy Koran but, once he had married, Aziz promptly broke his vow and escaped to his village, refusing to let Shirin even see Gol Dasteh. She spent a year fighting to win her back.

It was a complicated case because Shirin needed to obtain three divorces in order to release Gol Dasteh. The first stumbling block was her own husband, Sultan, who did not want to give up his second wife, whose name was Hanifeh. Why on earth had Shirin agreed to let him take a second wife, I wondered? She told me that he had insisted she would be just like Shirin's servant and had even sworn not to touch her (an empty promise, as it proved). Shirin needed someone to mind the children while she was out at weddings, and reasoned that a co-wife could do all the housework and look after things at home. However, Sultan fell in love with Hanifeh and refused to divorce her, although Yaqub was willing to give up his wife in order to retrieve Gol Dasteh.

Shirin was determined. Every day she took taxis out to the law courts and pressed for a hearing. She said the Lord God answered her prayers: a crucial change occurred when Sultan fell ill. She sold all her gold jewellery to pay for doctors to treat him, and stayed up at night nursing him. During that time they became closer, fighting together to save his life, whereas Hanifeh was powerless and ineffectual. One day Sultan really thought he was going to die. He was crying and suddenly realised that he might never see Gol Dasteh again, yet if he died Hanifeh would just return to her brothers in the village. What then would have been the point of resisting the divorce? At that moment he agreed to it.

In private Shirin told me how she had persuaded Aziz to agree to the divorce: she accused him and his brothers of a criminal plot. She admitted to me that there had been no truth in her allegations, the details of which she kept secret, but she guessed that they had things to hide and were afraid of rumours or an enquiry. They knew Shirin was going to the law courts every day and they lost their nerve. They realised Shirin would never give in, and that Gol Dasteh was unhappy anyway. Aziz submitted, the three divorces were signed at the Governor's office, Sultan's relatives took their sisters back to the village, and Shirin triumphantly brought Gol Dasteh home.

Although there were several offers for her, Shirin was in no hurry to have her married again, and could see that she savoured the independence and variety of her present life.

Shirin was quick to take advantage of the skills, contacts and knowledge of people she met, and soon after I got to know her she taxed me on the subject of birth control. Had I never become pregnant? What did I use?

'You must show me your pills,' she said seriously, asking exact details of their colour and provenance. 'I don't want any more children. I conceive every year and it's wearing me out.' She was quite sure of her decision, and had no qualms about contraception being sinful. 'I tried those pills from the hospital – they give them out free, you know – but I took one and it made me ill, so I refused to take any more. Maybe yours would be better.'

She explained that she had been to consult the best women's doctor in Herat, Ziba, whom she had met at a wedding. Ziba worked in the hospital and had a surgery in the new city. She had prescribed and fitted an IUD, but Shirin said it had hurt her kidneys and she had had it removed. What else could she try?

'What about those *puftunak* – "things you blow up"?' I asked, grinning. The sheath was widely available in the bazaar and cost only one *afghani*, but it was rarely used for its intended purpose; adults bought them for their children as balloons.

'Balloons?' she laughed. 'Our Afghan men won't use those, you know. I tried to get Sultan to wear one, but he took it off half-way through. He said it was bad for him!'

We were sitting alone discussing these matters when Nadieh came and joined us, but Shirin went on, unconcerned at the intrusion. She questioned me about the diaphragm, a method that was little known but which Ziba had apparently mentioned, although unfortunately spermicide cream seemed to be unavailable in the pharmacies. They listened to my explanations about correct fitting and spermicide with interest.

'But when do you use them?' asked Nadieh, puzzled.

'You have to put it in before you want to make love!' I said, laughing.

'What's the use of that?' she asked in amazement. 'How do you know? You wake up in the middle of the night and find him there!'

We laughed loudly, agreeing that it did present problems. Shirin ordered me to bring her some of my British pills, but after taking one she did not proceed with the course, saying it had made her feel weak and faint. She was afraid of side-effects, if not of sin.

Although she was open-minded in some ways, Shirin was essentially very traditional. She wore written prayers as a cure for ailments and a tiny Koran as a protection against dangers at night. Musicians were vulnerable when walking home late and she was afraid of *jinns* (not muggers or rapists, who did not lurk in the streets). Because of the demands of their work, the Minstrels had to adopt a relaxed attitude to purdah, but they followed religious customs like everyone else, cooking *nazr* once a year, observing the fast and visiting shrines. Shirin had a strong personal faith and she talked to me about Islam and told me stories of the Prophet and his family. She was wary of breaking the code of modesty and exposing herself too much in public. When a music shopkeeper wanted to sell recordings of her singing, she refused to let him put her picture on the cassette, uncomfortable at the prospect of revealing her face.

One night she invited me and John to supper, and Hakim, Sultan's nephew, an engaging character and a very good raconteur, described the occasion when he had taken her to the radio station in Kabul. She had been on her way back from a pilgrimage to Maraz-i Sherif and he had met her in Kabul and suggested that she went to make a recording.

'Ooh no, I couldn't go there. It's dishonourable for a woman to sing on the radio!' she said, but in the end he persuaded her, although she was nervous about performing in front of the *ustad*s and female radio stars.

In telling the story Hakim made a great play of her modesty and shyness, and Shirin laughed, enjoying his anecdote, which was amusing and affectionate. Eventually they had set out for the radio station, but she insisted on wearing her veil right to the door, although in Kabul the custom of veiling was not nearly as widespread as in provincial cities such as Herat, Kandahar or Mazar-i Sherif. Hakim reeled off a long list of the famous musicians who had been at the radio station that day, and described the rapturous reception her singing had received. All the *ustad*s had praised and congratulated her, and the female vocalists had stood up and clapped, saying she was a better artist than they were because she could also accompany herself on the harmonium.

'Her *charbeiti* broke their hearts,' said Hakim. 'She went there with her face covered, but then outshone them all!'

Unusual opportunities had transformed Shirin's life and given her worldly experience far beyond the average expectation. Although she had received no formal education and was not free from misconceptions and prejudices, she had a generally wider and more informed view of her own society than most women I met. She had the opportunity to meet women from very different walks of life: from the ultra-religious to the emancipated, and from the relatively poor to the very rich. Her music took her into households all over the city. Occasionally she went to villages or inside nomad tents where women had never seen a harmonium, and ultimately she was even broadcast on the radio. She had privileged access to the thoughts and ideas of a wide range of people and she put this to advantage in determining the course of her own life.

25

Learning Music

Each time I visited Shirin we spent part of the time working on my songs, and gradually I began to make progress. She was a generous and patient teacher, and we worked well together. I was the first outsider to take lessons from a Minstrel; they had no tradition of the formal adoption of pupils. Among the male professionals in Kabul it was customary to imitate the Indian guru system with a ceremony, presents, and the ritual tying of a thread around the disciple's wrist, but this was rarely performed in Herat. A formal discipleship would have been quite inappropriate between us as Shirin had no classical training: there were no systematic teaching sessions among the Minstrels and she had learned her musical skills through participation in performance.

She was a natural teacher though, and understood the importance of patience and encouragement. Her method was one traditionally employed in many Asian music cultures: memorisation through constant repetition and practice. She would dictate the words of a song, and then we would sit together and sing them over and over again, until I had learned the melody. She used to lay down the rhythm on a *daireh* or a tray, and I found it helpful to mark the main beats over the relevant syllables in my notebook. She made no objection when I brought a tape recorder and used it as an *aide-mémoire*. She recognised that my task was not easy. Everything was foreign to me – the language and poetry, the *daireh* and its rhythms, and the Herati style of voice production and ornamentation. She felt that I was at a particular disadvantage in starting so late, and said it was much easier to learn young, when the memory functioned best.

Most of the songs were relatively simple in their structure, consisting of four-lined verses interspersed with choruses, some with refrains after each line. The rhythmic elements were often trickier; I found it hard to match them with the words, and as there was a variety of rhythms, stresses could fall in different places in the poetry.

Whereas male professionals employed musical terms based upon Indian classical music, the Minstrel women lacked knowledge of this jealously guarded theory, and a certain amount of vagueness hampered my initial progress in learning. Shirin had no precise terminology through which musical concepts could be expressed, for instance names for various rhythms, modes or structural elements within the music; nor did the women have any system of notation (unlike male professionals, who used the Indian system – orally, if they could not write). However, once I had become accustomed to the basic musical forms, I found that memorisation was a most effective method of learning.

Shirin's teaching had the great virtue of consistency. I had been disconcerted to find that Mother of Nebi's melodies and rhythms for one song varied from week to week. It was acceptable to perform different versions, but impossible to teach that way. Shirin was a professional, and leading a band necessitated sticking to a standard version of a song.

I adopted a more or less passive policy as regards the material I learned. At first Shirin taught me songs that were currently fashionable at weddings: Iranian popular songs, new songs from Kabul, or old

Herati folk songs that had been revived on the radio. Later she realised that I was interested in old songs, and she enjoyed mining deep in her memory and bringing out nuggets of gold, recalling songs that had long been forgotten. We made recordings together and sometimes she became impatient of interruptions and ordered Gol Dasteh to shut the door and prevent the children disturbing us. Gol Dasteh complained that we were like a bride and bridegroom closeted together in privacy!

My progress was constantly tested by performing to audiences of ever-increasing size and discrimination. It was one thing to sing along with Shirin in the familiar surroundings of her house, quite another to perform on my own for outsiders. I remembered what Shirin had told me at our first meeting: that a singer must conquer shyness. Often audiences met my efforts with delight and enthusiasm, which gave me courage to meet new challenges. (But ironically this drawing out of my personality as a performer worked in opposition to the subtle process of withdrawal through wearing the veil, and these contradictory transformations built into a real conflict, of which I became fully aware only later in the year.)

Sometimes I let Shirin down in these public tests. On one occasion we went to visit Parwin, a senior musician associated with Leila's band; she had a large gathering of relatives who had come to welcome her daughter home after several months' absence. Shirin boasted about the fine wedding where we had met, and recounted how I had sung for the Governor's wife. Parwin requested me to sing, so I had to perform two songs to a large audience of experienced male and female musicians. They clapped and congratulated me, but when we got back to Shirin's house she immediately took down the *daireh* and began demonstrating the correct way to perform the second song. She explained that I had put the wrong emphasis on the poetry, and we practised together for some time, although it was late and I could see she was tired. My error had humiliated her, and she wanted to iron it out.

When we eventually rested, she told me that she disliked the way people made me sing, particularly with so many men watching and admiring me. But how could she have refused to let me sing? If she had, they would have said to themselves, 'Obviously Shirin's pupil doesn't know anything!'

In March John and I paid a visit to Kabul, where we gave a radio interview and talked about our work with Afghan music. I sang three songs and John played the *dutar*. When we returned to Herat everyone seemed to have heard the programme, and they congratulated me warmly.

'Why didn't you choose all three songs from me?' asked Shirin, mildly annoyed that I had acknowledged the first song as belonging to Latif Khan; it was a wedding song that I had learned from a recording. 'You mentioned his name before mine,' she chided.

At my next lesson she was angry, and told me that Sultan had met Latif Khan in the bazaar; they had been discussing my radio perform- ance and he had said, 'Why doesn't Shirin teach Veronica to play the *daireh*?' She said that we had to work on my *daireh*-playing: it was all wrong, although she did not like to hear it criticised by Latif Khan, as this reflected upon her as a teacher. Naturally there was tension between the rival clans: Latif Khan and Salim Jan competed directly for work playing at weddings, and the Minstrels were aware of the fact that Latif Khan strove to dissociate himself from them on account of the reputation of their women. This made things awkward for me. Latif Khan was not pleased that I had 'joined the enemy camp' and become Shirin's pupil, although he was too tactful to say so. No doubt he felt that if I wanted to learn I should have gone to him, the acknowledged master in Herat.

Shirin decided we should concentrate exclusively upon the *daireh*, and forget about singing for the moment. Hard practice was the only way my hand would become 'fluent': my fingers were still stiff, the drum did not make a clean sound and the rhythms did not flow. She instructed me patiently, step by step, as she had never had to with her own girls, who picked up the drumming by themselves. She advised me to rest the drum comfortably on my knee, so my arm did not tire, and showed me how to position my fingers. She demonstrated heavy, damped strokes in the centre of the drum, and told me to space my fingers when I hit the rim, so as to obtain a high, clear sound. I learned how to make my first finger work separately from the second and third and to alternate them quickly. She taught me various rhythmic patterns to accompany my singing: several four-beat rhythms, various six-beat patterns with a strong cross-rhythm of three against two, and the infectious and exciting syncopated seven-beat, of which the circle dance rhythm is a variant. Her teaching was methodical and precise and she was able to break down the complex patterns so that I could understand how to make my own variations.

Once mastered, the *daireh* is easy to pick up and play at any time. It does not necessitate the athletic feats of training, memorisation and practice of the classical Indian *tabla*, with which I have wrestled in the past. It is a very versatile instrument and has many different regional styles. Given freedom and encouragement, Afghan girls absorb and play the rhythms effortlessly from a young age. At less than a year, Shirin's own baby banged on the *daireh* in time to music, and she could almost dance before she could walk. Shirin advised me to practise and practise. She also told me to cook *halwa* and make a holy wish for my hand to become fluent in drumming.

'In Kabul there's a shrine belonging to the Saint of Kharabat,' she said. 'Whenever someone becomes a disciple to a musician, he gives out *halwa* and raw sugar as charity. You should do that. You know how to cook *halwa*, don't you? It will bring merit and help your playing.'

I had visited the shrine of Kharabat, the gathering-place of Chishti Sufis, but there was no equivalent shrine for musicians in Herat. Shirin told me to cook at home and give out the *halwa* from there. I obeyed her and sent offerings to her, Mariam and Mother of Nebi, making a wish for my playing to improve.

When I had mastered the *daireh*, we resumed work on songs. The most intangible area of performance was the characteristic Herati mode of voice production, which it was essential for me to learn. In contrast to breathy, chest-resonant Western singing, it is rather 'forced', highly ornamented and nasal in quality, having the head and throat as the main centre of resonance. Shirin did not theorise about singing, she simply insisted that I should practise. She never corrected my voice or intonation, and gradually I learned how to achieve the right sound by imitation, how to attack and end a vocal line, and how to vary the melody with appropriate grace notes and ornaments. Decoration is an essential component of the Afghan style and a matter of refinement and delicacy.

After a while it became easier to learn new songs, and I built up a bank of poetry from which I could improvise: a singer needs to know poetry in order to select appropriate images and sentiments. Shirin dictated dozens of quatrains from the oral tradition. They were heavily romantic, expressing longing for a loved one or for home when far away, a longing linked to the spiritual thirst of the soul for God. Some verses recalled the famous lovers Leila and Majnun, and described Majnun's crazy, demented passion. Similarly there were verses taken from the real-life story of the shepherd Jalali's love for the beautiful Siah Mu. Some verses used imagery borrowed from Sufism, evoking the fatal attraction of the moth for a burning candle, or the nightingale singing for the love of a rose:

> *Dawn has broken: my flower has not come*
> *The sound of the nightingale's song has not come*
> *Let's go to the gardener of flowers and ask him*
> *Why the nightingale has not come to view the flower.*

Through poetry the heart poured out feelings of love which transcended the mundane world, and spirituality and emotion conquered the cold logic of thought.

There was also a lighter, humorous side to the women's music. Some songs were satirical, for example 'The Knife-sharpener's Wife', which Jamileh used to perform as a song-and-dance act. In each verse the wife said she would refuse to marry a man of a particular profession, slamming the tool of that profession down upon his head in defiance: the carpenter's saw, the *mullah*'s 'book', the tea-house proprietor's teapot, even the hash-smoker's pipe. The women loved the song because it claimed the lowly knife-sharpener as an ideal husband and made fun of the serious world of men. Another song specifically sung by women was 'The Widow', a variant of an ordinary love song. In it the widow flirtatiously shows off various parts of her body – lips, eyes, eyebrows, bottom – demonstrating that she is ready to marry again. There were songs that catalogued the various parts of an animal's anatomy, offering them as presents for a daughter- or son-in-law, as in the song 'When Will You Kill the Donkey?' In this the donkey's eyes become a mirror, his skin a long coat, his intestines a turban, his tail a broom, and his anus a spittoon!

Whether romantic or humorous, most women's songs dealt with relations between the sexes, although the lament of unrequited love merged into other less specifically sexual expressions of sadness. It was not unusual for women to sing verses which expressed a man's love for a girl, but equally men were known to sing songs of a girl's love for a man, and many songs were addressed to named people: 'Darling Leila', 'Cruel Yellow Flower', 'Dear Mullah Mohammad', and so on. It was an art to be able to improvise verses relating to particular occasions or people; addressing a prospective bridegroom, for instance, or naming a loved one far away.

There was a large overlap between what was performed by male and female professionals, although the women tended to learn songs after they had already become incorporated into the male repertoire. The main differences were that the Minstrel women did not perform classical or devotional music, which was a male preserve, and that, apart from the rarely performed folk theatre of the Jats, humour and satire were more commonly featured in women's music. No doubt this was because their music was performed in a private, domestic context, which provided an ideal chance for occasional facetiousness at men's expense.

26

Professional Life

That year Moharram, the Shiah month of mourning, fell during the winter, so there was very little work for musicians. Most of Shirin's clients were Shiah – she guessed that 90 per cent of her engagements were in Shiah households – and their ban on music and celebration started ten days before the anniversary of the martyrdom at Karbala and continued for two months.

Shirin was Sunni, and I wondered how she could recognise clients as Shiah? They were fair-skinned, well-dressed and usually looked clean, she said, explaining that many were from families of wealthy merchants who had money to spend on fine cloth and lavish parties. However, it was not surprising that, like many Sunnis, Shirin expressed some prejudice against Shiahs. Being the orthodox sect (and belonging to an overwhelming majority among the nation as a whole), Sunnis openly held the view that Shiah beliefs were heretical. They themselves recognise the Prophet's Four Companions, Abu Bakr, Omar, Osman and Ali, as the Caliphs that followed Mohammad, whereas Shiahs look upon the descendants of Ali as Mohammad's true heirs. In particular Sunnis abhor the Shiah mourning ceremonies and the associated custom of ecstatic self-flagellation. However, as is usually the case with cultural bias, Shirin's distaste for Shiahs focused upon differences in custom and matters of hygiene as well as doctrine. She confided to me that she could tell a Shiah household by its lavatory: she said Sunnis used clods of dried earth to cleanse themselves and you could see them put ready for use, whereas Shiahs used a ewer of water; but she felt it defiled water to pour it on to excrement. I questioned the validity of this and many other statements she made. The Traditions of the Prophet lay down details about every aspect of human behaviour, and prescribe three stages of ritual cleansing after defecation: wiping with dried earth, washing with water, and drying with a clean cloth. In practice (and contrary to her assertion) washing is the most common method among both sects. She also estimated that two-thirds of the inhabitants of the city were Shiah, whereas in fact Sunnis were in the majority by about six to four, and she told me, quite erroneously, that Shiahs called themselves Haji (the title for Mecca pilgrims) after they had merely made the pilgrimage to the shrine of Imam Reza in Mashhad.

There was mutual distaste between Sunnis and Shiahs, although in general I admired the Heratis for keeping it under the surface. Relations between the two sects were sensitive, and marriages between them still relatively rare. One tended to adopt the attitude of always seeking to establish whether a new acquaintance was Sunni or Shiah by picking up on small hints rather than asking openly (as Protestants and Catholics do in Northern Ireland). In the past conflicts had been flagrant, particularly during Moharram, and the mourning ceremonies were still held secretively so as to avert Sunni hostility.

The fact that most of her clients were Shiah was obviously a source of tension, and aggravated a relationship which was difficult at the best of times, but particularly delicate within the intimate context of weddings. Shirin strove to maintain good relations with prosperous Shiah clients, but the undercurrent of religious and cultural disharmony was an added problem in her work.

In the spring the party season began again in earnest. Shirin received most of her bookings at very short notice. Men would come to the alley to negotiate an agreement; she either spoke to them herself or sent one of the girls to make a preliminary evaluation. There could be long sessions of tough bargaining before a price was agreed and the deposit paid in advance. The fee for weddings varied considerably according to supply and demand and the clients' means: it could be as little as 1,500 *afghanis* or as much as 5,000. As well as paying cash, it was customary to give the musicians a set of material from the dowry and various gifts and tips.

Weddings lasted about twenty-four hours. The Minstrels would normally be collected at dusk and play until the early hours of the morning, when the guests were too tired to dance any longer. The musicians would snatch a little sleep (in very crowded conditions), then continue to play throughout the following day. 'Sweet-eating' parties were much shorter, and were usually in the afternoon; the band would be paid only about 500 or 600 *afghanis*, but they were virtually assured of a booking for the wedding.

Engagement parties and weddings were the bands' main source of income, but they could also be invited to play at picnics or private gatherings. They occasionally played at parties given for women during their last stages of pregnancy (when the women's stomachs were ceremoniously rubbed with fat), or to celebrate the arrival of a new baby. Competition was fierce, and the musicians took great interest in one another's negotiations.

Shirin had managed to reclaim from Golnar her two front rooms that overlooked the alley; we were eating lunch one day when a poorly dressed woman shouted up to the window, saying she needed a band for a 'sweet-eating' that afternoon. Shirin called down, asking how long the band would be required to play for and how much the client was prepared to pay. The woman replied that she wanted them from one o'clock until about five or six, saying she would pay 250 *afghanis*, plus fifty in tips. It was a tight bargain. Shirin could see that the client was not prosperous, and it was not usual to include tips in the negotiations. Once she had established that the woman would not go over 400, she turned away from the window, impatient to get back to her food. She told me that she would have sent Gol Dasteh and the girls for 500, but not for less.

As soon as she had finished eating, Ferideh went down to the alley to discover who had taken the booking, and reported back that Parwin had agreed on 400. Shirin wondered who she could be planning to take in her band, as she knew that Leila and the others had already gone out to play elsewhere. The afternoon was hot; we were just about to take a nap stretched out together on the floor, our bodies draped with veils as sheets, when Gol Dasteh called us to the window. Parwin was emerging down the alley, dragging Rokhshaneh, who was blinking in the sunlight and wailing bitterly at being woken. Why should she have to get up and play for a measly fifty *afghanis*, she moaned. Shirin chuckled and we settled back on our pillows, glad that we could doze in the heat of the day. Shirin commented that Parwin was so greedy that she couldn't resist a booking, no matter how much trouble it involved.

Shirin had a special relationship with some clients, rich families who appreciated her excellence as a singer and had patronised her for many years. She was infinitely polite with them, and never let a trace of unpleasantness or haggling enter into their dealings; moreover, she gave them precedence over all others.

Once I arrived at her house to find two women sitting in her front room. I had met Hakim in the alley, and he told me that they belonged to the family of an important Agha; they had come to ask Shirin to play for them and were waiting until she returned.

The Agha's wife was a self-assured young woman with a heavy necklace of gold coins and an enormous locket adorning her neck. She told me that she was arranging a marriage for the son of her companion, her sister-in-law, but that they were keeping it secret from some of the men in the family, who might disapprove. She wanted Shirin's band the following day. Just then Gol Dasteh and Jamileh returned noisily from an engagement, but as soon as Gol Dasteh saw their visitors she put on her most deferential manner, and very politely asked after the health of all the members of the Agha's family. She told the Agha's wife that they had a booking for the following day, but that of course they would change their arrangements to suit her. The Agha's wife, who had the unflurried confidence of a woman who is used to getting her own way, nodded and murmured that she would speak to Shirin herself.

When Shirin arrived, she respectfully kissed her visitors' hands and showered them with welcoming phrases and compliments. The Agha's wife responded to her flattery in like manner, pretending to take off her own massive gold locket as a gift, which Shirin hastily refused, declaring herself unworthy. The Agha's wife told Shirin about the wedding and requested that her band be ready to go out to the village the following afternoon. Shirin agreed, her hand on her heart, not even mentioning the problem of the double booking, and the Agha's wife rose to leave, apologising for not staying to drink tea.

Shirin made rapid calculations to muster enough musicians for two bands: she would have to ask Golnar to let her take her daughter, Sima, a young but competent musician. I was surprised that Shirin dealt with her hated sister, but she said they co-operated over musicians and in return she occasionally let Golnar take Jamileh. She decided that she would go to the Agha's village herself, taking Jamileh and Nadieh, which left Gol Dasteh, Ferideh and Sima for the original booking. I commented that she had not arranged a fee, but she said that it would be remiss to bargain with the Agha's wife: she was sure to pay them well. Really she disliked going out to play in villages, but couldn't refuse a request from such a client.

Sometimes Shirin even waived her fee, knowing the time might come when she wanted a favour from a powerful client. For instance, how could she ask the Governor for money? It was better to honour and please him and have him in her debt: that was far more useful than a few thousand *afghanis*. Good relationships, contacts and goodwill were all-important. I once heard Leila say that charm paved the way for future employment, and mattered far more than musical knowledge or expertise. This was the great paradox – musicians had a bad name for being like 'Jats', yet if they were treated well they had perfect manners. Very few people understood this, and they expected musicians only to be grasping and rude.

Shirin began taking me with her to weddings, at first as a pupil and onlooker, and later as an integral member of the band. I was grateful for the chance to see the musicians' lives from the inside and I became more accustomed to singing in public.

The first occasion was a wedding in the house of some rich Shiah clients where Shirin felt sure I would be treated with kindness and respect. Ferideh came to collect me in the morning, but the rest of the band had been there since the previous evening. We found Shirin sitting on a smart bandstand in the centre of the courtyard, which was crowded with women in dazzling new clothes. The walls were decorated with colourful cloth and the floor was spread with fine carpets. Jamileh was there with her new baby, a girl, who had been born only eleven days before. She seemed in excellent spirits and boasted that she had been out with the band on the seventh day after the birth, although Shirin quickly put in that she had not forced her to do so. Shirin described how she had sent for Jamileh's mother and sister once they were sure she was in labour; they had not brought in a midwife, but Shirin had assisted with the birth herself. It was remarkable that the musicians carried on playing at weddings with virtually no interruption for childbirth and the post-partum period. However, I did notice that tension built up between Shirin and her band-members during the final stages of pregnancy. When their babies were imminent, both Jamileh and Nadieh were reluctant to go out to weddings, but Shirin put pressure on them to continue working.

Throughout the morning we played music and the guests danced in turn. A woman dressed in blue and silver kept urging new dancers to take their place in the dance area. I played one of the *daireh*s, and thoroughly enjoyed the excitement of the occasion. When Shirin introduced me as her pupil I performed some songs, which were greeted with enthusiasm.

Before lunch Gol Dasteh and I brought in the bridegroom, who was to join his wife for an appearance on the 'throne'. She was waiting in a side room, a very pretty young woman in a white dress and veil, which were decorated with white artificial flowers, and she held a matching posy in her hand. We sang ritual verses as the bridegroom and his father appeared in the doorway, and then we slowly led the way out into the courtyard. It was exhilarating drumming and singing blessings and praises as the handsome couple moved solemnly behind us, hand in hand. They sat on their throne for about ten minutes, and then the bridegroom slipped away to help prepare for the serving of food, leaving a small girl to take his place next to the bride. Gol Dasteh whispered to me that the couple were happy and in love: they had been having 'engagement play' for six months, and she had played for their 'sweet-eating'.

We played music until after midday, when lunch was served. We ate on the band-stand and one of Shirin's sons arrived to collect an extra trayful of food, which he transferred into an enormous basin, tied up into a cloth and carried home for the family. Gol Dasteh explained that it was customary for wedding hosts to provide food for them since the musicians were unable to cook at home. I noticed that Shirin's children kept in contact while she was out at weddings, running errands or informing her when prospective clients came to hire the band.

Towards the end of the afternoon, the dowry was displayed. Shirin held up each item, calling out as she did so – ten, eleven, twelve dress-lengths! – almost like an auctioneer. The guests all crowded round to see, and once again the bridal couple sat on their throne, watching impassively. Afterwards the bride's mother sent Shirin to distribute gifts from the dowry to the bridegroom's mother, sisters and sisters-in-law, who had all worked hard serving the guests. She took them each a set of cloth laid out on a tray: in return they gave her tips, which she collected and thrust down the front of her dress. The last of the dowry gifts went to Shirin herself. The musicians were expected not only to provide music and a joyful atmosphere, but also to perform an essential role in the rituals, processions, and display and distribution of gifts, acting as go-betweens for the principal actors in the drama of the marriage.

The bridegroom's brothers sent a message that we should bring over our *daireh* so they could also put in their tips; *daireh*s were used for collecting money, just as we 'pass the hat'. Gol Dasteh seemed to appreciate their doing this, rather than obliging us to go and beg, but she ordered Jamileh to go. She refused, so Ferideh went over and coyly held out her drum. Transactions such as receiving money from strange men gave the musician girls a bad name.

We were about to leave when the bridegroom's father, who had been busy organising everything, asked Shirin if she would play an extra set. He said the family had all been working hard to serve their guests and now they wanted to enjoy some music.

'It's late,' said Gol Dasteh curtly. She had already shut the harmonium, but Shirin told her to play a little more, so she reluctantly sang two verses but then closed the instrument abruptly, almost rudely, making an unconvincing excuse about having to leave. Musicians never wanted to play for extra time: it meant further delay and they were never sure of getting paid for it. But the man was good-humoured and did not insist; he handed Shirin her fee, and gave her some money for our fare home. In the event we did not leave for another half-hour as Shirin got involved in negotiating a further booking. Gol Dasteh's excuse about being in a hurry was patently transparent.

Not all clients were as polite and good-tempered with the musicians, and there were sometimes ugly scenes on departure, when musicians contested the quality of the gifts they had received or argued for more money. At one wedding our host paid Gol Dasteh in a huge wad of small notes, which she had the humiliating job of publicly counting before we left.

It was remarkable that Shirin managed to run the band and organise her family and home all at the same time. Sultan went out to work in his barber's shop every day, and when he came home he expected someone to serve him tea. Men played no part in minding the children, so Shirin took the very youngest ones with her to weddings and left the others to play unsupervised in the alley at home. Alleys were safe: there was no traffic and everyone knew who the children were. Occasionally she left Zahra with Salim's wife, who also had a baby and could breast-feed her; she paid her for this service, but used her only when invited to particularly formal evening parties. Of her eight children, only the older boys went to school, and even then lessons took up only half the day, so all the children had a lot of time to play.

When Shirin was very busy, her eldest son, Yaqub, sometimes had to take charge of domestic affairs. Once he pulled a soiled pair of trousers off his baby sister's bottom, wrinkling his nose and laughing.

'I shouldn't have to do this sort of thing! It's not men's work. I have to help my mother far more than most boys of my age. It's hard for her: she works all the time. At night the children cry and she has to get up, and then often she's out all day playing at weddings. No one from my school knows she's a musician,' he added confidentially. 'I'd be embarrassed if they knew.'

Gol Dasteh cooked all the family meals, and Ferideh helped her tidy up and mind the children. Every few days they and Shirin did the family wash together.

'It would have been good if I'd had more daughters!' Shirin once remarked, contradicting the usual preference for boys. 'Then I'd have a bigger band and more help with the housework.' She had kept her girls out of school not through distrust of education, but because she needed them as musicians.

Although she worked hard and earned good money, Shirin was not well off and, unlike some of the other Minstrel women, she did not wear ostentatious gold jewellery. When Sultan had been ill she had sold all her gold to pay for treatment, and she had also spent a great deal on Gol Dasteh's divorce. Sultan was currently in some kind of business difficulty which involved a constant drain upon her funds. He needed to make trips to Kabul, which she had to finance, including giving him money to bring back lavish presents for all the family. One way or another he whittled away at her resources, whereas certain other Minstrel husbands invested their wives' earnings in prosperous businesses and made the money grow.

Nevertheless, Shirin was happy as a musician. Once when Leila was visiting us and complaining about her work, Shirin reprimanded her lightly.

'We've no choice: otherwise how would we live? After all, it's not that bad. We get out and enjoy ourselves, and they bring us *pilau* to eat. We play music and meet lots of women. It's entertaining work. I'd rather be a musician than be stuck in a dark room ruining my eyes making carpets all day!'

Late one afternoon I made my way to Shirin's house, still feverish from a chill. As I passed Soraya's house, I noticed a bustle of activity, with men giving orders and huge bubbling cauldrons of rice, and I realised that they must be making preparations for the wedding of the son of the house, Mohammad Ali. Two weeks before I had attended a big gathering for his relatives at a picnic spot in the countryside: they had brought carpets and instruments and had had a full-blooded music session and an expensive feast to celebrate the arrival of the bride from Kabul. She was the daughter of a famous musician, Ghafur Khan, and this was not the first marriage alliance between the Minstrels and the *ustad*s of Kabul.

Shirin immediately saw that I was not well, diagnosed my illness as 'hot-and-cold', and dictated a recipe for a beneficial 'hot' soup. Then I remembered Mohammad Ali's wedding and anxiously asked if it was going to be held that night. She told me the whole alley had been filled with the sound of rejoicing for the past week: their heads ached with the din coming from the bridegroom's house. The wedding was to take place that evening, so I hurried home to change.

An hour later Shirin and I entered the bridegroom's spacious compound, which had been gaily decorated and hung with strings of light bulbs. A number of women had already gathered and the party was warming up. Golnar's precocious fourteen-year-old, Sima, was up on the band-stand, trying to dazzle everyone with her latest songs. The musicians took it in turns to play, but Shirin stood rather aloof, holding baby Zahra on her hip and making critical comments.

Gradually the compound began to fill with smart young female guests; they were shown to their places on folding metal chairs arranged around the band-stand, and I concluded from their fashionable long maxi-dresses (called '*maksi*') trimmed with ruffles and flounces that they must be Soraya's rich clients. Some of them did not even wear prayer veils, and others draped them loosely around their immaculately coiffed heads as if to enhance rather than hide their ostentatious elegance. Puzzled, I asked Shirin if there was going to be a party for male guests. She thought they had some carpets spread out for men on the flat roof overlooking the courtyard, but said this was a gathering for Soraya's rich friends. Everything seemed upside-down: a wedding with music and splendour for women, where men peered down from the roof, out of sight, like secluded women!

Soraya, as eldest sister and band-leader, took charge of everything. When all the Minstrels performed a huge *atan* together, she pulled me up too. I danced and clapped in time, my head dizzy with fever, joining Soraya, her sisters, Parwin, Salim's wives, Negar, Rokhshaneh and others, who looked resplendent in their finest dresses and jewellery. Shirin did not join in, and Gol Dasteh and the band had gone to play at another wedding, although they much regretted missing Soraya's party. The guests smiled and sipped tea, enjoying our dancing, but no one invited them to join in. Then, to my great surprise, Rahim Gol, a famous Kabul musician, entered the compound with his accompanists. They hardly knew where to look, finding themselves surrounded by so much feminine beauty. Evidently the guests had expected their arrival, for there was no flurry of veiling or shielding of faces, only a little self-conscious smoothing and touching of curls. These sophisticated and emancipated women had been invited to a concert of male music!

Food was served late, after a dazzling performance by the musicians. The guests sat on carpets in groups of three, eating daintily with their fingers. Soraya and her sisters worked hard carrying the heavy trays of food, patches of sweat appearing under their beefy arms. They moved briskly and smoothly, never flagging, like a team of immaculately groomed carthorses ploughing a perfect furrow. The food was excellent: meat, *pilau*, aubergines and a dessert of cherry jam. The Minstrels were expert and professional in the art of celebration, and liked doing things on a grand scale. They were what Afghans call *kharabat* – indulgers, people who splash out. It is a generous characteristic which arouses admiration.

Late in the evening Shirin was asked to sing. Rahim Gol stepped down from behind the harmonium, politely inviting her to take his place. The *grande dame* of the women musicians, she had not sung until then. They urged me to join her on the band-stand, so I stepped up beside her, light-headed with excitement, and the *rubab* and *tabla* players smiled in encouragement. Somehow the lights and the audience did not bother me. I felt relaxed and secure sitting next to Shirin, used now to performing in increasingly large and awesome settings. We sang several songs together and were greeted by an enthusiastic response. Our voices echoed through the loud-speakers, sounding clear and disembodied.

Finally Salim Jan took our place for the ritual song 'We're Bringing Henna', and the bride and bridegroom sat on their throne, feeding one another sweet drinks and cake. The guests clapped at the end of each ritual and then graciously prepared to leave. It was after midnight, and their private cars and taxis were waiting to collect them. By the door Soraya handed them each a packet of sugared nuts from a silver tray and the guests left white envelopes of money in their place, discreet gifts for the bride. Smooth and sophisticated, Soraya bade them farewell, and they brushed cheeks. Yet how often on parting had she haggled over their gifts of cloth, or had they whispered malicious gossip against her once her back was turned? The difficulties of their business relationship were forgotten now that Soraya was not a hired musician, but a benign hostess. Indeed, who could have told that the elegant and well-mannered Soraya was really a common musician, who had walked home many a late night carrying instruments, a fat roll of bank-notes safely tucked away inside her ample bosom! It had been an entirely unexpected occasion. Times were quickly changing, after all, and rich

Heratis held weddings at the Park Hotel, where men and women mixed freely and waiters could see women's faces. The Minstrels had laid on a grand party, and their rich clients had condescended to set foot in their house and reinforce their relationships with gifts and polite expressions of goodwill.

27

A Member of the Band

The period immediately preceding Ramadan was hectic with weddings, and the musicians worked flat out. People came to the alley at all hours seeking to hire a band, all wanting to get their celebrations completed before the fast began. Merry-making and music were not prohibited in Ramadan, as in Moharram, but hunger and thirst killed the enjoyment of a festivity and sapped energy for dancing; and after Ramadan it would be too cold for evening parties. The demand for musicians was so great that band-leaders sometimes took double bookings and split their bands, sending a bare minimum of three players to an engagement. They also co-operated in lending less important members when necessary.

Shirin realised that I could pass as a musician, and began using me when she was double-booked. I was eager and willing to join the band, and very honoured. She would send messages to my house at short notice: 'If you can, come tomorrow at eight' or 'There's an engagement party at one this afternoon: can you make it?' Whenever possible I obliged her, delighted that I could repay her kindness as a teacher.

I even acquired a new name.

' "Veronica" sounds weird,' she said, pronouncing it 'Fa-ra-ne-ka'. 'I know: I'll call you Farahnaz! That's much prettier.' It was an Afghan name that she could conveniently use when introducing me to women at parties.

Other Herati friends were scandalised that I had joined her band: taking lessons was one thing, performing in public quite another. To them it was an unthinkable step; virtually a corruption of morals.

'You must take care,' counselled Mother of Nebi, not hiding her disapproval. 'Those women are shameless.'

'In England we don't consider music to be bad or sinful,' I replied, undeterred from my chosen course of action. 'This is a good chance for me to learn.'

'Didn't you see that little one wearing make-up?' she frowned, referring to Ferideh, whom we had seen at a neighbour's wedding. Herati girls did not wear make-up until their wedding day, so why was Ferideh painted like a little whore? I explained that the Minstrel women wore make-up because everyone was looking at them, but she remained unconvinced, obviously unhappy that I was always going out with Shirin. No doubt she was confused by my public alliance with such low-status people, as well as secretly envious of the parties and endless music-making.

I brushed disapproval aside and refused to countenance the idea that I might be doing something wrong. I vainly sought justification from the standards of my own country, and told people that I was carrying out research for the university.

'I know people say the Minstrels are tarts, but that's a lie,' I argued boldly, trying to explode their own myths in their faces. 'They play music for women: separate parties for women. There's hardly a man in sight.'

But people objected to the Minstrel women because they did not observe purdah strictly. They travelled with men in their cars and argued with them about payment; they were not modest – in fact they were dangerously free. Unlike other emancipated, professional women – bank clerks, or schoolteachers – they could not shore up their respectability with education. Sin was associated with music and dancing, and music was known to tempt one into forgetting religious obligations. Although it was an exaggeration to call the Minstrel women prostitutes (comparable to describing tourist girls as naked because they walked about with bare arms and legs), many ignorant people erroneously believed it to be true, so strong was their prejudice.

Usually I was merely irritated by people's remonstrations, but a conversation with Latif Khan and Mariam upset me deeply and made me intensely aware of the magnitude of my course of action. Latif Khan chose his moment carefully: the three of us were sitting drinking tea.

'You really shouldn't perform with Shirin,' he said sternly. 'I heard about it in the bazaar. It's unseemly: don't do it again.'

'But that's the best way to learn music – through practice,' I argued, alarmed at his directness.

'Practice at home or at her house, but don't go out with them. It looks bad,' he advised calmly. I felt it immodest to argue, but I had to defend myself.

'It's remiss for women to perform music in public,' Mariam said patiently, realising she had to speak out and explain her position. 'You know it's against our customs. Otherwise why wouldn't we do it ourselves?' she asked, suggesting the unthinkable.

'No, no! I know you shouldn't do that,' I protested, 'but it's different for me. I don't come from here, and in a few weeks I'll be leaving. When I go back to England, people will praise me for everything I've done and learned.'

'Shirin's taking advantage of you,' Latif Khan persisted. 'She gets bookings by advertising the fact that a beautiful foreign girl's in her band. It brings in the money – oh yes!' he said, making a gesture of counting bank-notes.

'She's my *ustad* and she's taught me everything I know,' I countered hotly. 'I should be pleased if she makes money through me, but in any case what you say isn't true; I only go with her if I'm free, often at the last minute. People never know she's bringing me.'

He insisted firmly that I was doing myself a disservice: it was harmful to my reputation. The other day a friend of his had remarked that obviously my husband had run out of money since he had begun sending me to play at weddings with the Minstrel girls! His words wounded me. No matter what the truth might be, people gossiped, and in Herat talk spread fast. My name and the name of Latif Khan, John's *ustad*, had already been muddied.

'But I don't take a penny!' I protested, suddenly desperate to leave Herat and escape this impossible conflict. I wished I could obey his command like an obedient daughter, and I felt I owed him this, but I was not prepared to give up being a musician. I had taken my place at Shirin's side.

I slipped easily into my new identity when performing with the band: Farahnaz, the musician girl, veiled and dressed like a Herati, but made attractive with eye make-up, lipstick and rouge. By then the veil had become second nature to me and I always wore Herati dresses and loose trousers; I did not look noticeably foreign. Each time we went out to play, the other girls painted themselves to look bright and garish; the make-up was part of the show, part of the performance.

'We won't tell anyone you're from England,' whispered Gol Dasteh, the first time I went with her as band-leader. 'They'll all crowd round and bother you. Let's say you're from Iran.'

It was easier to skate over the truth. Clients were usually inquisitive, and it was convenient not to arouse undue interest. Seeing my features were different, they would ask how I was related to the others. On a few occasions I lied glibly, making up whatever story came into my head: my mother was kin to Shirin, or I was from Kabul. They accepted my answers at face value, but whispered and stared. I had mastered the language and its colloquialisms, and had a good enough accent to pass. Anyway, the truth was too improbable: how could an English girl learn their language and songs, and if so, why would she ever choose to go out as a musician? Sometimes I was already known to the hostesses so there was no pretence. I took the tape recorder and recorded our performance. Once Shirin even made me lead the band, picking out the *atan* as the women danced. Nadieh played strong *tabla* at my side; I felt as if I had just learned to drive a car, but could not believe the machine was really moving under my own direction.

I noticed that the musicians were very concerned with comfort and refreshment, sizing up our new surroundings as soon as we arrived. Was there a band-stand for us? Did the people look prosperous? They took care in choosing where to sit: out of direct sunlight, near a cool breeze and away from gusts of dust and grit. Mostly we had to sit on thin mattresses on the ground, out in a courtyard or in crowded rooms, immediately smothered by eager children. If tea arrived promptly they brightened, and if we were served cool drinks, ice-cream or fruit – luxurious extra refreshments – they were even happier. Given these comforts and attentions we played far better, warming to our hostesses and striving to please them. Our more sophisticated clients knew how important it was to treat musicians well, and they served us first, seeking to gain our favour.

Another important factor was the mood of the guests, their degree of participation in the dancing and their appreciation of our singing. I enjoyed it if women asked me to sing duets with Shirin, and some even recorded us, but at other weddings people showed little interest in our performance, ordering us to stop and start up again like a record player. Even the most opulent wedding was tedious if no one danced: a wedding should be *'por jush'* – 'boiling' with excitement and atmosphere – and good spirits among the guests made the time pass quickly and enjoyably. Dance music gave our voices a rest and it was entertaining to watch and interact with the dancers. Naturally I was more conscious than the others of the effort of music-making: they played and sang with practised ease, but I had to concentrate on keeping to the rhythm and remembering the words of each new verse. My muscles were unused to such long periods of playing, and my voice became strained singing above the noise of children crying, women talking or shouting orders, and girls laughing and fooling. I found the hot afternoons the most trying, when one felt drowsy and heavy from lunch.

One of my last outings with the band was to a small village about half an hour's drive east of the city. Shirin was double-booked: Gol Dasteh, Nadieh and Jamileh had gone to another wedding; our band consisted of Shirin, Golnar's daughter, Sima, who would play *tabla*, Ferideh and myself. We were engaged to play for several hours at the bride's house before accompanying her to her husband's village. The Minstrels made sure they struck a highly lucrative bargain before agreeing to play outside the city: the journey was uncomfortable, conditions were always rough, villagers were notoriously uncouth in their dealings with musicians (men leered and insisted that the musicians danced), and there were no tips or gifts that merited consideration. Since they were further away from home, the musicians were also more vulnerable to abuse: Salim never allowed Leila to go out and play in villages at all.

I arrived early at Shirin's house, as arranged, but the driver was very late picking us up, and I became disgruntled at having to wait. Eventually he arrived in an impressive silver limousine, a small, dark-skinned man in a dapper suit, the bride's uncle but obviously not a villager himself. Ferideh and Sima simpered importantly from the rear window as we glided past the wide-eyed boys hanging around at the bottom of the alley, and Ferideh ordered him to turn up the radio so that loud music filled the car. He eyed me suavely in his mirror, but I resented his interested look and pulled my veil around myself, far too primly for a musician girl. Over the months I had become used to hiding myself from strange men, adjusting my veil more closely if I sensed that a glance was sexual. The veil could be used as a decorous rebuff, shaming men for their profane thoughts. But this was no place for modesty: Shirin and the others were free and easy, laughing and chatting openly with him. I realised that my response to his quizzical look had been inappropriate, motivated by bad temper at our long wait.

We left the cool shade of the pine trees lining the concrete highway and turned on to a bumpy dirt-track. On either side open fields of alfalfa and corn were broken up by irrigation ditches and occasional trees. Small groups of children played in the sun as we passed through a village, and little girls with grubby cotton veils put down their buckets of water to stare at our beautiful car. Shirin recognised the approach to the village. It was a big *qaleh*, wasn't it? The man nodded, expertly avoiding the numerous pot-holes and ridges. A *qaleh* was a very big compound: Shirin said about twenty families lived together there. She remembered having been there once before. I pictured a huge, square mud fortress with a tower at every corner, such as I had seen in other villages, but to my disappointment the house was modern, harsh with right-angles, and still partly unfinished. The yard outside teemed with unruly children, all swarming around the car as we drew to a halt. We struggled out and awkwardly made our way through the crowds, carrying our instruments.

We were told to sit in a dark hallway which gave on to several rooms filled with people. A very squashed and gloomy place to play, I thought immediately, having already developed a musician's instinct for comfort. A harassed-looking woman, who seemed to be in charge of the chaotic arrangements, dumped a few thin, worn mattresses unceremoniously on the concrete floor and brusquely ordered us to play. People surged around us, gawping and pushing, barely leaving us room to sit down. 'Play! Play!' they demanded rudely, impatient for a spectacle.

Shirin opened the first set, but we had to strain our voices to be heard above the din. Women and children pressed down upon us, staring avidly but showing no enjoyment of our playing. Then, after about ten minutes, another woman in charge ordered us to move, so we had to pick up our instruments and push through the crush. A girl followed, dragging our mattresses and shouting curses at women to clear the way. This time we were in a large dingy room filled with at least eighty people; there was absolutely no space for any dancing in the middle of the floor. We received no welcomes or smiles, only rude sullen stares. I felt tired and annoyed, but Shirin and the others seemed to accept our unpromising circumstances with bland equanimity.

'Have a go on harmonium,' Shirin offered Sima: evidently these villagers were not worth the effort of a polished performance. Shirin took a *daireh* and leaned comfortably against the wall, ordering Ferideh to take Sima's place behind the *tabla*. She had decided to take a break and let the others do most of the work, but without her leading the band I lost all motivation to sing. Ferideh played unevenly on the *tabla* – she had not really graduated to *tabla* playing – and it was hard to follow the beat. Our audience took little heed of our straggling performance, but stared at our city fashions and make-up.

'How much is that material a metre?' a hawk-eyed woman asked Ferideh, fingering her dress.

'Three hundred *afghanis*,' she lied, casting a disdainful look at the women's own garments, which were worn and old; none of the villagers seemed to have dressed up.

Sima finished her set and closed the harmonium. The women continued to stare, quite happy now that we had finished singing and they could question us. I was introduced as a guest from Kabul. None of them could tell that I did not speak like a Kabuli; they had never met anyone from Kabul and had only been to Herat city perhaps once or twice in their lives.

'And no children?'

'No, not yet,' Shirin replied, tacitly implying that I was infertile. I said nothing, unwilling to be drawn into the discussion.

There were more whispers and stares. Ferideh had begun fighting with girls who were tapping on her drums; some children deliberately shoved against us and Shirin cuffed the nearest offender, cursing them all loudly, but after a minute they began disturbing us again. She swore energetically, but did not become angry. Suddenly some women came rushing into the room shouting, 'The bride's become possessed! Play! Play!' Across the hall crowds of women were pushing at the entrance of another room, struggling to see the bride's fit. From inside a woman flailed her arms, beating them back, ineffectually begging them to give air and space to the hysterical bride. Sima struck up a fast dance piece: it was believed that when someone became possessed, loud exciting music would exhaust the *jinn*s and induce them to leave more quickly.

The day dragged on, becoming hotter and hotter. We were moved several times more, and eventually settled in a thin margin of shade outside the wall of the house. Flies buzzed around us relentlessly and children pestered us, but it was a relief to be in the open. At last we caught sight of women carrying trays of food, so we packed up our instruments and waited for lunch, but by the time they served us – last of all – the meat and rice were completely cold.

'Tasteless!' pronounced Sima, wrinkling her nose as she picked at the food.

'Village people can't cook,' said Shirin, stoically. 'They only know how to make soup.'

Afterwards it was time to lead the procession for the dowry display. The bride was very young and looked thin and unhappy; the bridegroom did not appear. Shirin and I sang and played energetically on our *daireh*s, and my spirits brightened at being on the move after so many hours of cramped sitting. When we stopped, the women pushed forward from all sides, eager to get a good view of the gifts. Shirin simply lay back against the crowd, as though floating on water, laughing at the screams of panic from the retreating mass. She cracked coarse jokes and began to display the dowry. I left and lounged gratefully with the others away from the din. When she joined us she said they had plaited the bride's hair, which was a village custom. She had tried to claim 'bride's-hair-plaiting' money but they had refused her. She told me I should have seen it, and I felt irritated to have missed something of interest.

At last it was time to set out for the bride's new home. She appeared wearing a *burqa* and a green shawl pinned over her head, which signified that she was the bride. She looked very slight beside her husband, a plump middle-aged man with a cataract in one eye. I had heard that she was his second wife, and guessed that she had become hysterical because she was unwilling to marry him. They stepped into the back of the silver car, while the rest of us clambered up into a big painted lorry. Its walls reached high above us, exposing the open sky, which was cut into sections by the metal frame for the tarpaulin. We crouched tightly packed, and lurched forward with a scream when the engine roared into life. Several women drummed loudly and others clapped, setting up a deafening processional beat as we clattered along the rough track to the bridegroom's village. The tops of trees flashed by and occasionally the high metal frame ripped off leaves, which fell like confetti as we swayed and jolted over pot-holes. It took about twenty minutes to reach the village. The bridal couple stood impassively by the car, waiting for us to assemble for the procession to the house. Drumming, clapping, pushing and shoving, we surged forward down the alley, with children worming between our legs to get further to the front. The crowds, the dust and the din were overwhelming.

Two stout women barred the entrance to the bridegroom's house, pressing the crowds back the way they had come. There was no room, they shouted: did we want the roof to fall in? Shirin grabbed my hand and argued our way up. We sang wedding songs and the bride and bridegroom stood on the narrow flat roof of the house, submitting patiently to another ritual. Shirin abruptly held out her *daireh* for a tip from the bridegroom, who fished grudgingly in his pocket and pulled

out a note. Our driver urged some other women to give her a tip, trying
to avert an ugly quarrel from breaking out, but Shirin threw down their
money, shouting that it was a poor wedding where musicians received
nothing from the bride's dowry. At that point our driver decided it was
time to leave.

'They don't know what a proper wedding is,' he said soothingly, as
we settled gratefully into the back of the car. 'They're ignorant people.
To them a wedding's just a get-together and a procession around the
village. They know nothing!'

He switched on a cassette of music to please us, and we sank back into
our comfortable seats, relieved to be moving. Ferideh sang raucously to
the music and Shirin chatted and cracked jokes; I realised that her anger
about the dowry gift had just been an act. After the rutted dirt-track,
the main road into Herat city felt like velvet, and the buildings appeared
massive, especially the imposing government offices. We were back in
civilisation, drinking in the bustle of cars and *gadi*s, the colourful shops
and elegant city-dwellers in silk *chapan* coats and expensive skin hats. I
felt euphoric to have escaped from the village. Exhausted, I begged
Shirin's permission to go straight home, but in less than an hour the
band were regrouping for their next engagement.

This village outing represented the low point of my experience as a
Minstrel. Previously I had thrived upon the excitement of new places
and the exhilaration of performance, but after a time these compen-
sations palled. No wonder the musicians were always asking one
another, 'What's the time? How much longer?'

Next time I visited Shirin I discussed my feelings with her; the fast
had begun and she had at last been able to rest at home. How could
people expect us to play and sing when they treated us like dirt, I
complained, recalling occasions when no one had brought us refreshment for several hours. Shirin quite understood: last night she had been
at a wedding and, as they had been fasting all day, she asked her hosts to
have food and drink ready for them at the sound of the cannon. To her
disgust all they had brought was warm water and a few pieces of bread.
Later on, towards midnight, she had felt tired and requested some tea,
but this had brought the bridegroom's father running angrily into the
room, shouting, 'Who are these people that want *pilau* and tea all the
time?' Obviously if people were rude and inconsiderate, musicians felt
disinclined to put on a good performance, and I could see that Shirin
was still sore at the insulting way she had been treated.

I aired another grudge with her: on repeated occasions our hosts had
not troubled to escort us home or even help us find transport. Once,
after a long day's playing, we had been forced to walk most of the way

back from a distant suburb where no taxis or carriages were to be found. I knew this type of treatment also applied to the men's bands: they would be attentively taken to the wedding in a taxi, but left to make their own way home, cold and tired, carrying heavy instruments. Shirin nodded, and simply said that people looked down on musicians; once they had played they could make their own way home.

It was only when I experienced the discomfort, rudeness, and lecherous glances myself that I realised how tough musicians needed to be. I understood what it was to be the butt of people's disdain and scorn and I cringed; but Shirin took it all in her stride.

28

Ramadan

The arrival of Ramadan, 'the holy month', brought a radical change in the pace and quality of life: the noise, excitement and frenzy of the past days of incessant music-making and activity gave way to the tension and boredom of long hours unbroken by refreshment. It took a few days for people's bodies to adjust to the rhythm of eating before dawn and after dusk, and to inactivity and starvation during the day: nerves were frayed by hunger and thirst, and petty arguments broke out easily.

When I visited Shirin on the third day, she cursed Ferideh for playing the *daireh*, and silenced her angrily. It was Ramadan; had she no shame? Surely music was not prohibited, was it, I queried, and she explained that it was immodest to play the drum when people were fasting and sleeping through the long hot afternoon. Besides that, she was aware that the sound of drumming would give people the impression that she and her family were not fasting, which would damage their reputation. I had brought my tape recorder, but she did not feel like working on our songs. Instead she sent out for a neighbour's religious tape and we listened to a long epic about a poor mother who sacrificed everything she owned to save her sick son. Shirin's eyes glistened and she sighed with pity. At the end, when a holy man saved the boy by a miracle, she wiped away tears: fasting all day had made her pious.

In the evenings there was an atmosphere of celebration and relief. The nights were balmy and people sat up late feasting and enjoying themselves. The moon waxed and gave increasing brightness. Around the time of the full moon gangs of excited boys roamed the streets knocking on people's doors and singing Ramadan verses, for which they received sweets or a few coins. Likewise, Shirin and her band visited some of their wealthy clients and received gifts; but they only sang inside, not out in the streets like the boys.

Ramadan was rich in evening entertainment. There was a circus (with comedy acts, acrobatics and music, but no performing animals), and special nightly performances of music at different venues. Enterprising tea-house owners hired caravanserais (large open-air enclosures) and commissioned prestigious bands of musicians to come from Kabul for the month, providing a rare opportunity for local people to enjoy listening to the famous *ustad*s and radio stars who never otherwise came to Herat. Many villagers came to the city for a few days and made the rounds of the different concerts, where they paid a modest entrance fee and spent all evening drinking tea and enjoying the music and convivial atmosphere. They could even buy a picture postcard and send it to the singer, requesting a favourite song. The profusion of public concerts during Ramadan was a new phenomenon, and it catered to a great hunger for urban music that stemmed from the wide availability of radios and cassette recorders. Previously men had simply socialised in the bazaar after the day's fast and gone to the mosque to hear the evening recital of the Koran.

There was a growing recognition that female audiences would enjoy these entertainments, if only they were provided with a suitable place to sit, away from unwanted stares. Until very recently, evening entertainment that took place all the year round catered exclusively for men, and in any case had an aura of sin attached to it. At the cinema the audience's chief interest lay in seeing women's faces and bodies (clothed) and enjoying the famous song-and-dance sequences of popular Hindi films. In the government theatre, where plays and music were performed, female actresses and singers had a worse name than the Minstrels for being courtesans; the atmosphere was highly charged with sexual excitement during the songs and dances. (Ironically, the favours of the girls who performed on the government stage could purportedly be bought at the end of the show; yet they were arrested and imprisoned for indecency if they were caught singing or dancing at a private party.) Despite the stigma of sin – or perhaps in an effort to counteract it – the cinema and theatre had begun providing screened-off seating for female spectators, and the Ramadan concerts imitated this trend towards secularisation.

I went with Gol Dasteh and some other Minstrel girls to hear Mahwash, a famous female Kabuli singer who had come to Herat with a band of excellent musicians from the radio orchestra. Shirin was shy at the thought of sitting alongside men, and would not come, although she admired Mahwash and bought a cassette pirated from one of the concerts. The venue was a modern hotel built for wealthy tourists; the band-stand and seats were arranged in the courtyard, in front of the swimming pool. Mahwash stood in a long evening gown, and her famous reedy voice echoed across to us through the loudspeakers. Her husband, formally dressed in a dark Western suit, sat close by, passing her drinks to soothe her precious throat, and her accompanists wore suits and perched on chairs rather than sitting on the ground in the traditional manner.

The concert was very polished; Mahwash was fêted in Herat and invited everywhere. She had recently been awarded the title 'Ustad' Mahwash, and was the first woman to receive this honour. Although the term *ustad* was used loosely to denote a 'master' or 'teacher' of music, art or calligraphy, certain excellent and knowledgeable musicians were awarded the official title as a prefix to their name. The example of Ustad Mahwash paved the way for other female performers to be accorded higher status, although it must be said that some people doubted that she had sufficient knowledge of classical music to be accepted as a true *ustad*.

Gol Dasteh had been going out every night, eager to learn new songs. A few nights later we went to another concert, this time accompanied by Sultan, Yaqub and Bibi Del, a female relative who was staying at the house. At the Mahwash concert women had sat right at the back, but at this venue there were some inadequate screens sheltering an area to one side. Chairs for about 200 to 300 men were arranged in a large semicircle in front of the band-stand and on balconies overlooking it, but provision had been made for only about thirty women. We arrived in plenty of time to be sure of a seat; Sultan and Yaqub sat separately with the men.

Bibi Del was a young village woman who had never been in such a public place before. Gol Dasteh showed her how to tuck her veil to one side, like a man's coat-tails, in order to avoid crushing its pleats, and she told her to raise the front panel and hold it like a screen so that men couldn't see her face while she watched the concert.

There was an atmosphere of anticipation and excitement. The audience sat packed together, their white turbans shining in the light of the electric bulbs that hung like bunting around the walls. Some young boys shinned up ladders carrying huge trays of tea to spectators on the balcony, and others walked along the narrow gangways selling cold drinks, nuts and fruit. On the decorated band-stand, which was festooned with pompons, frills and pictures, the musicians had begun tuning, a star-studded group rivalling Mahwash's band.

Soraya and her sisters arrived, greeted us haughtily, and sat separately. They were veiled in crisp, elegantly pleated *burqa*s with smart dresses beneath, and they wore shining make-up. There had been much talk in the alley recently about Soraya's love for Naim, one of the singers who was about to perform, and several days before I had witnessed a dramatic row between some of the Minstrel women as to whether she would marry him. Tonight he would sing for Soraya, Gol Dasteh joked.

When the music began, Gol Dasteh leaned forward and gave it her full attention, savouring this rare opportunity to learn directly from skilled musicians whom all the Herati professionals strove to emulate. Every night the local hereditary musicians – Latif Khan, Salim, and their clansmen – attended these concerts and gleaned new material, and they also took trouble to play host to the Kabuli musicians, inviting them home and promoting goodwill between their families. Evidently Soraya hoped that she might marry Naim, the handsome singer in a suit, red shirt and cummerbund; maybe a flourishing career as a singer awaited her in Kabul.

After several songs, Bibi Del became restless. She had never been out like this before in her life and she was not enjoying it. She was worried that her baby, whom she had left with Shirin, would be crying; the music was strange and unfamiliar; she disliked the men's stares from the other side of the screen, and she was unused to sitting on a chair. Gol Dasteh pulled a face at me, wishing she had not brought her, and then boldly hailed a waiter and ordered tea, hoping to cheer up the party with some refreshments.

The next time I visited the house, Gol Dasteh was singing songs she had heard that evening for the first time. Shirin became competitive and brought out the harmonium, saying she wanted to record a new song for me: she had been listening to Mahwash's concert over the loudspeaker and had decided to learn a song there and then. She picked out the new tune confidently, called Gol Dasteh to accompany her on *tabla*, and recorded it for me without a hitch.

It was ironical that Ramadan, the holy month during which people remembered their religious obligations and amassed merit, was also such an important source of input into Herati musical culture. *Mullah*s preached against music as a diversion from the true path, yet during Ramadan – for some at least – it acquired the character of a welcome and pleasurable reward at the end of a hard and trying day. The impact of the influx of Kabuli music was undeniable: the public cultivated new tastes and straight away demanded to hear local musicians play songs they had first heard from Mahwash, Naim and the other singers. The quality of the Kabuli bands – both in repertoire and standard of performance – attracted cultivated people as well as curious villagers, and often singers ended the evening with classical religious poetry. The concept that music was sinful was rapidly becoming outmoded.

29

A Musical Legacy

Ramadan ended: on the last evening the cannon fired many times, signalling the end of the fast. Three days of celebration began, and in every household cloths covered with ceremonial sweets were laid out in guest rooms. At festival times musicians called on their rich clients and played for them, and I accompanied Shirin on one of her 'festival rounds' to see what happened. We set out with two *daireh*s – *tabla* and harmonium were too heavy and cumbersome – and walked to a leafy residential suburb where we visited four or five houses. After we had sung a few songs we were brought refreshments and envelopes of money on silver trays.

Unfortunately, an incident occurred which caused me deep embarrassment and humiliation. On our way we met my teacher of miniature painting, who was just about to visit a nearby house. Since I had taken up with Herati women I had neglected him completely – the pursuit of his art and research into women's lives were completely incompatible – but I had never given him a proper explanation. During the whole year I, his erstwhile devoted student, had seen him only once or twice. We met in the dusty street and there I was, standing with some Minstrel girls who were patently out on a begging round, drum in hand. (Because of the traditional contempt for professional musicians, great shame attached to being seen carrying an instrument in public; Shirin never let me carry even a *daireh*.) My companions were veiled and he tactfully ignored them while we chatted awkwardly for a few minutes. I could hardly apologise for them or explain why I had forsaken his art to tramp the streets with common musicians, yet I felt ashamed and condemned in the public eye. He must have known that I sometimes played in Shirin's band, as a short time back I had seen his daughters at a wedding. They had been visibly surprised and shocked that I was acting as a musician, but at least we had the opportunity to relax and enjoy one another's company and they appreciated that I had learned a great deal from Shirin. My old *ustad* made no comment upon what I had done, and uttered warm phrases of goodwill, but at the end of the encounter I had a confused sense of guilt and betrayal of past hopes and promises.

Shirin and the rest of us stayed longer at the house of one of her patrons, where they brought out the family harmonium and asked to record us. Shirin boasted about me: I was her show-piece, her glittering prize, the foreign girl who had learned their language and songs and who had performed on the radio in Kabul. I smiled and made conversation, but I disliked the admiring looks of the young men of the family and felt falsely compliant for Shirin's sake. Occasionally I caught a strange look in their eyes as we talked, as though they wanted to ask what on earth a girl like me was doing with such people as the Minstrels.

I sang for them and they recorded me, but I drew the line at dancing. As a member of Shirin's band I had always firmly refused, saying no, my husband would not allow me to dance in public. At one of the first parties I attended as a musician, an old woman whispered to me, 'Sing if you must, but don't dance!' I also remembered Latif Khan's advice not to play in Shirin's band and felt this was the least I could do to protect his name. As we prepared to leave our hosts brought presents on an elegant tray; the usual money and sweets, and special gifts for me – a box of toffees and a black head-scarf with white embroidery and tassels. I thanked them but felt embarrassed at taking their gifts, as though I had been bought. My withdrawal into purdah had had a certain effect. I felt uncomfortable singing for men, highly conscious of their admiration and aware that I was granting a rare, almost erotic, delight. The fact that the words of the songs concerned desire and romantic longing emphasised a singer's identity as a sex object when viewed by men. I had become infected with a Herati sense of shame.

I felt humiliated by the 'festival rounds'. Shirin and her band did not play outside in the alley and go from door to door like *sazdohol* musicians, shouting praises for the charitable gifts they received, but the parallel applied. Although they visited only well-established clients where they were assured of a warm welcome and a polite reception – unlike the *sazdoholis*, who called on all and sundry – I was still aware that our envelopes of money were well-mannered tokens of dismissal, and that we were like grateful servants. My delight in Afghan music was unquenched, and my love and gratitude towards Shirin were undying, but I had tasted enough of the public role of the Minstrel.

Our stay in Herat was almost over. In a way I was relieved, yet grief-stricken at the prospect of parting. I felt like a conjuror who had performed astounding tricks but who now had to pack up the paraphernalia and get on to a bus; an anonymous passenger clutching a bag and staring into space. I had had so much exposure to new people and situations that I needed to retire into a corner for a while; the diversity of friendships and alliances that I had developed had forced me to adopt a different personality according to the company I kept, and I was feeling the strain. I needed to get home and see which aspects of my Herati self would wash away like make-up, and which were indelibly impressed upon me.

Our last days were impossibly busy and I became frantic with anxiety. There was so much work packing up the house and saying farewell to everyone, and we were showered with final invitations. Shirin counselled me not to fret, saying that everything 'happened in God's time'. When John came down with a mild dose of hepatitis, we had to delay leaving. Our food and water were here in Herat, she said: not elsewhere.

She came to my house the day before we left, realising that there would scarcely be time for me to visit her again. She brought only Zahra, a dainty little toddler with tinkling silver rattles around her ankles. We sat together in a back room among a disarray of possessions waiting to be packed. There were trunks and boxes in every corner, but she hardly noticed or took any interest.

'I'll make a last tape for you,' she said, with characteristic generosity. 'You sing along as you learn the chorus, and when you get to England you can copy down the words. I've remembered some lovely old verses for you: be sure to learn them.'

She sang for me and I joined her; they were beautiful songs that had not been sung for maybe twenty years. Her last gift to me was her music, her light, sweet singing.

'It's late,' she said finally, preparing us both for the shock of parting. 'Promise me two things: learn all the songs I've given you and sing them to your own people sometimes; and write to me every month or two, so I know how you are.'

We went out of the house and embraced by my front door for the last time. I told her it might be five years before we came back again, but we would return for sure. Little did I know that my wishes and promises would remain unfulfilled. She let out a cry of anguish, clutching my hands amid a flood of tears, crying, 'Oh, but you're like a daughter to me!' I wept, but had no sense of foreboding that our separation would be so complete. Resolutely she pulled down the front panel of her veil, grabbed her bewildered child in her arms, and swept out of my front door.

> *You went, and I was watching you, oh flower*
> *I was saying prayers for you, oh flower*
> *I didn't realise on that day of separation –*
> *Or I'd have sacrificed my soul for you, oh flower.*

During our association I collected more than seventy songs and at least as many quatrains of poetry from Shirin, and I made recordings at weddings and at her house. Words on paper and sounds on tape, tangible gifts from her to me: songs expressing the different aspects of love – excitement, pain, wonder, sleeplessness, longing; songs with humour, pathos or spirituality; lullabies for me to sing to my own baby. When I sing my songs from Herat they evoke a different world of emotion, recalling the shining moon in a clear sky at night, the soft cooing of doves in a shrine courtyard, or the rare beauty of a dew-filled rose at dawn. I riffle through my book of songs and sigh: faith, longing, hardship – they seem so removed from the experience of British life.

Before I left Herat I made a recording of my best songs, accompanying myself on *daireh*, and I gave copies to Shirin, Mariam and Mother of Nebi to remember me by. I imagine that they have played the tapes over and over again, and that others have copied them; they have spread to households throughout the city, like Chinese whispers, gradually becoming changed and distorted. Perhaps my voice has become unrecognisable; maybe stories have spread about the musician girl, Farahnaz, describing events that bear no relation to things I did. And now that Herat has been bombed and devastated and my friends are lost and scattered, what songs lie under the ashes, waiting to be rekindled?

Epilogue

The following spring, in 1978, there was a *coup d'état* in Afghanistan, and the first of the pro-Soviet puppets was installed. Resistance against Soviet domination began during that period and with it government suppression of 'anti-revolutionary elements', who were imprisoned, tortured or killed in savage purges. Even before December 1979, when the Soviet invasion of Kabul hit world headlines, the precarious government had already mounted a campaign to crush the growing resistance of the *mojahedin*, the 'holy warriors'.

Early in 1980 thousands of refugees began flooding across the borders, and by the mid-1980s over a quarter of the entire Afghan population had gone into exile, while within the country a high proportion of the people became internal refugees, forced to flee from their homes through bombing or imminent danger. The 5 million Afghans who have left their beloved homeland constitute the largest refugee group in the whole world.

The war has intensified into a long, bitter struggle backed by self-interested super-powers: Afghanistan is now a 'regional issue', inextricably linked to global concerns about arms control or distant conflicts in Nicaragua or Angola. Western media coverage has been scanty. Press and television crews have been denied access to the interior, apart from occasional carefully shepherded visits by pro-Soviet journalists who produce misleading films and news reports presenting the regime's own cosmetic version of reality. Freelance journalists go into Afghanistan clandestinely, but the terrain is difficult, conditions are dangerous, the political situation fragmented and extremely complex, and there are no guarantees of a 'good story'. The Afghan people's cause is forgotten or misunderstood.

After 1978 letters from our friends in Herat ceased to arrive and we did not dare write for fear of compromising them. The little news of Afghanistan that did reach the newspapers concentrated upon the eastern side of the country, filtering through Pakistan. Herat had become inaccessible to outside observers. In spring 1983 we had our first letter, from a schoolteacher we had known well in Herat. He had become a refugee in Mashhad, across the border in Iran. He told us

Herat had suffered severe bombing and thousands of civilians had been killed, and he gave news of specific deaths, among them that of Latif Khan. He said no one now lived in the area where we had rented our house – the resistance held that territory and it was bombed night and day – and that he had crossed the land between the ruined city and the border and seen that all the villages had been laid waste. More recent eye-witness accounts describe it as a lunar landscape: crops all burnt, buildings flattened, wells filled with concrete, springs and streams poisoned. The fertile valley is a desert and Herat city, once singled out by Unesco for restoration as a world treasure, has become a battlefield, defying government control.

In the spring of 1985 I went to Peshawar, on Pakistan's border with Afghanistan. The city had become the headquarters of Afghan resistance to the Soviet-backed regime and it sheltered the largest concentration of Afghan refugees in Pakistan. Some lived privately in the city, others in camps supported by government rations. I dreaded what I might hear and see.

John excitedly told me that he had found Hakim, who was working as a professional musician in a refugee band. Unfortunately he had left Herat years before and did not have fresh news of his uncle, Sultan, or of Shirin. I was delighted to see him again. He called me Farahnaz and greeted me like a sister, saying my face reminded him of his family in Herat, so much had I become part of that household. I was happy, but shocked at the change in him. His face was deeply incised with lines and his hair, which had been bushy and long, was thin, receding and dyed black. It emphasised the darkness of his eyes and altered his whole appearance. I hardly recognised him: weariness and suffering had been etched into his smiling face.

I asked about Shirin and the family. He thought they were still in Herat, but had heard nothing for years. He had left precipitantly, his life in danger. While he was still there one of Shirin's sons had been killed, caught in cross-fire and shot in the head. However he had some happy news: another refugee, Rustam, his friend from military service, had given his daughter to Hakim in marriage, and that very morning their first child had been born, a daughter. I promised to visit the house and meet his new family.

We reminisced about old times. Then he described the big uprising in Herat city in March 1979 when thousands of anti-government protesters, armed with spades and sticks, had been mown down by government tanks near the Kandahar Gate. He had witnessed the killings and seen the mob set light to several government buildings, expressing their violent hatred of the new regime. There had been retaliatory bombing. He said they had secured the door of Shirin's house and gone on to the roof to watch. He excitedly mimed planes dipping and wheeling in the sky, clearly upset by his vivid memories.

I added new images to my picture of Herat: soldiers firing guns from the tall blue minarets of the Friday mosque; the bazaar half dead, with whole areas reduced to rubble and most shops closed and abandoned; the long avenues of pine trees chopped down or blasted by bombs.

I felt ill in Peshawar. Hot feelings of panic rose from my stomach to my throat. The suffering of the Afghan refugees, especially the women, punched the wind out of me and I was left gasping for air; I felt anxious and lost my appetite. Many refugee women suffered from a state of clinical depression: their bodies ached, they slept poorly, and their minds were confused and distracted. Nights in the camps were regularly disturbed by women's nightmares of bombardment, and doctors working within Afghanistan reported many similar cases of psychological distress among women. Why women in particular? Because they, at the heart of the family, suffered most intensely at the insecurity of their new situation and because, as women, they were impotent to act against the powerful forces that had transformed their lives.

I spoke about it to Bilqis, an educated and emancipated Afghan woman who, fearing imprisonment and torture, had been forced to flee from Kabul soon after the 1978 coup. She told me she had accompanied a Western female doctor to the camps as an interpreter.

'She kept asking the sick refugee women, "Where does it hurt?" They said the pain was everywhere – in their heads, their legs, their whole bodies – nowhere in particular.' She insisted that their pain and depression were real, not imaginary, and explained that some of them had had appalling experiences that were impossible to forget. As an example she told the story one woman had related to her: the bombardment of her village had begun very early in the morning and she had awoken to find two of her children dead beside her. The village headman gave immediate orders for evacuation, but there was another child – a two-year-old – still missing. She had seen him run away in fright. They forced her to leave the village before she could find him. She simply could not forget that child she had abandoned and her mind had become deranged.

For women in particular it was impossible to erase memories of the harrowing experiences of bombardment, massacre or terrifying journeys into exile. Men had choices. They could take up arms and fight, they could go and find work in the city, meet new people and adapt to their new surroundings. Women had no options and nothing to distract them from the past.

In coming to Peshawar I had been interested in recording women's music, wondering what women sang about now. Maybe there were new songs about the war, about resistance heroes. Bilqis looked doubtful: it would be impossible to record music in the camps, which were control-led by the *mullahs* who would not allow women to sing or leave the camp with me to make recordings. Most of the inhabitants of the camps were women and children, many widowed or orphaned, some whose men were away fighting in Afghanistan. The sound of clapping and drum-ming was not appropriate to the new situation. Music, associated with happiness and celebration, was prohibited for those in mourning. Only the screams of women at night were now acceptable outlets of feeling. I began to see the women as guardians of Afghan pain. Someone had to remember the horrors and keep a sense of outrage alive.

Refugee women were not only depressed, they were far more isolated and confined than they had been at home, where there had been parties and outings and a wide family network to provide variety in their lives. Now, with the holy war, the Afghan people had become strongly imbued with a militant Islamic spirit and this was easily expressed in the stricter seclusion of women. Many women who had not previously covered their faces – nomads, villagers, emancipated city-dwellers – had come under pressure to adopt the *burqa* veil. Uprooted from their communities, women had very little reason to go out, which exacerbated their isolation. The city of Peshawar remained alien and unknown and they felt like unwelcome foreigners.

I met a middle-aged woman, Fatimeh, who seemed completely unable to adapt to her new surroundings.

'I'm so depressed here,' she said. 'There's nowhere for me to go, no one to visit. I stay at home day after day; I hate having to veil myself to go out. In Kabul I never had to cover my face.'

Her face was sad and her eyelids drooped. Throughout the evening she hardly smiled. Her daughter told me how they had fled from Kabul as soon as her father, a political prisoner, had been released from jail. She, her father, mother, two sisters and a two-year-old child had made their way on foot across the mountains from Jalalabad to the border. Her brothers were already in Peshawar.

'It was a very dangerous journey – one man and so many women! On the way my mother fainted. Somehow we carried her. The little one was crying with hunger. We left empty-handed so as not to look like refugees. At night some peasants took us in. They fed us and massaged our legs; they were so kind and sympathetic. Even though they were poor they looked after us. They do that all the time; they've given food and shelter to hundreds of refugees.'

Yet two summers running Fatimeh had made her own way back to Kabul alone, desperate to escape the heat of Peshawar and to breathe the air of home again. She stayed with her sister, who had remained behind.

'Please don't talk about it,' her daughter whispered. 'Don't remind her: we don't want her to go again.'

Her mother sighed. 'My body aches, my head aches, and I can't sleep at night.'

My feelings about purdah changed radically. Although I had previously seen it as potentially very harmful to women – witness Mother of Nebi or Fereshteh – it had still been possible to appreciate the security it provided for fostering family and community networks. For women in this new situation, however – uprooted, refugees – I could see purdah only as a stifling prison which prevented them from breathing fresh air which might heal their wounds. Seclusion was a device which kept women locked up, inactive and powerless.

I tried to assess the positive work being done for refugees and found the balance heavily weighted in favour of men. There were training schemes, income generation projects and various courses for them, but aid organisations were inhibited from setting up similar facilities for women. Trained female staff would have to be found and special premises set up if women were to be allowed to gather outside their homes. Because there was an Islamic tradition against professionalism in women, it was not considered desirable to teach them new skills. Trapped inside their houses and tents, the energies of the refugee women remained untapped. There were better educational facilities for girls, which boded well for the future, but few openings for mature women. Only in the area of health was there a positive improvement: often women were receiving medical care for the first time in their lives.

I went with a female friend to assess the feasibility of exporting needlework done by refugee women. Together we visited an Afghan Women's Association which organised a sewing project for women in refugee camps. Khadijeh, their leader, told me that they were strongly affiliated to resistance groups and that they also received funding from an international relief agency. They had their premises in a poor suburb of the city: a small courtyard and two modest rooms. Upstairs on the roof, in a narrow margin of shade, a group of teachers was receiving instruction in Koranic education. During their break they gathered downstairs and listened as I talked to Khadijeh about the activities of the group, of which the sewing scheme was a small part. Although there was not a single man inside the compound, the women were heavily clad in long sombre dresses and white trousers, and their heads and necks were tightly swathed with plain white cotton veils. Their demeanour was solemn and pious. They reminded me of nuns in grey habits and white coiffes. The room was stuffy and pungent with sweat.

Khadijeh told me that the group ran Koranic schools for girls, and courses in sewing and the Koran for married women, as well as working with resistance groups inside Afghanistan and campaigning to recruit new members. An article in their quarterly magazine caught my interest. Its title read, 'What can women do for the holy war?', a question I had asked myself. Khadijeh explained that women's work lay in bringing up children correctly and making sure they were good Moslems. She was composed and articulate, and tremendous energy and conviction shone out from her piercing grey eyes. Women had to maintain the purity of Islam and keep their minds free from heresy, she went on, citing the example of the Polish people who had held on to their faith in the face of the infidel Soviets. She told me how the group found foster families for orphans and gave out material aid, and she showed me photographs of the children, whose solemn faces stared back at me in black and white. Again and again the faces were replaced by new ones.

Then she began to describe the horrors that had been inflicted upon people in Afghanistan, still speaking evenly but holding my gaze so that I felt dizzy and overwhelmed. She spoke of villagers rounded up in buildings, doused with petrol and burnt – a commonly reported atrocity. She spoke of soldiers chopping children to pieces in front of their mothers, saying, 'They'll become *mojahedin*: that's why we're killing them'; and of tying children by the legs and head to two tanks and tearing them apart. Tears rolled down her face as she spoke, and the words poured from her mouth without pause. We all wept silently as we listened.

'Did you really believe all that?' people asked later, in Karachi, in London. 'That's just propaganda.'

But the pain of human suffering and hatred had cut through me and left no time for the questioning of facts and details. I knew well that atrocities had occurred and would still occur on both sides of the Afghan conflict. In Herat during the 1979 uprising that Hakim had described, fifty or so Soviet citizens were tortured and killed in public by fierce mobs, some flayed alive. During the summer of 1978, thousands of political prisoners were shoved into huge pits and buried alive right outside the gates of Kabul's Pul-i Charkhi prison. There have been numerous accounts of whole villages ruthlessly wiped out, and testimonies of barbaric torture in government prisons.

At last Khadijeh stopped talking. Shaking, I went into the next room to look at the sewing project. They showed me samples of embroidery done by women in the camps, much of it not highly marketable and over-priced. I felt depressed that this was all the group did: give cloth and thread to women in the camps and then pay them for their finished work. I imagined that the women were also told to stay at home, remain pure in Islam and be grateful that they could sew these tiny stitches for strangers. Although I was glad that women were organising themselves, I could in no way identify with this group's aspirations and with their fanatic fundamentalism. The heavy black uniform that shrouded their young pupils from head to toe spoke of repression and an excess of zeal. These women were missionaries preaching self-denial to women, advocating a very narrow and restricted role for the female sex. Although Khadijeh had said that women should study and work and should not remain idle at home, I could not see this idea being put into practice.

I felt refugee women needed help and encouragement of a different kind. They needed incentives to get out and learn new skills. There were many ways in which they could help the resistance – training to become nurses, doctors, teachers; learning to cut and stitch useful garments, to make boots or weave shawls. They could also learn to help themselves and receive basic training in infant care or midwifery. If they were to cease being crippled by harrowing memories of the past, women needed to form new social networks, to get outside and breathe fresh air.

I went to Hakim's house as I had promised, although by then my emotional strength was running out. I dreaded meeting Afghan women and encountering their problems; I was struggling against claustrophobic feelings of panic at the prospect of the pain I would feel for them. Together we made our way to the poor suburb where Hakim, Rustam and their families lived. Our rickshaw dropped us at the bottom of the alley. I drew my black veil more closely around myself to deflect curious stares. Although still early, it was very hot. Inside their small compound they had set up a ragged tent, providing privacy for the women when strangers called and shade to rest in during the day. Apart from the space around the tent, where the women cooked and worked, they had one room at the far end of the compound, accommodation for Rustam, Hakim and their wives and children.

I sat facing the door, which was the sole source of light, and took in my surroundings, smiling and greeting the family in turn. Despite being dark and cramped, the room was pretty. The walls were papered all over with newspaper and decorated with photographs and colourful posters. The ceiling was strewn with faded paper pennants on strings, left hanging from Hakim's wedding the previous year. There were two beds, a cradle, trunks and bundles of bedding, which gave little space for us to sit.

Meyna, Hakim's wife, was a pretty girl of fifteen, dressed all in pink with a wide pink and gold veil of thin shiny cloth. She was still weak after the birth, four days before, and she had been taken ill the previous night.

'Hakim and my husband were both out,' said Mother of Meyna, a vigorous, capable woman. 'I had to send someone to get the doctor. She was screaming with pain. He gave her two injections.'

I urged Meyna to lie down and rest, not to worry about having a guest, but she sat for some time before eventually agreeing to stretch out on a bed. She was quiet and spoke very little. The baby lay still under a thin gauze veil, which had been put there to keep off flies. She was swaddled and bonneted and her eyes had been painted with kohl. A *mullah* had found her a name by opening the Koran at random: she was Sadiqeh.

Hakim introduced me to Rustam's mother and father, who lived close by, simple, friendly people from Jalalabad. Throughout the day various people drifted in and out of the room; I was glad to see they had visitors coming and going. An old woman sat very quietly watching us, her yellow teeth protruding from between her lips. She was Rustam's grandmother, which meant that five generations were gathered. Hakim returned to John, giving the women elaborate instructions – serve me tea, keep the fan going, keep me happy.

Mother of Meyna told me they had married their daughter to Hakim so they could keep her with them. People had offered large sums as bridewealth for her, but it was more important for them to remain together as a family. She said Hakim was a good person, and Meyna assented with a smile when I asked if they got on well.

'You're lucky,' I told Mother of Meyna, 'at least you have your daughter with you and relatives coming to the house. I've seen other refugees who have no one. They get very depressed and lonely.'

'Yes, thank God,' she replied sadly. 'But these are all my husband's kin. I have no one of my own here. I miss my sister very much. All my people stayed in Jalalabad.' I realised that when families split up it was usually the women who suffered most because they followed their husbands. 'We haven't got used to living here,' she went on. 'We feel strange. We're ashamed to go out and we don't know our way around. We're not from here; we didn't grow up here.'

I asked if there was a shrine they visited to offer prayers, or a *hamam* where they could meet people. They sometimes went to a shrine but there were no *hamam*s. They washed in the courtyard behind a curtain.

It was obvious that, unlike Hakim and Rustam, they had very little possibility for integrating themselves into a network outside their own immediate family.

I left Peshawar abruptly, deeply affected by all that I had seen, panicky and depressed, overwhelmed by so much human misery. The war was very real and very close. I was continually meeting resistance fighters: old men, young men, even sick men. Some had haunted eyes and spoke very little. In the streets amputees walked on crutches, swinging their bodies along cheerfully. Refugees were still arriving with fresh stories of massacre and destruction.

A few days after I had gone, I learned that Hakim's baby had become ill. They took her to the hospital to be treated for jaundice and dehydration, but she died.

That day at Hakim's house I met a beautiful young girl of about eleven or twelve: Nazieh. Her mother was still in Jalalabad, but Nazieh was relaxed and carefree, refreshingly untainted by sorrow. She danced beautifully for me that day, her head veiled with a red shawl; her gestures were delicate, and her feet moved lightly as she sang. Her song was of love and longing and occasionally I caught the word *mojahed* in her verses. Instead of singing of sweethearts, people sang of holy warriors.

Let Nazieh take up the dance of my three women of Herat, now that they have been lost. What became of them? I have no news and I miss them desperately, not knowing if they are alive or dead, sick or well, yet being sure that they have suffered terribly. Let Nazieh take up their dance: she is innocent of sadness and has no shame at expressing the beauty of womanhood. She is young: may her life be long and happy.

Perhaps Mariam, Mother of Nebi, Shirin and my other Afghan friends heard me broadcasting in Persian for the BBC World Service, describing my impressions of Peshawar. I hope they heard the old Herati song I sang for them and know that I have never forgotten them. I chose verses appropriate to the feelings of all Afghans, expressing the pain of separation, the longing for home and loved ones, and looking to God for help and solace:

> One road has become two roads – alas!
> My friend has become separated from me – alas!
> My friend is separated, gone far away
> God ordained her place be far away – alas!

Glossary

afghani	unit of currency (then approx. 140 *af*s=£1)
Agha	'Father', holy man, sometimes spiritual healer
'Allah Hu'	'He is God'; Sufi incantation
ambejin	the relationship between the wives of brothers
arusi	(*arus*: bride) final stage of marriage when the bride goes to her marital home; wedding party
atan	circle dance performed at weddings
barakat	healing blessings or life-force emanating from a holy person, shrine, book, etc.
'Bismillah'	'In the name of God'
bridewealth	substantial sum of money given on behalf of the bridegroom to the father (or guardian) of the bride, payable before the wedding
burqa	traditional women's veil worn in cities, completely covering face and body
chador	Iranian veil (known as 'prayer-veil' in Herat), covering head and body but not the face
charbeiti	folk quatrain; style of highly ornamented folk singing
'cold'	category of food derived from Greek humoral medicine; watery, acidic
co-wife	the relationship between women married to the same man
daireh	large frame drum, usually with bells or rings fixed inside rim
dua	personal prayer expressed directly to God or through the intercession of saints
dohol	double-headed drum played with sticks, accompanying the *sorna*
dutar	long-necked lute
Eid	religious festival: Eidi Ghorban, the Festival of the Sacrifice, associated with the pilgrimage to Mecca; Eidi Ramadan, concluding the month of the fast
'engagement play'	courting visits to the bride by the bridegroom (on completion of the *nekah*)
gadi	horse-drawn carriage

hakim	traditional healer using Greek humoral medicine
halwa	sweet ritual food distributed as alms
hamam	public bathhouse
harmonium	free-reed keyboard instrument imported from India, pumped with one hand and played with the other, essential to the urban Afghan popular music style
'hot'	category of food derived from Greek humoral medicine; substantial, oily, sweet
Jat	derogatory name given to a specific group who work as barbers, *sazdohol* musicians, circumcisers, makers of sieves and drums, actors and puppeteers in their satirical folk drama
jinn	spirit belonging to Islamic and pre-Islamic Arab cosmology, thought to cause sickness, madness or death
khaneqah	Sufi gathering place
kursi	small table covered with a thick quilt to trap heat from a brazier of glowing embers beneath
maraz	'illness', specifically connoting fits of spirit possession
meleh	outdoor picnic; huge outdoor fair held during springtime
Moharram	lunar month during which deaths of Shiah martyrs are mourned
mojahedin	'holy warriors', resistance fighters
mullah	Islamic cleric; man with religious learning
namaz	ritual prostrations and Arabic recitations performed at the five daily prayer times
nazr	'vow'; sweet milky rice cooked according to personal obligation during the month of Safar
'needle and thread'	symbolic gift from the father (or guardian) of the bride denoting acceptance of a marriage proposal
nekah	religious marriage ceremony
pilau	oily steamed rice served on festive occasions
qadifeh	large gauzy veil worn by women to cover the head
Ramadan	lunar month of fasting during daylight
rowzeh	Shiah mourning song about the martyrs; Shiah Moharram sermon; shrine
rubab	short-necked Afghan lute
sazdohol	music of *sorna* and *dohol*
sheikh	holy man, healer
Shiah	minority sect of Islam, state religion of Iran
sorna	double-reeded oboe, accompanying the *dohol*

Sunni	orthodox sect of Islam
'sweet-eating'	engagement party
tabla	Indian drum pair played with two hands, essential to the Afghan urban popular music style
tawiz	healing or protective prayer worn as an amulet
ustad	expert, teacher; honorific title
'*Wah wah!*'	exclamation of delight and appreciation
zikr	Sufi remembrance of God; ritual gathering

Reference List of Main Characters

Part One—Mariam

Mariam	housewife and mother
Latif Khan	her father, leading musician of Herat
Mother of Karim	her mother
Karim	Mariam's eldest brother, musician
Zahir	her second brother, musician
Fereshteh	her elder sister
Hossein	her younger brother, musician
Parwaneh	her second sister
Nassimeh	her youngest sister
Hassan	Mariam's husband, carpenter
Simin and Mahmood	her children
Tayereh	Karim's wife
Mohammad Omar	Fereshteh's husband, musician
Ustad Sultan Khan	deceased father of Mohammad Omar, musician
Mother of Rahim	Mariam's uncle's wife
Zainab	Latif Khan's sister
Azizeh	Mariam's maternal cousin
Aisheh	girl engaged to Zahir
Mother of Sekhi	Aisheh's mother
Mother of Ghani	Mariam's neighbour, traditional midwife

Part Two—Mother of Nebi

Mother of Nebi	diviner, housewife and mother
Shemsaddin	her husband, caretaker and gardener
Nebi, Abdullah and Nadir	her sons
Mah Gol, Meri Gol and Zia Gol	her daughters
Mother of Farouq	her mother
Sadiq	Mother of Nebi's stepfather, shopkeeper
Farouq	her elder brother, shopkeeper

Timor	her younger brother, shopkeeper
Firuzeh	her younger sister
Habibeh	her second sister
Bassireh	her youngest sister
Zuleikha	Farouq's wife
Peri	Timor's wife
Resul	Habibeh's husband, engineer
Anar Gol	Shemsaddin's sister
Agha Mohammad Ali	deceased spiritual healer
Agha Seyed Osman	Agha Mohammad Ali's son, spiritual healer
Sherifeh	girl engaged to Nebi
Ghulam Mohammad	Sherifeh's father, sharecropper
Mother of Nassar	Sherifeh's mother
Mother of Gol Shah	Mother of Nebi's neighbour, traditional midwife

Part Three—Shirin

Shirin	bandleader, housewife and mother
Gol Dasteh	her eldest daughter, musician (Shirin's band)
Ferideh	her younger daughter, musician (Shirin's band)
Khalifeh Sultan	Shirin's husband, barber
Yaqub	her eldest son
Hakim	Khalifeh Sultan's nephew, musician
Nadieh	Shirin's uncle's wife, musician (Shirin's band)
Jamileh	Shirin's brother's wife, musician (Shirin's band)
Minstrel Amin	deceased Minstrel patriarch, musician
Shahzadeh	deceased fourth wife of Minstrel Amin, bandleader
Salim Jan	son of Minstrel Amin, musician
Leila	sister of Salim Jan, bandleader
Golnar	Shirin's sister, bandleader
Sima	Golnar's daughter, musician (Golnar's band)
Soraya	Shirin's neighbour, bandleader
Negar	Shirin's neighbour, musician (Leila's band)
Parwin	Shirin's neighbour, musician (Leila's band)
Rokhshaneh	Negar's daughter, musician (Leila's band)

Acknowledgments

Without my husband, John Baily, this book would not have been written. His inspiration took me to Afghanistan and led me into Herati research, and his generous grants from the Social Science Research Council gave me the official residence status necessary for such an undertaking. His ideas and specialist knowledge have enormously enriched my understanding. Informal participation in Professor John Blacking's Department of Social Anthropology at The Queen's University of Belfast gave me much insight into problems relating to ethnomusicology and fieldwork. Various others have encouraged me and read sections of early drafts of the book: Anne Barry, Eve Bell, Bob Boakes, Mary Boakes, Karen Brignall, Joanna Lowry, May McCann, Marly Morgan, Mahboob Takapou and particularly Arian Misdaq, Margaret Mills and Nancy Tapper, who gave detailed informed comments. Norma Weller helped and inspired me with my illustrative drawings. My brother, Oliver Doubleday, provided two colour photographs. Liz Calder, Karen Lewis and Mandy Greenfield gave invaluable help in the editorial process, and special thanks go to Tony Colwell for his patience, wit and understanding in overall supervision of the book. Finally, I am deeply grateful to all the individuals and families in Afghanistan who looked after me and initiated me into their rich and precious culture.